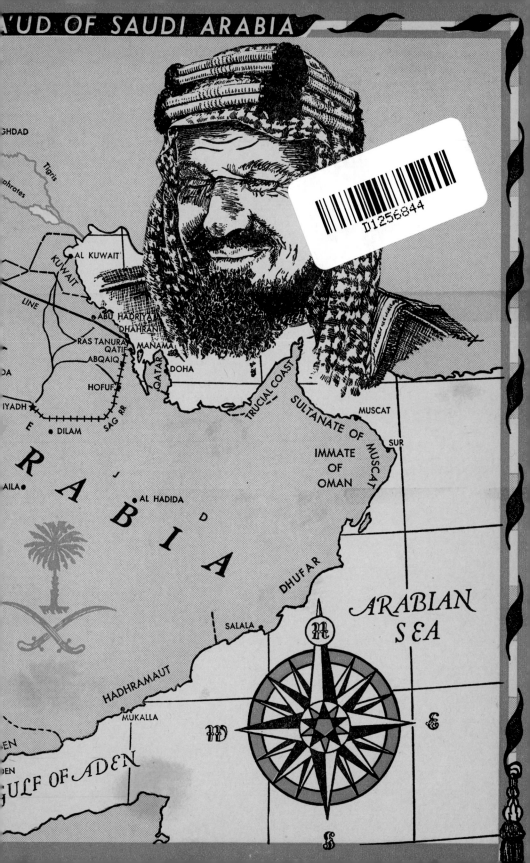

*ARABIA
REBORN*

ARABIA REBORN

GEORGE KHEIRALLAH

Drawings by
CHARLES O. NAEF

THE UNIVERSITY OF
NEW MEXICO PRESS

Preface

King Abdul Aziz ibn Sa'ud is remaking Arabia.

A man who would have stood out among men in any generation or country, he rose out of adversity by the strength of his arm and the oneness of his purpose; he welded the warring tribes into a united nation and his wisdom is directing it on the road of modern progress.

Fourteen centuries ago, under similarly bleak conditions, an orphan boy, unlettered and untutored, gave the world a religio-social system which today governs the lives of one-fifth of the human race. Out of Arabia Deserta, the mother of many nations, came a civilization that fertilized the mind of man and initiated modern progress.

Now, the importance of the Sa'udi oil reserve is beginning to penetrate the consciousness of the American people; the requirements of our Navy and Army, of the Marshall Plan for the reconstruction of Europe, and an ever increasing world need for the commodity are served in part from Sa'udi Arabia.

Yet Sa'udi Arabia's greater potentiality and importance is due to its position as the Sacred Land of Islam, where, at present, three hundred thousand Muslims—and in the foreseeable future, one million—gather annually from the reawakened and strategically situated Islamic countries to worship and confer.

As guest of H.R.H. Amir Faisal at the Pilgrimage of 1948, and through graciousness of the King and Crown Prince, the writer traveled considerably over Arabia Deserta, the safest country on earth, and feels that some knowledge of its background, touching casually upon certain highlights and retelling a few personal stories, may facilitate a better general understanding between Americans and Arabs.

In a befuddled and fast-changing world I have avoided the present political travail of the "Arab family at large," hopefully awaiting parturition.

The careful reader may note that the same word is occasionally spelled differently in these pages, such as the word for "Father of," which occurs as: Abu, Aba, and Abi. This is due to the Arabic syntax. The impossibility of trans-literating the delicate shadings of Arabic gutturals and aspirates into the English alphabet decided the use of the current accepted spelling as in Koran, Mecca, Souk, etc.

I thankfully acknowledge my indebtedness to the Arabic writings of my friends: Their Excellencies Sheikh Hafiz Wahba and Sheikh Fuad Hamza, the Honorable Fuad Shakir, Ustath Ahmad Abdul-Ghaffour Attar, Ustath Shekib Amaway, and, above all, my friend the late Ameen Rihani, whose untimely death was a loss to the Arab World.

To Professor Dr. Nabia Abbot of the Oriental Institute of the University of Chicago for permission to quote from her *Lady of Victory* and *The Two Queens of Baghdad*; to Mr. Raji Ali Saleeby for the composite diagram of the greatest dam of antiquity; to Mr. K. S. Twitchell, and Dr. George Miles, Curator of the American Numismatic Society of New York, for operational and historical references pertaining to the Cradle of Gold mine. To the Arabian American Oil Company for making available their operational data and photographs; to Miss Lucile Gillet and to my wife for their labor in proofreading and transcribing this manuscript.

GEORGE KHEIRALLAH

Contents

[vii]

CHAPTER ONE

Of Dreams and Deeds

Through the blackness of the desert midnight, forty men trudged silently toward destiny.

Leading them was a tall, powerfully-framed youth who had been warned by his father: "Return home lest you perish."

And he had answered: "Perish we may, but we shall go forward."

At the edge of a sleeping town, the youth signaled his men to halt. Before them, the houses and the citadel stood hushed against the darkness. It was there that destiny waited.

The young leader instructed thirty-three of his men to remain where they were. Six were to advance with him into the town.

"At the right time," he told those who remained, "we shall send for you."

It was two o'clock in the morning. At four o'clock, one of the six went for the others. At five o'clock they prayed.

The battle began a few moments later: the Governor and his eighty soldiers against the forty. Within an hour, it was all over. Forty of the defenders and two of the attackers were dead, and the criers were out in the streets of ar-Riyadh proclaiming: "The Governor is killed, and the rule belongs to Allah first, and to Abdul Aziz al Sa'ud next!"

The date: January 15, 1902.

*   *   *

Across the face of Europe, and over the vast Pacific, the world's great powers were locked in mortal combat.

Through the ancient waters of the Red Sea, a destroyer of the United States Navy churned northward . . . through the Gulf of Suez and the south section of the Canal . . . into Great Bitter Lake, in Egypt.

There, it drew alongside the U.S.S. Quincy, and a regal figure, six feet five inches tall, was piped aboard with full naval honors.

Abdul Aziz ibn Sa'ud had come to meet with Franklin Delano Roosevelt at a solemn moment in the life of the world.

It was after luncheon when they began their serious discussions, and it was far into the afternoon when they finished: the man of Groton and Harvard, born to wealth and reared a cosmopolite; and the man of the desert, born to insecurity and reared a nomad, who had never been outside his native land until this very occasion.

Fifteen days later, President Roosevelt had occasion to speak of the frank man of the East, who had scorned conventional diplomacy, and he was saying: "I learned more about the Arab question . . . by talking with Ibn Sa'ud for five minutes than I could have learned from the reports of dozens of commissions."

The occasion: the President's report on the Yalta conference, before a joint session of the Senate and the House.

The date: March 1, 1945.

*　　*　　*

When the 21-year-old Abdul Aziz led his forty companions through the desert, in 1902, his friends had already begun to speak of him as "The Youth With a Purpose." Yet, he was, as far as anyone knew, just a gallant young

[2]

man whose only well-defined ambition was to recapture the town of ar-Riyadh, long the Sa'ud family capital, but held at the time by the Rasheeds.

When he boarded the Cruiser Quincy, forty-three years later, he was the undisputed ruler of the Arabia he had united; the King who was leading his five million people out of the poverty and lawlessness and inertia which for so long had blighted their lives.

One may thus span the years with two paragraphs, but for Abdul Aziz the spanning required unfaltering courage and patience, and a full fund of wisdom. It required well-planned strategy, and a willingness to accept temporary set-backs and unwelcome compromises in the interest of the ultimate goal. It required, above all, faith.

For the Arabia that Abdul Aziz knew in 1902 was a land of scant promise. For four centuries it had lain in almost full eclipse, except for brief periods of partial resurgence. Gone were the glories of the ancient days, when the Arabian Empire swept from the boundaries of China to the heart of France; when the Persian Gulf and the Red Sea were the centers of the world's trade. Vanished was the age of Arabia the Civilizer, the Mother of Culture and Learning.

Instead, Arabia was in a state of seemingly permanent blight, imposed by the sword and the torch of invaders and oppressors. The camel herders and shepherds were continually warring with one another for possession of the insufficient oases. When they were not fighting, they were wandering endlessly in search of vegetation, or in quest of those few places where the limited water supply would permit the growing of meager crops.

They had no money. They had no education. They knew no trades. If they failed to reach an oasis, they went

[3]

thirsty. If they failed to raise crops, or to rob them from others, they went hungry. If they became ill, they suffered without medical aid. In brief, they seldom knew anything but want and hardship.

Life in the towns and villages was little better. Sometimes, indeed, it was worse.

Such was the land that Abdul Aziz saw about him in 1902.

Then, one moves forward . . . to 1950. Is *this* the *same* Arabia? The answers are two: It is the same *land,* yes. But that is all. This is *Ibn Sa'ud's* Arabia. In the difference lies the story of one of the truly great men of our time.

Most of Ibn Sa'ud's people are still camel herders and shepherds, but their warring has stopped. The King saw to that. No longer do they have to wander endlessly in search of water, for wells now dot the desert. The King saw to that, too. And he has seen to other things:

Agriculture, for example. The great irrigation and agricultural experiment project at Al Kharj marked the start of a whole series of similar undertakings. Sanitation facilities are constantly increasing. Education is expanding. Roads are being built, and electrification facilities, and all manner of urban improvements. When illness strikes today, there are modern hospitals to give the proper care; and traveling medical units are being formed to carry assistance to the hinterland. Malaria is being combated successfully, and doctors have turned their weapons on trachoma.

By the spring of 1951, the great new port at Dammam, with its seven-mile pier to deep water, was nearing completion; and, the 350-mile railroad from Dammam to Dhahran, Abqaiq, and Riyadh was scheduled for operation over its entire route by year's end.

On the Red Sea coast, the city of Jiddah has been so

[4]

transformed that it would not be recognized by those who knew it a half-century ago; and, beside the Persian Gulf, there are sights such as could not even have been envisioned when Ibn Sa'ud began building his career; acres upon acres of industrial installations, where before there had been only sand; great clusters of modern homes, dormitories, office buildings, schools, hospitals, recreation buildings. There are paved streets, electric lights, taxicabs. In brief, there are modern American communities.

For there, on the edge of the Persian Gulf, is the center of the petroleum operations which the King, in his wisdom and foresight, brought to Arabia to fulfill the dream which sustained him during the thirty-five years of war that were the price of Arabia's unity.

Unity and independence had been only part of Ibn Sa'ud's dream for Arabia as he fought the desert tribes to achieve the one, and resisted the great outside powers to insure the other. The rest was Arabia with enough to eat, Arabia adequately clad, Arabia with permanent homes for its wandering tribes . . . with schools, mosques, hospitals, roads, water wells . . . with protection against the lawlessness which had harassed his own people and those who came to make the pilgrimage to Mecca.

All of these things Ibn Sa'ud is achieving, though the task seemed hopeless in the beginning. There was resistance to change, and suspicion of motives. There was ignorance and prejudice. There were internal jealousies and external covetousness. There were two world wars to impose their staggering impacts. Yet Ibn Sa'ud never acknowledged the possibility of failure.

These were the things that called for the unfaltering courage and patience, the full fund of wisdom, the acceptance of setbacks and compromise, and, above all, faith.

[5]

These were the things that required a *man*: A Man With a Purpose; the things that required, saying it another way, Abdul Aziz al Sa'ud.

And this is his story . . . and the story of his people, and their land, and *their* Faith . . .

CHAPTER TWO

The Greater Arabian Family

Two factors may, perhaps, be considered predominant in giving form to the Arab way of life, and in making possible its development and expansion. One is the physical nature of the region: its topography, its soil, its climate. The other is its isolation.

In its topographical aspects and its arid climate, the land of the Arabs is more akin to eastern Africa than to western Asia. Its vast expanse of desert basin, fringed by mountains, is manifestly a continuation of the African continent.

Its deserts occupy the heart of it, and continue as sand and limestone plateaus far into the northern portions of Syria and Iraq. Only along the edge of this sea of desolation and in the mountains and their valleys, are water and fertility encountered, except for an occasional oasis, sandwiched between the *nufuds,* or sands.

Thus, there are the verdant mountains of the extreme south, where the rainfall of the monsoons refreshes the land. This is the Yemen, which the Latins named "Arabia Felix," or "Happy Arabia." In the extreme north are the well-watered, productive plains of Shinar, which we know as Iraq; and the small but rich valley of the Orontes, which is Syria.

In between, skirted by barren mountains, is the great expanse of desert and dry plateau which has become Sa'udi Arabia. Blocking off this region from the rest of the world

[7]

is a circle of natural barriers. From the head of the Persian Gulf southward to the Arabian Sea, westward to the junction with the Red Sea, and northward to what we know today as the Bay of Alexandretta, the Arabs were isolated by water, fringed in great part by steep mountain shores, except for the small strip of desert which connected them with Africa.

In prehistoric times, the Persian Gulf extended 135 miles north of present-day Basra, surrounded by marshes and flanked on the east by the steep and rugged Zogros Mountains, forming a barrier which separated Iraq from the Persian plateau, and diverted the Indo-European and Mongolian migrations northward.

On the north, the Taurus Mountains completed the barrier around Greater Arabia, or Jezirat-ul-Arab (the Island of the Arabs).

In this protective isolation, back in the remote darkness of time, a branch of the Caucasian race established itself. These primitive hunters learned, thousands of years ago, to domesticate animals; and led the lives of nomadic shepherds, their livelihood depending upon their sheep, goats, dogs, and, later, camels. Rarely did they have cattle.

They lived on milk, and fresh and dried meat. From goat's hair, they wove their tents, rugs, and ropes; and from the wool of sheep and the hair of camels they made their garments. They moved south in the winter and north in the spring, for the rains brought a short season of pasturage to the desert plateaus, and pasturage meant life to their flocks, and hence to them. To this pasturage, the friendly visitor or the traveler could come without fear, and be sure of hospitality, but he who came with pre-emption in mind could be certain of trouble.

Consequently, since the means of sustenance were never

[8]

sufficient for everyone, fighting was virtually unceasing. Those who had no pasturage or no watering place raided those who had; those who had no herds fought to gain a share from the more fortunate.

In these circumstances, individual self-reliance was not enough for survival, so brother was in duty bound to defend brother, and relatives banded together in firm fealty for protection. Next to this blood obligation was the responsibility of neighbor to neighbor, and thus the tribal organization had its beginnings.

Often, the smaller and weaker tribes would align themselves with others and those combined groups would fight for the water courses, wells, and pasturage which had been denied to them before.

This practice of "ghazu," or raid, was born of necessity, but it grew into the game and sport of the Arabs, and, in some parts of the Island of the Arabs, it so remained until very recent times. The raids, being snatch games, were not particularly bloody affairs. They consisted of single combats, or melees, which ended with an appointment for another battle in the future.

Not so harmless were the blood feuds; for, when a man was killed, except in the normal course of battle, his tribe was in duty bound to avenge him, or to compel a ransom if it chose. These blood feuds, in contrast with the ghazu, would sometimes evoke such deep enmities that they would evolve into wars lasting for decades, for no Arab rests until his blood feud is settled; and, in the process, the original cause is often magnified.

The arms of these early Arabs consisted of wooden spears and lances, and bows and arrows. Not until a much later period did they obtain bronze, then iron swords and spearheads. But, whatever their weapons, their basic reason

[9]

for war remained unchanged. Except in the case of blood feuds, it was almost always prompted by the unceasing struggle for the grass and the water.

Inevitably, the weaker tribes plagued by scarcity and hunger, were forced to the fringes of the desert, and to the less abundant pasturage of the plateaus, there to fight, in turn, among themselves for the means of survival.

Inevitably, also, those who were able to do so began to settle permanently in the more fruitful locations: in the mountains and valleys of the Yemen, in the few valleys of Hadramut, around the water pits of Yamama, the grassy plateaus and valleys of Najd, the shores of the Tigris and Euphrates, the valleys of northern Syria, and down to the edge of the Mediterranean and the Gulf of Aqaba.

Throughout the course of history, these settled communities were continually replenished from the deserts of Arabia, sometimes in waves of mass migration, and endlessly by infiltration. Thus, in spite of the conquest of Syria and Iraq by Hittite, Persian, Greek, Roman, or Crusader, the foreign element was ultimately absorbed.

* * *

There can be no doubt that the nomadic life, with its dangers, its hardships, and its constant insecurity, sharpened the wits of its disciples, and made them hardy, resourceful, alert, and self-reliant. But, a career of wandering is hardly conducive to the development of civilization.

It was only when the nomad settled down in a favorable locality that he had the time or the compulsion to put his mind at work on the reasoning that was to mean progress. It was then that he had to think about such things as when to plant and when to harvest; how to build a permanent shelter; how to make suitable clothing; how to conserve his

[10]

livestock, his pasturage, and his trees; how to carry water to where there was no water, in order to make things grow.

He learned to measure time by the reappearance of the moon; to breed better varieties of his domesticated flocks; to select the edible plants, to propagate them, and to develop better varieties from the wild ones; to watch causes and effects; to observe, to study, to speculate, and thus to accumulate, over the years and the centuries, an expanding knowledge of objective nature.

This progress, starting as it did from complete lack of knowledge, must have taken thousands of years, but out of it we owe the development of barley, wheat, and millet from the wild grasses; and from it came the invention and development of spinning, weaving, and dyeing, the plow, and the wheel.

The details of this early history of the settlements along the water courses and the fertile spots on the fringe of the Island of the Arabs are lost in the mist of time. But, reasonable conclusions are possible on the basis of what existed at the fruition of this long period, and on the strength of the art traces of the ancients.

The art which they left was manifestly a development that came after the nomads had become adjusted to living in a settled location. The settled life confined this early man to a limited space, and tended to permanence: to home. This permanent possession, and the seasonal leisure of the farmer's life, prompted him to improve his domicile and his surroundings. He developed a feeling for harmony, and art began to express itself in the media at hand.

These art traces have become the best guides to the millennia of speculative history. They show clearly that civilization and progress were built upon an agricultural foundation. From this foundation, man advanced from his status in the stone age to that of man, the thinker, whose eyes, mind, and spiritual senses were quickened to solve his specific problems, individually, and in community with his neighbor, whose help he utilized in exchange for his own labor and products.

The major branches of the people who inhabited this region attained distinctive historical entities in the pre-Islamic days: the Akkadians, Amorites, Babylonians, Phoenicians, Ma'inaens or Sabaeans, Canaanites, Hebrews, Chaldeans, Assyrians, and Arameans or Syrians, after whose country, Shem, the word Shemite, or Semite, was applied to all branches of the Arabian family.

The language developed by these early peoples gradually assumed a number of variations, as groups held clannishly together, and the difficulty of communication localized their spheres of operation. Thus, the sister languages spoken by the Babylonians, Assyrians, Phoenicians, Hebrews, and Arameans, were all derived from the same Semitic root, yet are no more similar than the languages spoken today in Italy, France, and Spain.

Present-day Arabic is nearer the original root than any other Semitic language, yet this very classical Arabic of today is but the dialect spoken at one time by the tribe of Quraish, and stabilized by the written Koran of the Prophet Muhammad (570-632) in the same manner as Shakespeare stabilized English, or Dante, Italian. Even today, while the grammatical or literary language is standardized, the spoken language, or vernacular, differs greatly throughout the Arabic-speaking world.

While the language was in its early stages of development, and while those early Arabs were evolving from hunters to nomadic shepherds to farmers, the human race was distributed all over the face of the globe, on all continents,

and on many islands. Man lived on the shores of lakes and
seas, roamed over fertile valleys, and took shelter in forests
and caves. Yet, under all of these varied conditions, he did
not shed his primitive mode of life, and his elementary
thinking, until a late period, *except in the valleys of the
Nile and the Euphrates.*

CHAPTER THREE

Civilization Is Born

It was in the valleys of the Nile and the Euphrates that man first stepped forth onto the stage of progress; it was here that civilization blossomed into its first rich luxuriance.

It is still a moot question whether the beginnings were in the one valley or the other, but there is sufficient honor for both. Egypt has been the more fortunate in the abundance of its traces, because stone was available as the medium of expression. The Euphrates Valley had only mud and clay with which to build, and so the things which they built and wrought, except in the highlands of Assyria, were relatively perishable.

Happily, in both cases, a dry climate and the accumulated dust of centuries have, in good measure, preserved the story for us. Records of stone and libraries of baked clay tablets lift the achievements of these brilliant ancients once more before our eyes.

From these records, we know that these peoples, here in the Island of the Arabs, speaking varying dialects of the same basic language, produced such civilizations as the Akkadian, three thousand years before the Christian era; the Amorite civilization of Babylonia, which produced Hamurabi, the Law Giver, in the 1900's B.C.; the Assyrian, which left us libraries, one of which, containing 22,000 tablets, is now housed in the British Museum; and the second Babylonian (Chaldean) era, the mother of sciences, beginning 604 B.C.

[14]

Thus (as Prof. A. I. Olmstead wrote): "When Cyrus entered Babylon in 539 B.C., the world was old; most significant, the world knew its antiquity"; for Cyrus entered by default, because Nabonidus, the king, was preoccupied with his archaeological studies, and was, therefore, the first known archaeologist in history.

Our first civilization, then, was Arab-created: Sumar-Akkadian,* Amorite Babylonian, Assyrian, Chaldean Babylonian, all were *nomadic desert Arabs who had settled along the water courses;* and so, too, were the Canaanites, and likewise the Phoenicians, originally from al-Hasa, Bahrein, and possibly farther south along the borders of the Empty Quarter, Rub'al Khali. Arab, as well, was the civilization of Ma'rib and Saba, with its great dam of antiquity (800 B.C.), its imposing system of irrigation, and its buried cities; and Hadrumut, the mother of skyscrapers, and the Yemen, as described by Hamadani, were Arab countries populated by Arab people.

Old Persian was written in the Aramaic alphabet, and the Sanscrit alphabet is derived from the same source. As late as the Roman and Byzantine period, the Nabateans and the people of Palmyra were making contributions of value.

Instead, then, of grouping these people as Shami, or Semites, which actually is accurately descriptive only of the inhabitants of present-day Syria, one may more properly call them the "Greater Arabian Family."

Five thousand years ago, in this land, accounts were written with the stylus on clay tablets which are preserved to this day. The Babylonian calendar is still used by the Oriental Jews and Muslims. The Babylonians early devel-

---

* Of Sumar, little is known. Future archaeological findings in southern Arabia are likely to place us on a surer footing. At present, views are far apart.

MEANING	PHOENICIAN	S. SEMITIC	GREEK	LATIN	ROMAN	ARABIC
1 OX'S HEAD	⋉ ('a) ALEPH		ΛA (a) ALPHA	A	A	ا
2 HOUSE	9 (b) BETH		B (b) BETA	B	B	ب
3 CAMEL	1 (g) GIMEL	٦	ΓC (g) GAMMA	C/G	C/G	ج
4 FOLDING DOOR	⊿ (d) DALETH		Δ D (d) DELTA	D	D	د
5 REJOICE HIGH	⋺ (h) HE		ΞE (ĕ) EPSILON	E	E	ه
6 SUPPORT	Y (v) VAU	Φ	F(w)/Y(u) WAU/UPSILON	F/V/Y	F/Y/U / V/W	و
7 NICE	I (z) ZAYIN	8	I Z (z) ZETA	Z	Z	ز
8	⊟` (ch) CHETH		θ H (ē) ETA	H	H	ح
9	⊕ (t) TETH		⊕ (th) THETA			ط
10 HAND	Z (y) YOD		⅄ (i) IOTA	I	I/J	ي
11 CUFF-? PLANT	⋎ (k) KAPH		K (k) KAPPA	K	K	ك
12 CORD	6 (l) LAMED	7	⅂Λ (l) LAMBDA	L	L	ل
13 WATER	ヅ (m) MEM	8	↑M (m) MU	M	M	م
14 SNAKE	7 (n) NUN	Ч	↑N (n) NU	N	N	ن
15 FISH	‡ (s) SAMEKH		⅂X (x) XI	X	X	س
16 EYE	O (ʽa) ʽAYIN	O	O (o) OMIKRON	O	O	ع
17 MOUTH	⁊ (p) PE	◇	ΓΠ (p) PEI	P	P	ف
18 HUNT	ⱶ (ys) TSADE		M (s) SAN			ص
19	φ (q) Q'OPH	φ	ΦΨ (k) KOPPA	Q	Q	ق
20 HEAD	٩ (r) RESH	)	Ρ (r) RHO	R	R	ر
21 TOOTH	W (sh) SHIN	3	≤Σ (s) SIGMA	S	S	ش
22 CROSS	+ (t) TAU	†	T (t) TAU	T	T	ت
6 ARABIC LETTERS ADDED	ظ	غ	ض	ز	خ	ث

oped a decimal system, but later discarded it for a system based on sixty, because of its convenience in the representation of fractions. We still retain their sixty system in our measurement of angles and time, and follow their division of the year into twelve months and the week into seven days. Their "Mina" has descended to us as the pound weight. They developed methods of indirect measurement in geometry.

The Era of Hamurabi

King Hamurabi was the greatest patron of the arts and sciences that Babylonia had produced up to his time. Under his rule, civilization became cosmopolitan, and commerce flourished. By promulgation of a proverb, "He who excels in tablet writing shall shine like the sun," his people evolved a civilization whose grandeur and richness retain their lustre nearly four thousand years later.

Hamurabi is, of course, most widely remembered for his code of laws. Though the code was based to a certain extent upon earlier codes, the complexities of a commercial and scientific civilization stimulated the judges of King Hamurabi to establish a superior legal system.*

By 2,000 B.C., the day was divided into twenty-four hours; and time was kept by sun dials by day, and by water clocks at night. Treatises on medicine were written, showing a remarkable acquaintance with chemistry and pharmacology. Compendiums on flora and fauna were made on clay tablets.

These people not only had a complete mastery of fractions, but could solve problems involving equations of the

* *The Code of Hamurabi,* by Prof. R. F. Harper, Chicago University Press, 1904, contains the 282 laws in original script, its transliteration, with English translation.

[17]

first, second, third, and fourth degree; and prepared tables of reciprocals, and squares, cubes, and other powers and roots. In short, they laid the foundation of algebra. Their geometry was sufficient that they knew the theorem later ascribed to Pythagoras, and they were able to compute the areas of triangles, polygons, circles, truncated pyramids, cones, et cetera.

Their art and architecture represented advanced conception and execution, marked by magnificent sculpture and superb skill in the lapidary art, as exemplified by the Ishtar Gate with its glazed tiles depicting animals in color, the Tower of Babel (Ziggurrah), the Temple of Murduk, the beautiful Hanging Gardens, and the elevator used in the Palace.

The use of bronze and iron weapons, the siege apparatus, and armour, all point to the development of the crafts. They gave us the wheel, the basic methods of road building, the postal system, and the oldest musical notation of record.

Such was the civilization of Babylonia.

Phoenicia

The city-kingdoms of Phoenicia were the peaceful civilizers of the Mediterranean shores, occupying the coastal area of present-day Lebanon, and playing a role of distinction for two thousand years before the Christian era.

Two thousand years before Europe (in 1498) celebrated the sailing around the Cape of Good Hope by Vasco da Gama, of Portugal, the Pharaoh Nikhus (609-593 B.C.) commissioned a band of his Phoenician mariners to circumnavigate the African continent, and they did so. The Portuguese explorer, incidentally, had an Arab navigator, Ibn

Majid, who, according to the records of the voyage, had superior maps, charts, and instruments.

The Phoenician sculpture, as shown by the sarcophagus of Ahiram (1,300 B.C.), points to the etiology of early Greek sculpture; and it was these same Phoenicians who gave the Greeks the phonetic alphabet, and tutored them in the Babylonian sciences.

The Dam of Ma'rib

At an elevation of thirteen hundred meters—165 kilometers northeast of San'a, bordering the Empty Quarter —lie the buried ruins of the city of Ma'rib and the remains of the greatest dam and irrigation project of antiquity. The dam was built in the eighth century B.C. and served a flourishing agriculture for thirteen hundred years, to the sixth century A.D. The bursting of this dam is supposed to have caused the ruin of the Sabaean Kingdom and to have scattered the survivors far and wide over the peninsula. This dispersion of the Sabaeans is mentioned in the Koran and throws a light on the magnitude and extent of the irrigation system developed. Pliny referred to the dam as "The Royal Lake."

In modern times it has been the ambition of archaeologists to verify the tradition; and, of the Europeans who attempted to reach it, a number perished in the quest. It was in 1888 that Von Eduard Glaser (1855-1908) was spirited in to the new Ma'rib by the influential Sadah, disguised as an Arab Faqih (learned religious lawyer). He spent a month in the neighborhood and had to be spirited out to save his life.

Only two moderns freely examined the dam and the ruins. One was Nazih M. Azmi, a Muslim Arab, of Damascus, who visited Ma'rib escorted by the governor of the province and a company of soldiers by order of the late Imam Yahyah, of Yemen. From his pen we received the first comprehensive description of the dam, its conduits, and sluices, in 1936. Nazih Bey partially quenched our thirst for knowledge, but, lacking photographic experience, his reproductions were poor.

Dr. Ahmed Fakhry, Bey, Egyptian Director of Desert Antiquities, made an archaeological survey at the request of the Yemenite Government in 1947, and is now preparing a comprehensive book on the antiquities of the Yemen. The diagram here reproduced is a composite by Raji A. Saleeby from the drawings of both authors.

The concept and execution of this project points to an advanced knowledge of scientific engineering. The dam was built with a broad base so as to resist water pressure. The grade between the top and the base measured over two meters giving it the appearance of a hill; the cement (*qadhadh*) employed is hard to chip 2,800 years after building; some of the dressed granite and volcanic stones are interlocking and have the appearance of new construction as the joints are hardly visible. The northern outlet, which is better preserved, has five spillways and a solid building at the middle of the conduit to break the force of the water. The exceptional and advanced engineering skill apparent in the building of the conduits and distribution of the waters, built in the eighth century B.C., was not a spontaneous development of that century but must have been a development of the Ma'in predecessors.

In fact, history shows that a glorious civilization had flourished in the land of the Arabs for thousands of years before the Greek learned his alphabet, or chiseled his first block of marble. Yet, the contrary has so often been re-

[20]

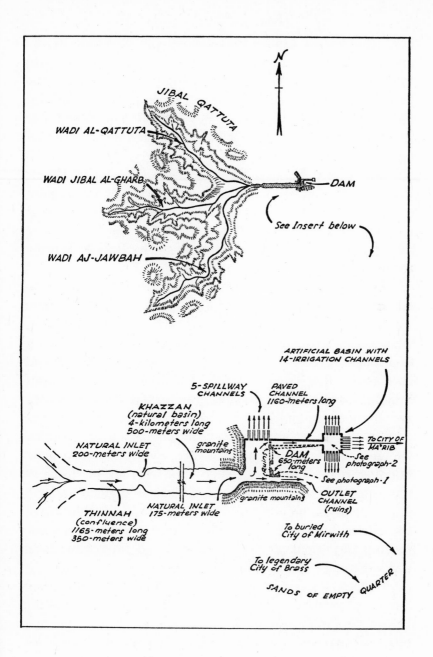

N

JIBAL QATTUTA

WADI AL-QATTUTA

WADI JIBAL AL-GHARB

DAM

See Insert below

WADI AJ-JAWBAH

ARTIFICIAL BASIN WITH
14-IRRIGATION CHANNELS

5-SPILLWAY
CHANNELS

PAVED
CHANNEL
1160-meters long

KHAZZAN
(natural basin)
4-kilometers long
500-meters wide

granite
mountains

To CITY OF
MA'RIB

NATURAL INLET
200-meters wide

DAM
650-meters
long

See
photograph-2

See photograph-1

THINNAH
(confluence)
1165-meters long
350-meters wide

NATURAL INLET
175-meters wide

granite mountains

OUTLET
CHANNEL
(ruins)

To buried
City of Mirwith

To legendary
City of Brass

SANDS OF EMPTY QUARTER

peated that, today, these historical facts are heard with surprise.

Aloys Springer tells how the Greeks gained their knowledge and culture from the East and took their mythology from Babylon:

> They personified their idols after the Babylonia formulae, invented fables in explanation of the reasons, and produced poetry which, like their arts, personified their idols. It was the old Oriental Fable in a new and more pleasing garment. . . . Natural philosophy they gained from the Chaldeans and Egyptians, for Aristotle alludes occasionally to these sources; half of their medicine and plants had names of Arabic or Persian origin . . . they adopted Babylonian chronology and sciences; therefore, when the Arabs came into their own, they found their own Semitic thoughts beautifully arranged.

Shakespeare was to write many centuries later, in *Julius Caesar,* that "yon Cassius has a lean and hungry look; he thinks too much." Perhaps this is partial explanation of the mental agility of the early Arabs: their life of hardship and self-dependence prevented superfluity of fleshing and so quickened their perception that, when they found themselves possessed of a fertile soil, an abundant water supply, and a sunny climate, they were quick to utilize their opportunities and develop a great civilization.

When they waged war because of city jealousy or greed for spoils, as often happened, they would destroy a city or a section, only to replace it with another, as was the case with the Assyrians (originally nomads of the Syrian desert): Sennaherib destroyed Babylon but built Nineveh; Ezarhaddon destroyed Memphis and rebuilt Babylon; Ashurbanipal sacked Thebes and devastated Elam, but he collected a library of 22,000 volumes, which has been preserved for us.

These were the cruelest and most destructive warriors of the Island of the Arabs, yet each in his turn kept Iraq flourishing as the center of civilization.

It remained for the touch of the Macedonian, Alexander (330 B.C.), to wither and blight this center of science, culture, and commerce, and to lay it fallow for nearly a thousand years. It was he who burned magnificent Persepolis and destroyed Tyre, the civilizer of the Mediterranean basin; and only by the providential covering of the desert sands were the ruins preserved for our present-day archaeologists to enrich our knowledge.

In Egypt, the highly developed craftsmanship and the learning of an old and glorious civilization made the port city, built there by Alexander, another center of culture; but the plight of the Arabs had started with his depredations. With spotted exceptions where a flicker of culture lingered, advancement lost its momentum and the countries and peoples deteriorated into disorganization and inertia.

During the Roman period, the greedy eyes of the West were directed toward the fabled riches of southern Arabia. Accordingly, Augustus equipped magnificent legions, under the leadership of Aelius Gallus, for the invasion of that section. His defeat and failure were decisive.

The Romans then directed their efforts toward the Nabateans, originators of the famous dry agricultural development, who hewed and sculptured their superbly beautiful capital city of Petra (Sala') out of the rose-colored cliffs of an all-but-inaccessible canyon. Their country was then the center of the caravan trade between East and West.

After repeated setbacks, the Romans conquered the Nabateans and destroyed their capital (106 A.D.) and, there-

[24]

after, the caravan routes shifted to the Arabian principality of Palmyra, sixty miles northeast of Damascus.

By this time, the known world was divided between two contending powers: the Persians and the Romans. The Arabs, finding themselves sandwiched between the two, as they are today between Soviet Russia and the West, sided mostly with the Western power.

In the first Persian-Roman encounter, the Persians were victorious, and they celebrated by making a prisoner of the Roman Emperor, Valerian, and then skinning him, tanning and stuffing his skin with straw, and then hanging up their grim trophy in a temple as a symbol of their triumph.

But, then, Adanathius (Ibn 'Uthainah) came to the aid of the Romans, with his wife, Zenobia (Al-Ziba: she of the long hair), daughter of a Bedouin chieftain. They and their forces were so effective in the defeat of the Persians that the Roman Senate voted Ibn 'Uthainah the title of Caesar.

After Ibn 'Uthainah's death, Zenobia succeeded him on the throne, and she brought to it not only grace but greatness. For truly unmatched were the women of the "Island" in these pre-Islamic days: Semiramis, the desert nymph of Iraq; Julia Domna, daughter of the Priest of Baal, of Hims, Syria; and Zenobia, daughter of the Syrian desert.

Zenobia annexed Egypt. Thereupon the Romans, as jealous as ever of competition, set out to destroy Palmyra. They were fought valiantly by Zenobia, who led her armies in person, but ultimately she was defeated near Hims (272 A.D.); and, taken prisoner, she was bound in golden chains to grace the victorious entry of the Emperor Aurelius into Rome (274 A.D.).

Thus, another effort of the Arabs failed before the power of the West, and the Island of the Arabs gradually sank into the shadows. Eclipse had come to the towns, and it had come, as well, to the nomads, the source of all settlements and nations in the peninsula. These wandering Bedu found their lives disrupted by the chaos all about them. Raids and blood feuds were continuous, and tribal disunity became general.

In such a state of haplessness was the Island of the Arabs when a son of poverty came upon the scene, and the Miracle happened.

CHAPTER FOUR

The Miracle of Muhammad

One must go back nearly fourteen hundred years to find the beginnings of the religio-social pattern of life and civilization which today is the guide to one-fifth of humanity: Mohammedanism, as it is known to the Western world; Islam to its faithful.

The scene of its origin is fifty miles inland from the Red Sea, where a small valley, hemmed by barren hills, became a caravan center, due to its strategic location, its good water well, and a temple, the history of which is irrevocably lost in antiquity. Situated at the intersection of the natural routes from south, north, and east, it became a trading post for the nomadic tribes, and there they established their idols around the House of Worship. This was Mecca.

The Quraish, a small clan, pre-empted the settlement, and made themselves its lords and administrators, and the guardians of its Temple.

The house of Abdul-Muttalib, though held in esteem, was among the poorest in the clan. Its younger son, Abdullah, joined a commercial caravan to Syria in order to better his financial condition, but he was stricken ill and died at Yathrib on the return journey. As earthly possessions, he left five she-camels, a small flock of sheep, and a slave girl named Um-Ayman.

He left, also, a son, born after his death (570 A.D.). His grandfather named him Muhammad.

[27]

Muhammad's childhood started out much the same as that of any other born to the lean life of the desert in this era of darkness. Then, when he was six years old, his mother died. Two years later, his grandfather followed her in death, and he became the ward of his uncle, Abu-Talib.

Muhammad's life, thereafter, was that of a shepherd boy for his uncle and other Meccans. The hardships which he experienced, seeking desert thorn or shrub for his flock, can well be appreciated by those who know Mecca, even today.

Muhammad never learned to read or write. At the age of twelve, he went with his uncle on a caravan trip to Syria and back. The journey was repeated in his early twenties, and his uncle found employment for him with a caravan owned by Khadija, a well-to-do Meccan widow. She paid him for his services with four she-camels.

At the age of twenty-five, Muhammad married the lady (595 A.D.); and their union brought him love, companionship, and comfort. She bore him one son, who died in infancy; and four daughters.

No longer was Muhammad to know financial worries, for Khadija managed her own commercial ventures. So it was that, soon after their marriage, Muhammad saw a young slave for sale, and requested Khadija to buy him. He then immediately freed the youth, and adopted him as his son. Thereafter, Zaid was called Zaid ibn Muhammad, the son of Muhammad.

Now possessed of security and leisure, Muhammad gradually became a man of solitary habits and pensive moods. He began spending a great deal of his time in fasting and contemplation, trying to understand the riddle of the universe and the mystery of creation. In this quest, he frequented a natural cave atop barren Mount Hira, a few miles north of Mecca.

It was at the age of forty, in 611 A.D., that he commenced to preach to the Meccans concerning the Oneness of God, without partner or associate, presenting a noncorporeal conception of God, whose grandeur was manifested only in His creation. This is the cornerstone of Islam.

Surah 2-255: "Allah, there is no God save Him, the Alive, the Eternal. Neither slumber nor sleep overtaketh Him. Unto Him belongeth whatsoever is in the heavens and whatsoever is in the earth. Who is he that intercedeth with Him save by His leave? He knoweth that which is in front of them and that which is behind them, while they encompass nothing of His knowledge save that what He will. His throne includeth the heavens and the earth, and He is never weary of preserving them. He is the Sublime, the Tremendous."

Surah 6-104: "Vision comprehendeth Him not, but He comprehendeth all vision. He is the Subtile, the Aware."

Surah 42-11: "Naught is as His likeness; and He is the Hearer, the Seer."

As for himself, he emphasized from the beginning that his role was simply that of messenger and warner; that he possessed no miraculous power, and was subject to error, fallability, sickness, and death, just like other human beings.

Say for myself I have no power to benefit nor to hurt, save that which Allah willeth. Had I the knowledge of the Unseen, I should have abundance of wealth, and adversity would touch me not. I am but a warner, and bearer of good tidings unto folk who believe.

[29]

This was his position at the beginning, and so it remained at the height of his success: it had been revealed to him to act as messenger; nothing more.

He brought his people no teachings which were not acceptable to reason, and imposed no duty which was beyond their ability to perform. He advocated prayer to God only for forgiveness and grace.

Muhammad's preachings, and the written Koran which embraces them, qualify the Creator with all sublime attributes, but the one ever-repeated aspect is that of Al-Ruhman, Al-Rahim (The Merciful, The Compassionate). At the start of every chapter, and often through it, and throughout the prayer ritual, the designations are so often repeated that, should any Muslim be suddenly asked to qualify Allah, his spontaneous response would surely be: "The Merciful, The Compassionate."

Out of the Prophet's religious teachings came practical precepts which were so far in advance of his time that they are astonishing to those who are unfamiliar with his life and work.

He became a law-giver, establishing a code of greater universal application than those of Justinian and Napoleon.

He was perhaps the greatest sanitarian in history, for he obligated his followers to pray at five stated intervals in the twenty-four hours, and, before prayer, to perform their ablutions, bathing the face, arms, legs, feet, and loins. Before prayer, as well, he prescribed the rinsing of the mouth three times in succession, and cleansing of the nostrils thrice by snuffing water.

The prayer ritual, therefore, called for cleansing five times daily, and for oral and nasal rinsing fifteen times daily. Has any present-day American or European physician or dentist advocated such rigorous sanitary measures?

History records that Cordova, Spain, had nine hundred public baths when the Arabs lost the city back to the Spaniards. During the Inquisition that followed, a clean person was suspected of heresy, which was a capital crime. One wonders how many public baths can be found in Cordova today.

One wonders, also, whether the present-day advocates of the "daily dozen" do not seem ineffectual, compared with Muhammad's program for the physical well-being of his followers. His prescribed method of genuflections during prayer are certainly such that they keep the body supple, and prevent the muscular atrophy commonly noticeable in the aged.

The Arabian Prophet was the first teacher and reformer to raise his voice against the practice of slavery, and the first to take practical steps to mitigate the evil. It was thirteen centuries ago that he set the example by freeing his own slaves, and he recommended the same course to his followers. He looked upon slavery as destined to disappear with the enlightenment of his converts. Meanwhile, he insisted upon decent treatment for those who remained in bondage, instructing, in his final sermon:

And your slaves: see that ye feed them with such food as ye yourselves eat, and clothe them with the same stuff ye yourselves wear; and if they commit a fault which you are not ready to forgive, then part with them, for they are servants of the Lord and must not be ill-treated. Slaves who say their prayers are your brothers.

This and other admonitions gave the slave in Islam three distinct rights never attained under any other religious or governmental system:

[31]

First—An abused slave could oblige his master to put him up for sale.

Second—A slave could purchase his freedom by borrowing the necessary price from the Muslim treasury and gradually repay it without interest (for interest is forbidden in Islam).

Third—If a slave woman bore a child to her master, her status became changed, and the child was recognized by the father as a free person, and not a chattel to be sold by his heirs.

Muhammad made the freeing of slaves an atonement for many sins. In like manner, he prescribed to the slave only half the punishment meted out to a free man for a sin or offense.

All of these reforms, it may well be remembered, were instituted more than thirteen hundred years ago, while we in the United States freed the slaves only in the latter half of the nineteenth century.

Centuries ahead of his time, also, were Muhammad's precepts concerning women. He made the status of women that of *femme sole,* whose possessions, inherited or acquired, were her own; and he forbade encroachment by the husband on her property, goods, or adornments. She could not be held responsible for the actions or debts of her husband.

In the light of our occasional smugness about our modern social outlook, it is perhaps the more interesting to note that, until the very recent past, woman in the Western world was considered her husband's chattel, in law and in fact; and, in some places, is to this day, to all practical purposes.

Muhammad advocated the marriage of the physically

and mentally fit regardless of station or possessions; and made marriage the foundation of society, on which permanent responsibility is built.

As to polygamy, which had been practiced from the dawn of history among all peoples, can one find evidence of any teacher, prophet, or reformer before Muhammad who limited the polygamy practiced by the Christian and Hebrew prophets?

Yet, although Muhammad raised and safeguarded the status of womanhood, the presumably enlightened Western world of the twentieth century is unaware of the fact, and holds him responsible for the institution of polygamy.

Muhammad's stand on learning was apparent in the first battle which he and his followers fought against the idolators of the Quraish, when he made the ransom of the literate prisoners the teaching of ten Muslim children to read and write. Among his sayings:

> Seek ye learning unto China. He who travels for knowledge walks in the path of the Lord.

In this religio-social system instituted by Muhammad, individual initiative for the acquisition of the good things of this world, and their enjoyment in moderation, is encouraged, but not permitted to run a rampant course.

By way of illustration, an annual tax of about 2½ per cent is exacted against a Muslim's capital for the benefit of the community. Thus, an inactive fortune is liquidated in about forty years.

But, if capital is risked in trade or employed in constructive projects, whereby it is mellowed by human sweat and gives employment and enjoyment to others, it is permitted unlimited gain, *except:* it is forbidden to compound by interest—usurious or otherwise.

[33]

The Prophet did not reach his objective easily. He was ridiculed and personally abused during the first ten years of his mission, for he struck against the foundation of his clan's position and prestige by preaching against the veneration of idols, telling the nobles of Quraish: "The noblest among you is he who is righteous."

His handful of followers were persecuted to the point where a group of them, consisting of men, women, and children, had to leave their native land and migrate to Abyssinia in 615 A.D.;* and, at last, Muhammad, himself, had to escape to Yathrib, present-day Medina, where many of his followers had already fled. From this migration, 622 A.D., the Hijra, or Muslim era, is dated.

Quarrels, raids, and battles between Muhammad and his followers and the Quraish and their allies went on for a period of twelve years, until the forces of the Prophet achieved ultimate victory, including the capitulation of Mecca (630 A.D.).

Such, in very brief outline, is the story of the Miracle of Muhammad; the career of the poor orphan boy, unlettered and untutored, who emerged from bleak and wild surroundings, among even wilder men, to become the spiritual leader who was able to unite the unruly tribes and weld them into a nation; far more important, was able to found a religion which has guided a major segment of humanity for more than thirteen centuries.

So clear and simple were his teachings that they were understood by the simplest and most ignorant, as well as the most sophisticated and learned; and so deep an impression did they make that Islam remains today impervious to the proselyting of other faiths.

---

* This was the first migration to Abyssinia; a second group followed in 616 A.D.

Muhammad, whose conduct earned for him the title of Al-Amin (The Trustworthy), had begun with nothing, and lived to see the full triumph of his mission, and his full dominance of the Arabs. Yet, he lived more humbly and in greater humility after achieving pre-eminence than he had at the commencement of his mission; and he passed away, 632 A.D., impressing upon his followers his own limitations.

During the following fourteen centuries, there never arose a faction or sect, among the billions of human beings who embraced Islam over that period, who dared to ascribe to Muhammad any divine attributes, or any role beyond his own modest claim of messenger and warner.

He had claimed nothing, but he had wrought a miracle.

CHAPTER FIVE

Flaming Sword
and Benevolent Empire

One recalls that Arabia had fallen into decline and seeming hopelessness when Muhammad came upon the scene to bring a renaissance to this land of proud tradition.

Having united his people, and welded them into a disciplined entity, his eyes turned beyond the nation's borders to the places where other Arabs were held in oppression by the Byzantines and the Persians.

Before his death, he had organized an army for the liberation, and had placed it under the general command of Usamah, the twenty-one-year-old son of his former slave, Zaid.

After the Prophet had passed on, his successor, Abu-Bakr, prepared to launch the campaign, not dreaming that, before the Arab drive had ended, it would create the greatest empire which the world had ever known; and give the world its most lustrous civilization up to that time.

When Usamah and his army were ready to leave for their invasion, Abu-Bakr gave them this parting admonition:

Betray not, nor take anyone unaware; practice no excess, nor retaliate in kind; kill not a child, woman, nor a man who is old; cut not a fruit tree, destroy not a planted field, and never kill a goat, cow, or camel except for food.

[36]

Imbued with such a soldiers' creed, the Muslim armies swept out of Arabia like a flaming sword, and slashed through the legions of the Byzantines and the Persians with phenomenal skill and power; but always they conformed with the admonition of Abu-Bakr, and soon they found themselves welcomed by the subjects of the invaded countries.

Faithful to the just and tolerant spirit preached by Muhammad and his successors, they conquered the Persian Empire to the east, the Byzantine-Roman Empire to the west; and, in less than a century after the Prophet's death, they had won an empire that reached to the borders of China, the gates of Byzantium, and the Atlantic Ocean, and was larger than Rome's at the height of her glory.

Then, under the leadership of Tariq, after whom Gibraltar (Gebel Tariq) was named, they launched their hazardous invasion of Spain. The leader was well fitted for the ambitious venture, and his armies overran the greater part of the peninsula in 711 A.D.

The world had begun to experience a philosophy and method of colonization such as it had not known before, and such as it has rarely, if ever, known since. For the Arab method was based upon justice, mercy, and tolerance.

The primary purpose was the spread of Islam, and all other considerations were secondary. Those who joined the Faith immediately became brothers, and enjoyed all the prerogatives of the colonizers. They participated in all Muslim activities, occupied offices on equal terms with the Arabs, and assumed equal responsibility in civil and military functions. In fact, valiant opponents of the invading armies became, upon their acceptance of the Faith, high officers in the armies and holders of top civil administrative posts.

Christians and Jews were accepted as brothers in the

[37]

worship of God, and were treated as wards of the Faith. Although non-Muslims were required to pay the Jizya, or poll tax, this exempted them from military service unless they desired to serve; and they were full participants in all civil activities, occupying at times some of the highest positions in the Khilafah.*

Certainly one must agree that this system is infinitely superior to the treatment which Muslim countries have received from those who have come to dominate them; and, as a matter of simple fact, much easier and less costly for the dominating power.

During a thousand years of undisputed supremacy, when Europe had no voice whatsoever in Muslim lands, and in spite of the incitement of the uncouth and barbarous Crusaders, the Muslims continued to protect and deal kindly with their Christian and Jewish wards.

Indeed, the Arabs so protected the sacred precincts of the other faiths that today, thirteen centuries later, one finds the Chaldeans of southeastern Iraq, the Syrians of Mosul, the Maronites of Lebanon, the Copts of Egypt, and the Greek Orthodox and Catholics of Palestine still established and flourishing, with their churches, monasteries, and convents just as they were before Islam. The Muslims ruled India for nearly a thousand years, yet the Hindu sacred places bear witness to their tolerance.

Surah 2-255: "There is no compulsion in religion. The right direction is henceforth distinct from error. And he who rejecteth false deities and believeth in God hath a firm handhold which will never break. Allah is Hearer, Knower."

In contrast, the Christians of Europe have completely wiped out—annihilated—the millions of Muslims in Spain,

* The leadership in direction of Muslim affairs.

Portugal, southern France, Italy, and Sicily, by such means as the inhuman Inquisition and other refinements of cruelty.

When the Arabs entered Europe in 711 A.D., the northern barbarians, the Goths, had spread over the continent and despoiled the faded civilization which the Romans had created or borrowed. As a result, the Latin tongue had fallen into disuse, arts and sciences were neglected, and the moral standing was that of a dark continent.

But the invading nomads from the desert were avid for learning; so, after conquest with the sword, they turned to book and pen, and the world witnessed a flowering of the arts and sciences, and a spread of culture, such as never before.

These knowledge-hungry people devoured and digested the remnants of Chaldean, Greek, Persian, and Hindu learning, and then proceeded to search, study, and innovate on their own account. They were the custodians of learning for hundreds of years. Damascus, Baghdad, Cairo, Fez, Cordova, and Palermo each became a lighthouse of scholarship and a center of civilization at its highest level.

In truth, had it not been for the advent of the Arab civilizers, Europe's progress would certainly have been far slower. It took three hundred years from the coming of the Arabs to open the eyes of Europe to learning, and it took another three hundred years of tutoring by these same people to bring about Europe's rebirth.

As soon as the Arabs had taken possession of Spain, they set themselves the task of civilizing the country. As Henry Smith Williams writes in *The Historian's History of the World:*

The people of Spain were rewarded, after the advent of the Muslims, with a gentleness and tolerance and a growth of intellectuality and commerce that lead one to question if the Arab domination of Europe would have been the horror it is usually imagined.

The Arabs introduced advanced methods of farming, including their system of irrigation, and the use of silos and windmills. Agriculture thereupon flourished. Artisanship and industry were established; commerce prospered. The invaders instituted universities and libraries, hospitals and asylums, pharmacies and public baths.

Three hundred years of this fruitful labor culminated in the "Glories of Cordova." Europeans came to the schools of Spain, Tunis, and Morocco to study medicine, surgery, chemistry, higher mathematics, astronomy, and philosophy.

Among the students were Pope Sylvester II; Roger Bacon, of England; Albertus Magnus, of Germany; Robertus Anglicus, the first translator of the Koran; Adelard, of Bath; Michael Scott; Daniel Morley; Gerard, of Cremona; Ramondus Lullus; Arnold Villa Novanus; and many another great scholar.

Arabic became the classical language of learning, and Arabic textbooks the great source of knowledge. It was Europe's demand for translated Arabic works which later re-established Latin as the language of learning in Europe, and made possible the Renaissance, "for Greek philosophy had blossomed in the gardens of Arab thought, while it had withered in the stony soil of Rome."

The net result was that Arab learning and teaching established two salients of enlightenment toward the citadel of darkness in Europe: one across the Pyrenees from Spain to southern France, and the other from Tunis into Sicily, Italy, and the heart of Switzerland to the German border (906-980 A.D.).

It was only when the influence of the Muslim schools had been filtering for several centuries through these sali-

ents, fertilizing minds and imaginations, that Europe began
to develop into a modern civilization.

It is one of the great ironies of history that the Arabs,
having shown Europe the way to progress, then fell, themselves, into decline: victims of their own conquests.

The basic reason is that the youth and manhood from
every corner of the peninsula competed for the opportunity
to carry the message of Islam in each wave of invasion: to
Sicily, Italy, Switzerland, southern France, and Spain; to
the islands of the Mediterranean; to north, west, and equatorial Africa; to Persia, India, Tartary, the Asiatic steppes,
and the islands of the Pacific. These, and the wars of Byzantium and the countries of the Caspian Sea, all took their toll
of casualties.

Beyond the losses caused by the actual fighting, thousands upon thousands of the soldiery going into these foreign lands married, settled, and became absorbed into the
countries they had conquered. This was a natural thing for
these men, coming from the meager existence of the desert,
and finding themselves in green lands of opportunity such
as they had never imagined.

So many of them settled in southern Iran that the Persians, themselves, came to know it as Arabistan, "the Land
of the Arabs"; and, during the early centuries of Islam,
Arabic became a popular language in Khorasan, Afghan-
istan, Bokhara, and Samarkand. In India, many thousands
have kept tenaciously, to this day, the genealogical and
tribal traditions which had their origins in the days of blending with the messengers of Islam.

This process of emigration has continued, on a smaller
scale, of course, to the present day, particularly from the
countries of Lebanon and Hadramut. In fact, the Lebanese
abroad today outnumber those at home. In the United

[41]

States, Lebanese and Syrian immigrants and their families are estimated at 500,000; and they have blended so well into American life that they are lost to the parent country.

The emigration of Hadrumutans into Indonesia is likewise continuous; and smaller numbers have settled in Singapore, the Malayan mainland, Hyderabad, and elsewhere in Asia.

The last historic mass migration was that of *banu* (tribe) Hillal into the Maghrib in North Africa during the Fatamite period (969-1171 A.D.); and the descendants of those migrants are now found in the cities, towns, mountains, and deserts of Tunisia, Algeria, Morocco, and Rio del Oro.

While Arabia's sons were migrating en masse, and making their homes in other lands and greener pastures, the Abbaside Khalifahs brought in mercenaries of Turkomen and Persians to serve as palace guards, military officers, and administrative officials. But the mercenaries became such masters of intrigue that the point came where they could enthrone or dethrone the Khalifah. Thus, the ties of the Empire, already weakened by the outpouring of the soldiers, had their disintegration accelerated, and every section began drawing away from the central government.

The Crusaders from Europe, carrying forward their ravages for two hundred years, exacted a toll hard to estimate; and, obviously, hastened the ultimate downfall.

But, the most telling factor of all was the invasion of the Mongols (1256 A.D.), who, in Baghdad alone, murdered one million persons; and later sacked and destroyed Damascus, thus striking, at two of the most brilliant Arab centers, a blow from which they have yet to recover. It was here, and not at Poitiers, that North Africa and southern Europe were saved; for the Arabs eventually defeated the

Mongols and stemmed the tide of conquest, while the Pyrrhic victory of Charles Martel has been exaggerated beyond bounds.

By 1492, the Arabs had been driven from Spain; and, by this time, the Turk had come into ascendancy, and had established himself as religious and secular head of the Near East. He was a valiant warrior and a cunning diplomat; and his suzerainty, like that of the Romans, lasted for four hundred years. But, again like the Romans, he had neither the temperament nor the aptitude for science, culture, or benevolent colonizing.

He neglected not only agriculture, the arts, the sciences, and the crafts, but also his subjects; and, so, he missed his opportunity: A hundred and fifty years ago, he had the human resources to keep pace with the progress of any European nation. Instead, he and his domain became afflicted with dry rot; and when, in his last days, he looked to the prostrate subject countries of his empire for help, they neither found him worthy, nor had they the knowledge or ability to assist him.

Like the Arabs whom he had dominated, he fell into decline; like the Arabs, he could not know then that his rebirth lay ahead.

CHAPTER SIX

Najd: Mother of the Sa'uds

While the Hijaz is the Qiblah * of four hundred million Muslims who face it at prayer time, Najd has always been the symbol of cherished memories: of poets and warriors, battles and love stories.

Here Imru'l Qais, the "Wandering King," was reared among the banu Assad; here this joyful blade pursued his tireless amours, and, in the environs of Riyadh, fought the battles which are described in his verse.

Here, still visible, are the foundations of the first mosque, built by Khalid Ibnul-Walid, the "Sword of Islam," who pacified the region and eventually humiliated the battle hosts of the eastern and western empires.

Here, about twelve kilometers south of Riyadh, is the old town of Manufuhah, where one still may see the ruins of the home of Al-A'sha, most prolific of the pre-Islamic poets, whose verse was unexcelled in its smoothness. South of Hofuf is another landmark of the golden but turbulent days: the graveyard where that other great poet, the gifted but indiscreet Tarafah ibnul 'Abd, lies buried.

Sheltered city dwellers, far removed from the barren hills and sandswept camping sites of Najd, have always sung of its legends; and lovelorn maidens have sighed their lyrics to its romance from the gardens of Damascus to the henna-scented bowers of North Africa and the rose-blown rendezvous of Seville. Toward Najd, and not to the Hijaz,

* The direction faced by Muslims in prayer.

[44]

schoolboys wandered in their dreams; and to it came the early philologists, grammarians, and traditionalists of Cufa and Basra to verify the meaning or usage of a word or expression.

Today, these high, dry limestone plateaus and *nufuds,* with their relatively few oases and *wadis* (valleys or dry river beds) still influence the sedentary Arab to remain a nomad at heart. The sagas of the tribes, with their adventure, their chivalry and their poetry, nourish his dreams and mould his ideals: though Najd did not produce a civilization, it assuredly produced poets and fighting men.

The fighting came first. It was the inevitable result of the unceasing quest for a meager livelihood amidst perpetual chaos. But people could not fight all of the time; and, eventually, two rules became established and generally accepted by the ruhhal, or nomads:

First—To mitigate the effect of perpetual insecurity, and to permit safe travel and trade, they instituted four months of the year as "Holy Months," during which a truce was observed, and wars, feuds, and even the sport of ghazu were forbidden. These were the eleventh, twelfth, and first months of the year, and another month in mid-year. Commerce was the underlying necessity; religion furnished the opportunity.

Second—The vicissitudes of the desert brought forth, also, hospitality, refuge, and the sacredness of trust. These were so highly regarded that they grew into a creed, in defense of which a tribe might sacrifice its very existence. People vied in hospitality to the extent that they would impoverish themselves rather than be remiss; and, conversely, no greater shame could befall an individual or a tribe than to be stigmatized as inhospitable. Proud tribes kept an all-night fire, "Narul-Qura," the fire of hospitality, that wanderers might find their way to their hospitality.

When Islam came, these practices were mellowed with tolerance and mercy, and there came into being the institution of "muruwa," or chivalry. The Muslim influence was a factor in the development of this institution in Europe, and there followed the period "when knighthood was in flower."

The establishment of the holy months gave the first great impetus to the development of poetry and oratory, for it brought the nomads together in the market places for barter *and* conversation.

The Hijaz, itself, was uninviting in its lack of pasture and water, but it had a prime point in its favor: accessibility, from south, north, and east; and so, from time immemorial, it had been the gathering place of the tribes for religious and commercial purposes. The ruhhal, who led a drab and precarious existence, looked forward to visiting its wondrous *souks,* meeting the notables of other tribes, and learning the news of Hira (Iraq), of Yemen, of Syria, and of far-off lands like Abyssinia.

While Mecca was the principal market place, and while Dhul-Majas was a popular souk for a few days, the real "Market of Intellect" was Souk 'Uqaz, situated above Mecca on the road to Tayif. There the bards and the orators gathered with their tribal groups to compete for acclaim under the presidency of renowned judges.

Great occasions these were, for, paradoxically enough, Arabia Deserta produced its classical poetry of all times during the Jahiliyah, or "Days of Ignorance," as the pre-Islamic period was called. While the ruhhal of those days were primitive in their mode of living, their language was highly developed. Limited in their physical circumstances,

[46]

they found outlet in their freedom of expression and their range of imagery.

Culture for them did not, nor does it now, consist of table manners or drawing room niceties, but was solely and strictly a matter of the tongue; and the tradition has been cherished to this day. An Arab traveling in any Arab country needs no letter of introduction, for his manner of speech places him where he belongs: "A man's tongue is his mount; it may carry him to safety, or stumble with him."

Naturally, then, poets were held in highest esteem by the ruhhal. When a good one was produced, his tribe and its allies made it an occasion for celebration, for he was the one who would record in verse the valor of his people, immortalizing their heroes in war and their hospitality in peacetime. He was the propagandist par excellence.

So, whenever men gathered during the months of truce, whether for religious purposes or for trade, the tribes brought forth their most brilliant performers to recite and to declaim. Then, to every corner and pasture range of Arabia, the approved poetry and oratory would be carried by these marvels of memory, the rawies, or narrators.

It is to the rawies that we are indebted for the little knowledge that has reached us concerning the pre-Islamic era. With their prodigious capacity for remembering, they could repeat and retain a poem after a first hearing. Some of them specialized in the genealogy of their tribes, and became the walking-talking encyclopedias of their time.

For obvious reasons, then, a poet was usually accompanied by his rawie; and, when he extemporized, the rawie memorized the verses and could readily repeat them. Both men were likely to have been unlettered.

It is, perhaps, not surprising that, of the four great poets of the Jahilyah: Imru'l-Qais, the foremost of them all (died

560 A.D.); Al Nabigha, Zuhair, and Al-A'sha, all but Al Nabigha served an apprenticeship as rawies; and that many another rawie later won fame as a poet.

Though rated fourth in poetic stature, Al-A'sha (the Nearsighted) was hardly excelled in popularity. At Souk 'Uqaz, he was repeatedly acclaimed, and became known as Sunhajet, or "Tambourine of the Arabs." He greatly enjoyed belittling unworthy nobles and elevating the humble.

It is related of Al-A'sha that he once stayed as a guest with Muhallak, a poor man who had to endure the calamity of having eight unmarried daughters. The poet was so pleased with the dignity and hospitality of his host that he sang at 'Uqaz of Muhallak's nobleness and generosity. It is said that, by virtue of these praises, all of the eight daughters were married within a year to noble suitors, and Muhallak's condition was bettered.

Al-A'sha lived to a ripe old age; but, in his latter days, became totally blind. When he heard of Muhammad's teachings, and of the reforms advocated by him, he composed a poem in his praise (it is still preserved), and set forth to visit him.

However, the Quraish, enemies of Muhammad, heard of this, and feared the effect of the poem upon the Arabs. So they met him and bribed him with a hundred sorrel she-camels to go no further. He therefore returned home.

Much briefer were the days of Tarafah ibnul A'bd, who, like the Sa'uds, was a descendant of the tribe of Bakr ibn Wa'il. Though he died violently at the age of twenty-seven, his Qassidah (Ode) of 107 verses is considered indispensable reading for the student of Arabic.

Tarafah made the mistake of ridiculing 'Amru ibn Hind, the King of Hira, although he had been in the habit of visiting the ruler and receiving his largesse. This came

[48]

to the notice of 'Amru. It was not long afterward that Tarafah and his maternal uncle, Al-Mutalammis, also a poet, made another visit to the King. They were received cheerfully; and, when they departed, 'Amru gave each of them a document of award to deliver to the Governor of Bahrein, which was then the name of the province of al-Hasa.

The poets, delighted, started for al-Hasa. Since neither of them could read or write, the uncle's curiosity prompted him to visit a scribe enroute. To his dismay, he discovered that he was carrying a death sentence.

Terrified, the uncle fled to the protection of the Ghassanide Amirs of Syria, and so saved himself; but Tarafah, unenlightened, continued his journey to al-Hasa and to his execution by beheading.

The greatest poetess in the Jahiliyah and Islam was Tumadhir al-Khansaa. When she first recited at 'Uqaz, the Nabigha who presided said: "Were it not that Al-A'sha preceded you, I would have declared you the best contestant of all."

Jarir, whose home was at Hijr (present day Riyadh), declared her the greatest of Arab poets.

Al-Khansaa lived to see and meet the Prophet after embracing Islam. Muhammad used to beckon her to his side and request her to repeat to him some of her verses. In 646, she was present with her four sons at the decisive battle of Qadisiyah at which the Muslims defeated the Persians. On the eve of battle, she delivered to her sons an eloquent oration admonishing them to persevere. When she was told of their martyrdom she said: "Praised be Allah, Who honored me by their sacrifice and I beseech Him to reunite us in the abode of His Mercy."

Such were the days of the Jahiliyah. So firmly did the

[49]

profession of the rawie become established in the life of the Arabs that the development of memory is a path to esteem right up to the present. There are today thousands who have learned the Koran by rote; and, should a chanter or reader mispronounce a word while reciting in the Mosque, voices will immediately be raised to correct him.

Americans of Arab descent in New York witnessed a striking demonstration a few years ago, during a visit by Dr. Habib Estafan. The Doctor, who spoke many languages, had such an amazing memory that he could repeat, word for word, lengthy and newly-composed poems which he heard recited for the first time. Dr. Estafan gave further demonstrations of his remarkable gift to his fellow nationals in many South American countries.

In less formal surroundings, we find rawies and troubadours in our own times, frequenting the souks and the cafes, as well as the tent fires of the nomads, to declaim in the vernacular and dialect of the various countries and tribes.

They accompany the recitation with music on the rabab, a one-string instrument, the forerunner of the violin, in order to give emphasis and drama to their verses. The audience usually squats around the rawie in a semicircle, forming tier after tier, as in an amphitheater, maintaining respectful attentiveness. Only when the rawie waves the bow of his rabab to punctuate the stroke of the hero's sword, or the end of a combat, do they give vent to their feelings with a lusty chorus of "Ya Allah!"

To the rawie and his institution, then, our gratitude is still in order. To him we owe what we know of that symbol of cherished memories: Najd.

CHAPTER SEVEN

The Sa'ud Ascendancy Begins

It was the Tunisian, Ibn Khaldun (1332-1406), greatest Arab luminary of his century and perhaps the world's most philosophic historian, who made the emphatic observation: "It is only by religious issue that the Arab is aroused."

It was, as we know, by such an issue that the Prophet Muhammad performed the seemingly impossible in uniting the warring tribes, and setting in motion a chain of events richly fruitful in social, cultural, and scientific progress, whose impact continues to influence humanity.

And it was not long after the establishment of the Khilafah (632 A.D.), that the Purist movement arose in what is now Iraq to keep the Faith pure of interpolations, and to adhere strictly to the teachings and examples of the Prophet.

Since then, Purist movements have recurred frequently in the history of the Faith, whenever its integrity has been threatened by a great prevalence of heresies, deviations, and superstitious practices, such as tend, in the course of time, to creep into the propagation and application of religion. At such times, groups of influential men have united to restore the teachings to their original purity and simplicity, as set forth in the Holy Book and in the sayings of the Prophet, recorded and interpreted by the early Khulafa ar-Rashidune, or the "Right Guiding Khalifahs."

[51]

The success of such efforts and admonitions was usually localized, although the reform of Ibn Taymiyah, of Damascus, at the end of the thirteenth and the beginning of the fourteenth centuries, enjoyed for a time a favorable reception in the neighboring states of Egypt and Iraq.

The two most influential and far-reaching reformations since the days of the Prophet Muhammad were those of Ibn Tumart (1078-1130 A.D.) and of Sheikh Muhammad ibn Abdul-Wahhab, the latter stoutly and effectively supported by Muhammad ibn Sa'ud, ancestor of the illustrious present King of Sa'udi Arabia.

The influence of the Wahabi reformation has continued to make itself felt to this day. It is the basis, for example, of the reformation movement in Egypt, sponsored by the late Sheikh Muhammad 'Abdo, former rector of al-Azhar; and the present Purist movement in the Maghrib (North Africa), which originated at the University of the Karawiyine, at Fez, when Moulay Abu-Shu'aybe ad-Dakkali, a former Minister of Justice and an alumnus of the University of al-Azhar, took up the propagation of such a reform.

Upon his retirement, ad-Dakkali was succeeded by Muhammad ibnul-'Arabi, an 'Alawite, a member of the Sultan's family, and Minister of Appeals, whose leadership greatly stimulated the movement. It has become firmly entrenched in Fez, Meknez, Rabat, Marakish, Casablanca, and Tangiers, and has spread rapidly over the rest of the Maghrib.

In Algeria, the modern Purist movement was headed by the late Abdul-Hamid ibn Badis, one of the greatest Muslim progressives whom the writer has had the good fortune to know. Ibn Badis was ably assisted by the learned ulama, al-'Okbi and az-Zuhrawi. This religious movement

[52]

is today sponsored by the most modern, progressive, and enlightened teachers and literati of Algeria, and has the enthusiastic support of the student bodies.

In Tunisia, the late 'Abdul-Aziz 'ath-Tha'alibi launched and promulgated these reforms.

All of these efforts were indirectly influenced by the Najdi Reformation, and followed its teaching in fighting Sufism.

As for Sufism, the subject is too complicated to define or describe in these pages. Suffice it to say that the various Sufi doctrines, which have appeared at many different times as a great many different cults, tend, in general, to superimpose upon the teachings of orthodox Islam various more or less esoteric concepts and ideas, and are, in general, more preoccupied with the special development of a few "enlightened" individuals than with the welfare of the masses. They usually lead to the development of Tariqas (paths) or brotherhoods, devoted to a special way of life, and are, of course, considered heretical by orthodox Muslims.

Ibn Tumart's program, initiated in Morocco at the beginning of the twelfth century (1121 A.D.), resulted in the establishment of Al-Muwahhidine (which became corrupted in the Spanish transliteration to "Almohades"). These Al-Muwahhidine, or Unitarians, wrote one of the most brilliant pages in the history of Islam: their emperors, scientists, philosophers, and artists constituted a galaxy unexcelled in any other period.

Ibn Tumart, a theological scholar of the Masmudah tribe in the Sous Mountains and the sub-tribe of Hurgha, had traveled to Egypt and to far-away Baghdad in search of knowledge. It is said that, in Damascus, he attended the courses of Al-Ghazzali, the greatest theologian of his time.

He returned to the Maghrib, fired with zeal for the reformation of Islam as practiced in the West. His one determination was to denounce the schismic innovations, to admonish against current evils, and to call for a return to the Sunna (practice) of the Prophet and the Right-Guiding Caliphs.

Landing at Bajayah, Algeria, he lost no time in launching his campaign: a task made easier by the fact that, in those days, every mosque of importance was open to all Muslim theologians for lecturing and teaching.

However, Ibn Tumart's zeal and vehemence aroused the displeasure of many of his listeners, for his admonitions ran counter to current practices; and, in consequence, local populations often invited him to leave. In Marakish, the capital of Ali ben Techfine, there was quite a delegation who wanted to kill him, but Ben Techfine was a high-minded and benevolent ruler, so he refused to listen and, instead, allowed Ibn Tumart to make his way to the Sous and return to his tribe.

At Tinmallal, he won great success. All of the tribes of Masmudah responded affirmatively to his orthodox teachings and became his devout followers. This, as usual, gave impetus to the Jihad to spread the reform, so Ibn Tumart set about to provide himself with the means.

He had been able (like Muhammad ibn Abdul-Wahhab was to do six hundred years later) to enlist a disciple with an alert mind and a strong arm: 'Abdul-mu'min ben Ali, an Algerian youth who claimed descent on his father's side from Fatimah, daughter of the Arabian Prophet. He became attracted to Ibn Tumart in the very early days of his teaching; and followed him to Tlemcen, Fez, and Marakish, attending him in his travels and following his courses.

So, when Ibn Tumart formed an army, 'Abdul-mu'min

was its leader. It was then that Ibn Tumart considered himself ready to reform, by the sword if necessary, the people of Marakish who had wanted to kill him for his teachings. He sent word: "Forsake your innovations or be attacked." They chose to be attacked, and they defeated 'Abdul-mu'min soundly, sending him and the remnants of his followers fleeing back to Tinmallal, where Ibn Tumart assured them of ultimate victory.

But Ibn Tumart was not to live to see his prediction fulfilled. He died in 1139 A.D., after making his chiefs pledge allegiance to 'Abdul-mu'min (1139-1163 A.D.), whom he designated Amir al-mu'minine, or "Prince of the Believers."

Ibn Tumart had prophesied correctly: Under 'Abdul-mu'min, the Al-Muwahhidines gradually extended their rule and their doctrines over Morocco, Algeria, and Tunisia, and over the Spanish peninsula as well.

But it is the other great Purist movement which holds most significance in relation to modern times, for out of it the Sa'uds emerged into prominence for the first time. It was this movement, originating in the eighteenth century with the sermons of Sheikh Muhammad ibn Abdul-Wahhab and the discipline of his sponsor, Muhammad ibn Sa'ud, which was destined to eventuate in the unification of a reawakened Arabia in this twentieth century.

When Ibn Abdul-Wahhab entered the scene (1703-1791), Arabia was an agglomeration of small states, whose principal leaders were the sherifs in the Hijaz, banu Khalid in al-Hasa and its environs, banu Mu'ammar in Najd, the Sa'douns in Iraq, the Imam of San'a in the Yemen, the Sadah in Najran, and a Sultan in 'Oman.

Each of these states expanded and contracted continually, according to the aggressiveness and ability of its lead-

[55]

ers. Lines of geographical demarcation were meaningless, because these provinces, and the people who inhabited or pastured them, were like the sands, shifting from place to place, settling for a while, and then moving on again. The ruhhal changed fealty as often as they migrated, in small groups or en masse, seeking pastures.

No better illustration of this shifting status of the inhabitants of the Island of the Arabs can be given than the fact that the Sa'uds, themselves, who have been domiciled in Najd for the last three hundred years, are direct descendants of the Masaleekh branch of the 'Anaza, who today range north of Hims, Syria.

As to the state of their faith, the people of Najd and other provinces, and across North Africa, were praying at the tombs of holy men, practicing fetishism, wearing amulets to ward off evil, following all manner of innovations, and putting their trust in oracles, soothsayers, fortune tellers, and astrologers who flourished on the meager earnings of the credulous.

Intelligent men at all times raised their voices against such practices, but there was no lack, among the public, of those who heeded the charlatan and listened not to the voice of such as Abul-'Ala (973-1053 A.D.):

> Could I command obedience, never in life
> Astrologer had shamed the causeway's crown. . . .
> To pelt o'er deserts with a caravan
> Is trade more honorable than gains like these
> Of one who, were he stoned, would justly die."

Thus, Arabia was ripe for the reformation: ripe, but unwilling to be plucked. So, when Ibn Abdul-Wahhab commenced his career, stirred by the urgency of his mission, he found scant sympathy for his discourses in his native Najd. Neither the people nor their teachers took kindly to his admonitions, and few indeed were the disciples he was able to win. In fact, he was compelled by the hostile attitude of his listeners to move again and again, from one center to another.

And then, at last, he converted Muhammad ibn Sa'ud (1744 A.D.).

The two formed an alliance, determined to accomplish, with the twin instruments of persuasion and compulsion, those things which had been beyond the power of persuasion, alone. Their goal: to propagate the reform, and turn the Muslim stream back to its true channel; to force the people into purification of their practices from the accumulated superstitions which had shrouded the Faith.

They wrote to the leaders of the different Muslim countries, calling upon them to "worship the only God, the One, the Ancient Truth, the Merciful, Who rewards the obedient and punishes the rebellious." They exhorted the Muslims to follow the Koran only, disregarding the interpolated additions.

"Muhammad," they wrote, "is the Messenger of God and His Beloved, but none must qualify him with attributes of praise and greatness, as these only befit 'The Ancient One.' "

Such a message was sent to Moulay Sulayman, then Sultan of the Maghrib, calling upon him to subscribe to this truth, to which Moulay Sulayman answered that this was exactly what he and all Muslims in the Maghrib believed and he, therefore, found no ground for difference or argument.

In considerable measure, Ibn Abdul-Wahhab and Ibn Sa'ud succeeded. The Sheikh, with the Koran in his hand, and Ibn Sa'ud, with his sword, combined to destroy the then-revered shrines of the so-called saints, to level all

monuments to the dead, and to cut down the venerated trees and other objects of fetishism.

Expanding their power rapidly, the combination very quickly extended the Amirate of Ibn Sa'ud and the teachings of Ibn Abdul-Wahhab throughout southern Najd, and among the ever-moving ruhhal.

It was in consequence of the partnership of Muhammad ibn Abdul-Wahhab and Muhammad ibn Sa'ud that the Sa'ud family developed a special meaning for the title, "Imam," which means, literally, a leader during congregational prayer. It is thus distinguished from the secular leader, who is known as "Sheikh" or "Amir."

In the case of the Sa'ud amirs, the essence of whose rise and advancement was the religious cause, he who took the helm of state was called "Imam" as well as "Amir," and he was the leader in prayer, in the Jihad, and in the administration of the affairs of the faithful.

During the Imamah of Muhammad ibn Sa'ud, peace and security were established in the domain which he controlled, and it seemed as though the Island of the Arabs was on its way to revival and an orderly existence. As events were later to demonstrate, this prospect was unduly optimistic; for, except for the brief but distinguished reign of Sa'ud the Great (1788 to 1813) and other brief interludes of recrudescence, the Sa'uds were to have many a reverse, and the Island of the Arabs was to have many a dreary year, before they were to reach the great era of today.

Nevertheless, Ibn Khaldun had been vindicated in his judgment that "only by religious issue is the Arab aroused"; for Wahhabism was purely a movement of religious reform. And so, regardless of the circumscription of the movement and its apparent eclipse at times, its effect upon the Muslim world has been to stir it out of its lethargy. And, it gave to the Sa'ud family the impetus that was to carry it to supremacy, to the great good of their people.

CHAPTER EIGHT

Trials Before Triumph

Largest of the Arab tribes of today is the 'Anaza, descended from Bakr ibn Wa'il, with branches in Najd, Iraq, and Syria. The Sa'uds are of the Masaleekh branch of the 'Anaza, who range the plains in the environs of Homs, in northern Syria; but the most numerous are the Ruala, embracing about 100,000 souls.

The Ruala have established their pasturage from northern Syria to the Oasis of Jauf in Najd; from Tudmor (Palmyra) to Hauran, and south to Jaulan. They are horse and camel breeders, as distinguished from sheep breeders; for, regardless of the introduction of motor vehicles, the camel remains the "Ship of the Desert": the carrier of its cargo. Pedigreed horses and zalul (racing camels) are the pride of the Ruala.

Those who followed the narrative of Lawrence may remember that he did not become sure of success in his campaign until he concluded an alliance with Nuri Asha'lan, chief of the Ruala. The friendship of Ibn Sa'ud for the Western Powers had a great influence on the attitude of Nuri.

A scion of the Ruala gave me an excellent illustration of the phenomenal adaptability of the Arab in bridging the remote past with modernity. It was in New York, where I saw a handsome, debonair, and meticulously groomed young man making his way through the lobby of the Waldorf Astoria. He was none other than Fuaz Asha'lan, grandson of Nuri, and present titular head of the greatest nomadic tribe in northern Arabia. No one could have guessed that this dapper youth was a Bedouin of the desert, bred to endure its hardships, to raise its best horses and swiftest camels, and, not too long ago, to lead its raids (ghazu).

Fuaz had come to the United States to purchase drilling machinery, pumps, et cetera, in order to tap the artesian basins underlying the limestone plateau of the Syrian desert, and thus to make the water available to the Ruala livestock as it migrates southward in winter and northward in summer.

To those interested in the life of the nomad, especially the Ruala tribe, we recommend the works of Carl Raswan, who was adopted by the Ruala and lived as one of them for years.*

The banu Bakr ibn Wa'il, from which all of the 'Anaza are descended, is famous in the genealogy and tradition of the pre-Islamic period. Like other great tribes of the Jahilyah, they produced gifted poets, including Amru ibn Qumay'a, Tarafah ibnul 'Abd, and Al-Harith ibn Hilzah. And, like other great tribes, they produced warriors by the score.

The most celebrated of the pre-Islamic hostilities of Bakr ibn Wa'il was Harb al Bassous, the Forty Year War (494-534), against its sister tribe of Taghlib; a struggle that started over a withered old woman and a mangy camel.

The woman had sought the hospitality of Jassas, of banu Bakr. By mistake, her repulsive beast was turned to pasture where Kulaib (440-494), of banu Taghlib, hero and leader of both tribes, grazed his prized stud camel.

Kulaib happened to pass, and, when he saw the old woman's wretched animal near the pride of his stock, he was so infuriated that he ordered his attendant to dart an arrow into it. Then, when Jassas learned what had hap-

* *Black Tents of Arabia,* Creative Age Press, N. Y.

[61]

pened to his guest, he was so enraged that he killed Kulaib.

The blood feud which developed from this single episode grew into a war of forty years, during which single combats, melees, and full-scale battles raged over the pasture lands of Arabia. Like many a modern war, it did not settle anything, nor did it add to the stature of either tribe.

The Sa'uds in those days, and, in fact, until the eighteenth century, had not yet come into prominence. Farming settlements and nomadic tribes had minor leaders who would extend their sway, or lose it, according to their strength and those of their rivals. There were no giants. The Sa'uds, like others, were groping through the dark centuries which had followed the golden era of empire. Indeed, in their strife for a meager livelihood amid continual chaos, the Najdis, as a whole, evolved no orderly communal state before the days of the Sa'uds, although, in the fifth century of the Christian era, the tribe of Kinda formed a loose confederacy.* One of their Kings invaded Palestine in 496 A.D., and exacted "a great tribute" (according to the records) from the Roman Emperor of Byzantium as the price of withdrawal from the country.

A brief period of moderate success had come to the Sa'ud family about the end of the fifteenth century, when Rabi'ah ibn-Mani', direct ancestor of the Sa'ud line, was invited by his cousin, Ibn Dur', to give up his residence at Dur'iyah, near Qatif, and to settle in the neighborhood of al-Mulaibid and Ghasaibah, near Riyadh. Here, Rabi'ah and his children diligently commenced to plant crops where well water was obtainable; and, for generations, the family continued to increase its holdings and broaden its influence.

* The tribe of Kinda gave the Arabs of the Islamic era their greatest, and possibly the world's most philosophic, historian, Ibn Khaldun; the first scientist, Al-Kindi (830); and the greatest poet of the Jahilyah, or "Days of Ignorance," Imru'l Qais.

However, it was not until Muhammad ibn Sa'ud strode upon the scene to become the sword of Wahhabism that the family's ascendancy had its noteworthy beginnings. Imam Muhammad died in 1765, but he left an able son: Abdul Aziz, and he not only consolidated his father's gains, but continued the expansion. He became, in actuality, the real founder of the dynasty.

Abdul Aziz reigned for thirty-eight years, but, in 1803, he was assassinated while at prayer. His assassin, a man from Karbala, whose name has been forgotten, perpetrated his deed in reprisal for the destruction, two years before, of the monumental dome of Al-Hussein, the martyr of Karbala: an act performed in conformity with the teachings of the Wahhabi Purists.

But Imam Abdul Aziz had sired a son who was destined, in his brief reign, to be one of the truly distinguished Arab leaders: Sa'ud ibn Abdul Aziz, who is still known as Sa'ud the Great. Fifteen years before his father's death, he had been nominated as heir and Imam.

Sa'ud was the greatest warrior and the most tireless expansionist of the dynasty, from the beginning until the reign of the present King. In his day, the domain of the Sa'udis included all of the Hijaz, the Syrian desert to the environs of Damascus and Aleppo, a substantial portion of Iraq and Oman, and into Zubaid in Yemen.

It seemed as though Sa'ud the Great would soon liberate Syria and Iraq from the Turkish yoke; and, in fact, had it not been for the exaggerated rumors of the ferocity of the Wahabi Ikhwan,* the people of Syria and Iraq might have assisted in making the dream of a free Arabia a reality.

Of all the Sa'uds, he most resembled today's King Abdul Aziz: in generosity, in courage, and in strategy in war; but

* Literally, "the brothers."

[63]

he did not have the King's diplomacy and far-sightedness. So he was led into setting himself up against the Turks and Egyptians in an effort to stop their pilgrims from bringing into the Hijaz, practices which he considered to be religious innovations.

Sa'ud wrote to Salim III, the Turkish Sultan of Sultans, and Vicar of the Muslims, the following:

"From Sa'ud to Salim: I entered Mecca on the fourth of Muharram 1218 (1803) and have protected the inhabitants and their possessions after destroying what resembled idolatrous shrines, and abated all but the correct taxes. I have confirmed the judge appointed by you according to the Shar' (Koranic law). Now it is up to you to stop the Governors of Damascus and Cairo from coming to this Holy City accompanied with drums and fifes, as these have no place in the Faith. May the mercy of Allah and His blessings be upon you."

The Turks could not let this challenge go unanswered: In claiming the Khilafah, or Vicarship, they were content with the nominal rule and protection of the Holy Land; but they could not afford to lose face in the Muslim world by outright defiance of this leadership.

In 1805, the Governor of Syria, escorting the mahmal (the cover for the Ka'ba) toward Mecca, brought with him a substantial soldiery, determined to have a showdown with Sa'ud. The showdown came, but it was Sa'ud who emerged the victor. He beat the Syrian forces badly; and, in the following year (1806), expelled all Turks from Mecca, and defeated all Turkish troops sent against him by the Governors of Syria and Iraq.

Humiliated by the repeated setbacks, and unable to cope with the situation themselves, they asked their Governor of Egypt, Muhammad 'Ali, founder of the present dynasty, to discipline the Sa'uds (1811).

This assignment turned out to be easier given than consummated, even though Sa'ud, at sixty-five, had passed the age of military activity, and so had to leave the leadership of the armies to his son, Abdullah, who was later to succeed him as Amir and Imam. Abdullah was a man of excellent mind and kindly character, beloved by his people, but he lacked his father's military talents. Even so, he made the invaders pay heavily for the discipline which they had set out to impose.

The Egyptian army, commanded by Muhammad 'Ali's son, Prince Tussoun, was composed of eight thousand Albanians and Turks, and had a number of French and Italian officers who had been with the armies of Napoleon before transferring their services to Muhammad 'Ali. Landing at the Port of Yanbo' in the Hijaz, they began their march toward Medina.

Ordered by Sa'ud the Great to drive back the foe, Abdullah executed a surprise attack upon Tussoun's army in a narrow pass called al-Khaif. The battle failed to give either side a decisive victory.

Abdullah then retreated toward Medina, and arranged an ambush in the pass of Judaidah, where the Egyptian Army was allowed to advance far along the narrow defile before they were attacked. The result was a rout for Tussoun and his forces. He lost five thousand men and had to lead the rest back to Yanbo' in disorder.

It was here that Abdullah made his first strategic blunder. He had suffered only six hundred casualties, and had captured a great stock of booty, consisting of cannon, small arms, ammunition, money, and other spoils. But, in-

[65]

stead of pursuing the beaten and disorganized Egyptians, and thus completing their undoing, he let them go their way, and returned with his forces to Medina. Not being one to pass up such an opportunity, Muhammad 'Ali utilized it to re-equip his son's army.

Thereafter, the war continued for three years, with victories alternating between the two sides, and with each suffering heavy losses. During part of the time, Muhammad 'Ali personally led one of his armies into the mountains of Hijaz and Asir to no worthwhile result.

Finally, on May 2, 1814, Sa'ud the Great died. Shortly thereafter Abdullah made another mistake in strategy: he agreed to a truce with the Egyptians, after Tussoun's armies had reached the town of al-Rass, thirty-five miles southwest of 'Unaizah, and had taken it without a fight.

The Egyptians, who had suffered large casualties, thus were given time to replenish their strength and supplies. Prince Tussoun returned to Alexandria, and died there soon afterward. But, to lead the Egyptian armies, Muhammad 'Ali now selected his intrepid son, Ibrahim Pasha.

Well equipped with men, cannon, ammunition, and supplies, Ibrahim Pasha moved into Yanbo' in September, 1816. With abundant gold, he was able to buy the support of the three tribes of the Hijaz: Harb, Mutair, and 'Utaibah.

He then marched with his allies to Rass (February, 1817), but this town, which had surrendered to his brother without fighting, now resisted desperately. In his first attack, Ibrahim Pasha lost 800 men, and it was three and a half months before he could take the town, at a total cost of 3,400 men.

Here, Ibrahim Pasha first showed his ruthlessness: he killed all of the male inhabitants of Rass when they surrendered. Then he pushed on to Shaqra, and again met

[66]

fierce resistance. Again, after taking the town, he killed all of the male survivors.

From then forward, no city or town dared oppose him more than a few days until, in April, 1818, he reached and laid siege to Dur'iyah, the Sa'udi capital. Five months of savage warfare ensued, with repeated cannonading of the town, until finally the inhabitants begged Abdullah to spare them from further casualties.

He agreed, and surrendered himself and the town. But, if the people of Dur'iyah had expected to win mercy by surrender, they should have known better. Ibrahim Pasha destroyed Dur'iyah's buildings, homes, and places of worship. He cut down its palm trees and destroyed its water wells. He dealt out death wholesale.

Finally, in 1819, he went back to Egypt, taking with him Abdullah and his principal supporters, who were then moved to Istanbul, paraded through the streets, and beheaded in the city squares, Abdullah in the Square of St. Sophia.

Many historians believe that the culmination would have been different had Sa'ud the Great been in his prime during the campaign, for it is doubted that he would have made the strategic errors which the gallant but less skillful Abdullah committed.

For example, after agreeing to the unwise truce at al-Rass, Abdullah compounded his troubles by waging a frontal attack against the re-invigorated and re-equipped Egyptians. Such tactics were contrary to all Arab strategy from time immemorial: the Arab advantage had always been his mobility, his skill at sudden onslaught, strategic retreat, and renewed attack at the most propitious opportunity. This had been the strategy of Sa'ud the Great, who invariably kept the well-equipped Turko-Egyptians off balance by continual raids, harassing them with his mobile forces and thus permitting his allies, the heat and sands of the Arabian peninsula, to weaken the foe until he was sure of success.

This was the method of the Arabs in their war with the invading Roman Legion under Aelius Gallus. When the Arabs moved against a fortified city, they never tried to take it by assault; rather, they preferred to lay siege to it for a long time. During their two hundred-year struggle with the Knights of the Crusades, it was the Arabs' mobility, unhindered by heavy armor, which was their greatest asset.

But, whatever might have been, Abdullah was defeated, and Ibrahim Pasha inflicted untold calamity upon Najd, destroying the order and moral decency which had been established by the Wahhabis. The country reverted to the worst chaos that the Island of the Arabs had witnessed since the Jahilyah.

Abdullah's execution by the Turks brought to an end the direct line of Abdul Aziz, the son of Muhammad ibn Sa'ud, founder of the dynasty. However, fortunately for Arabia, another line was to come from the founder's second son, Abdullah ibn Muhammad. Abdullah ibn Muhammad's son, Turki, established the second branch of the Sa'ud family, and was the direct forbear of the present King.

Turki's son, Faisal, was the most adroit of King ibn Sa'ud's direct forbears. He had a distinguished and adventurous career, struggling against the Turks and the Egyptians in his effort to re-establish the Amirate of the Sa'uds. Indeed, the story of his life has in it much of the romance and heroism of his grandson, the King.

He had been taken prisoner at the capitulation of Dur'iyah to Ibrahim Pasha in 1818, and was taken to Egypt with the others, but he escaped to regain Najd, which he ruled from 1830 to 1839. He was then defeated in a new Egyptian invasion, and retaken to Egypt. Once more, he escaped, and returned to rule Najd from 1843 to 1865.*

But, in spite of Faisal's brilliant efforts, the decline had set in, and no hand was strong enough to stay it. After Faisal's death, his children began fighting over the succession, and eventually managed to lose Najd to their able agent, Muhammad ibnul-Rasheed of the Shammar tribe, who made his capital at Haiel, in the north of the province.

Abdul Ruhman, father of King Ibn Sa'ud, made some efforts to regain the family power and position, but he was unsuccessful, and ultimately became a refugee with his family in Kuwait, as guest of its Sheikh and ruler, Ibn Sabah.

The day of triumph was not yet at hand.

* Among those who held the chieftainship briefly were: Mushari ibn Sa'ud, 1818 to 1820; Khalid ibn Sa'ud ibn Abdul Aziz, 1839 to 1841; Abdullah ibn Thunian, 1841 to 1842; Abdullah ibn Faisal, 1865 to 1869; Sa'ud ibn Faisal, 1869 to 1874; and Abdullah ibn Faisal for a second term, 1874 to 1884.

CHAPTER NINE

Enter: Abdul Aziz ibn Sa'ud

Abdul Aziz, son of Abdul Ruhman, son of Faisal, son of Turki, son of Abdullah, son of Muhammad ibn Sa'ud, the founder of the dynasty, was born at Riyadh on December 2, 1880, or by the Muslim calendar, on the twenty-ninth day of Dhi-l-hijjah, 1297 A.H. (After the Hijra).

At that time, the fortunes of the Sa'uds were at their nadir, in consequence of the losses and havoc inflicted by the Egyptian and Turkish armies of Ibrahim Pasha, and, further, as a sequel to the quarrels of the children of Imam Faisal over the succession.

The father of Abdul Aziz, Imam Abdul Ruhman, was a man of peace, and did not take part in the family dissension; but, on the contrary, disclaimed any personal rights in an effort to unite his people. But, defeat and adversity had so loosened all ties that the Rasheeds of Shammar were able to take advantage of the disorganization of Najd to gain complete domination.

In 1890, at the age of ten, Abdul Aziz accompanied his father when the latter gathered some partisans and started to the assistance of the people of al-Qasim, the district of Middle Najd, situated between al-'Arid and Jebel Shammar, with 'Unaizah and Buraidah as its principal cities. These people were being attacked by Muhammad ibn Rasheed. At night, during the journey, the boy would be placed in a saddlebag arrangement, lest he fall asleep and be thrown from the camel's back.

The journey was never completed: before he could reach al-Qasim, the father learned of Ibn Rasheed's complete triumph; and he, therefore, returned to Riyadh, assembled his family and the remnants of the other Sa'uds, and migrated southward into the desert. He well knew that Ibn Rasheed would follow up his victory by marching against Riyadh, and that there was no power left to stop him.

In 1891, he sent Abdul Aziz to the Island of Bahrein to ask permission of its ruler, Sheikh Isa al-Khalifa, to send the women and children there for safety. This sanctuary was readily granted.

With the women and children thus safely sheltered, Abdul Ruhman assembled a small force with which he raided and occupied Riyadh. From there, he advanced to Huraimalah to do battle with Ibn Rasheed's main forces. He was badly defeated, and had to flee southward again.

Abdul Aziz was not present for this battle, because he had been lamed in an accident, and had been sent to Bahrein with his cousin, Abdullah ibn Jlewi. He rejoined his father in the southern desert after three weeks of convalescence.

In the same year, the youth was again commissioned to seek refuge for his family, this time at al-Hasa. But the Turks, who were then occupying the province, refused them asylum; so he traveled northward to Kuwait, also then dominated by the Turks. Sanctuary was once more refused. There was nothing left to do but return to the desert: mother of the Arabs.

It was during the following years that Abdul Aziz endured the hardships and acquired the experience and skills which were to serve him so well in the years of war that

[71]

lay ahead for him. Certainly he could have had no more rugged an existence than that which he lived along the fringe of the Empty Quarter, among the untamed banu Murrah, the most famous trackers among the Arabs. Abdul Aziz lived, hunted, and fought in their ranks. He lived, as well, with the 'Ujman tribes, famous for their valor.

This training in the midst of continuous hardship and danger gave him a never-forgotten aptitude in the art of desert warfare, and in the reading of the signs and mysteries of the sandy seas. It matured him far beyond his years.

In 1895, with the desire to provide a counter-balance for Ibn Rasheed in Najd, the Turkish Government invited Abdul Ruhman to make his home in Kuwait, and allotted him sixty pounds a month to maintain himself and his family. Here they lived in a three-room house, but the sixty pounds monthly could hardly feed so many mouths, even if it had been paid regularly, which it wasn't. And there was no other source at hand. In fact, so lean was their situation that, when Abdul Aziz reached manhood and his father brought him a highborn bride from the desert, the ceremony had to be delayed for forty days until a friend, Yusuf al-Ibrahim, came to their financial assistance, and the wedding was consummated.

The nobles of the Bedu, as well as those who are settled and keep their tribal affiliations, do not marry or permit their daughters to marry except to those of equal lineage regardless of their wealth or position. They look down upon the families of craftsmen, regardless of their standing. Right through the medieval period and up to the present day, many instances have been recounted where tribal women have refused to be wed to nobles or rich officials whose maternal lineage was unknown, valuing pedigree, according to their own standard, above any other consideration.

[72]

A poor Bedouin is quite content to be a camel driver for a pittance, but he refuses to be employed as a workman at a better salary. A pearl diver in the Gulf never works for wages; rather, he gambles for a share.

Sheikh Hafis Wahba, Sa'udi Ambassador to the Court of St. James and author of *The Island of the Arabs in the Twentieth Century,* recounts a story told to him by the late Sayed Rajab an-Naqib: how, during his sojourn in Baghdad, he requested one of his intimates to find him a wife from among the noble families of the city. Whenever this friend mentioned the well-known houses such as Bashajji, Jadirji, and others, the Sayed would always refuse and say: "I wish to marry into a noble family."

The friend continued his search to no avail. At last he was out of patience and said: "I have proposed to you the best families of Baghdad and you have not been pleased."

The Sayed repeated: "I wish to marry into a noble family and you have only mentioned the names that denote craftsmanship, while I seek lineage."

"Ah," said the friend, "had I divined your wish I could have brought you every day the names of twenty uncouth Bedouins, instead I have offered you families of culture and position. Now I wash my hands of the matter. Go and seek for yourself in the desert."

But, to return to our narrative . . . It was in 1900 that the Turks began encouraging Ibnul-Rasheed in his ambition to control Kuwait as an outlet and port of entry for Najd. Directly opposite ideas were being harbored by Kuwait's ruler, Sheikh Mubarak as-Sabah: he wanted to be ruler of Najd.

Mubarak exerted an early and lasting influence upon Abdul Aziz. Concerning those early years, the writer was fortunate in meeting, at the King's court, one of the ruler's old friends, who had been a playmate of Kuwait days, a fellow student, and a companion in his first campaign in 1901: Abdul-Latif ibn Abdul Majid. He was purser of Abdul Aziz's first campaign, and later was for twenty years collector of customs in Kuwait.

The details of Abdul Aziz's youth, as given to me during those visits with his boyhood companion, formed a picture of the king-to-be as a serious minded boy with a *set purpose;* and, as the tale unfolded, he became, for the writer, the man with a firm objective.

"In build," the King's old-time friend related, "Abdul Aziz was overgrown but sinewy; agile and alert. His desert life fitted him so that none of our town group could compete with him. Therefore, he was conceded the leadership; in fact, he assumed it as a natural right.

"He was not fond of school or book-learning, but in the knowledge of horses, camels, arms, and war games, he excelled all others.

"His cousins, the Jlewis and Ibn Nasir, although some were older in years, deferred to him, except 'Abdullah ibn Jlewi, to whom he respectfully listened, and from whose hand he occasionally felt the stick, but never resented it, for between these two there existed a deep affection and understanding.

"I, myself," continued the friend, "am older than Abdul Aziz, and my impressions are unforgettable. As a youth, he had a great sense of humor, and quickly responded to what was funny. Today, he retains this, and often in his moments of ease, he bedevils his companions in the Majlis (court). As a matter of fact, he never misses an occasion to embarrass some over-serious and stolid counsellor."

Ibn Abdul Majid recalled how, from his school days onward, Abdul Aziz attended the Majlis of Mubarak. He

[74]

continued: "The old Sheikh was exceedingly pleased with the serious and alert youth, so that, whenever he absented himself, Mubarak, the old fox, missed him, and asked: 'Why is my son not here?'

"You must have heard, my friend, that Mubarak was the cleverest and trickiest diplomat among the Arabs during his lifetime. He was as sharp as the edge of a sword, and uncanny in divining things and evaluating men. He saw great promise in his young warrior protege, and subsequent events justified his intuition.

"Mubarak was the petty chieftain of an insignificant domain, yet he played with the Turk, German, Englishman, and Russian so as to make his little sphere of great importance. Finally, when the Turks determined to get rid of him, he called the English to establish a protectorate over Kuwait, thereby assuring himself of absolute stability, and serving the English to thwart the ambition of the Germans, who desired it for the terminus of their projected Berlin-to-Persian-Gulf railway.

"I personally feel that the silent, observant, and respectful Abdul Aziz acquired more wisdom and statecraft by attending his 'father,' Mubarak, than he could have gained in any other school of diplomacy. But he has never for a single moment lent himself to the tricky ways of Mubarak, nor has he ever in his long career broken faith with a single soul."

This, then, was the Mubarak who stood in the path of Ibnul Rasheed's covetousness of Kuwait; who yearned, instead, to usurp power in Najd. As a first step, he commenced to organize a force to invade Haiel, the Rasheed capital; and he induced Abdul Ruhman to join him, knowing that the latter's call would bring prompt response from the tribes of the south: the Mutair, Murrah, and 'Ujman.

[75]

From the north, Abu-'Ujaymi as-Sa'doun joined Mubarak, and brought the tribes of the Muntafiq.

Thus, when Mubarak marched toward Najd, with the secret receptiveness of the people of al-Qasim, he had ten thousand men with him, including the "Young Man With a Purpose," who was eager for action. Along the way, Abdul Aziz begged to be permitted to invade Riyadh, the Sa'ud family capital.

Approval was granted, and the twenty-year-old warrior led a thousand Bedouins over the desert for the gamble. They won the city, but the Governor and his soldiers established themselves in the citadel, which, ironically, had been built by Imam Abdullah. For four months, the attackers continued their siege, but they had neither the men nor the equipment to force capitulation.

Meanwhile, Mubarak and his army advanced toward the Qasim, while Ibn Rasheed, with his smaller force, retreated until they arrived at a place called as-Sarif, fifteen miles north of Buraidah.

It was February 16, 1901, when Ibn Rasheed attacked, and the results were devastating. He overwhelmed the allies, shattered their ranks, and sent Mubarak in flight, leaving his brother and his son among the killed. In all its history, the Kuwait had never suffered such a disaster; in fact, it is said that almost every home in the sheikhdom was left in mourning, for the ferocity of Ibn Mu'tib (Abdul Aziz ar-Rasheed) led him to kill both the wounded and the prisoners.

When the news reached Abdul Aziz, he knew that Ar-Rasheed would now drive south to relieve the garrison, so he wisely decided to withdraw from Riyadh, dismiss most of his Bedouins, and return to Kuwait in the hope that fortune might grant him another chance.

In 1902, he decided the time had come to try once more. Unmindful of the intense summer heat, he left Kuwait with two hundred silver riyals, thirty camels, and forty men, including his brother, Muhammad; his cousins, Abdul Aziz, Fahd, and 'Abdullah, sons of Jlewi, and Nasir ibn Sa'ud; and their retainers.

Their first objective was southern Najd, where the family had many followers among the Bedu and town dwellers; and their plan was to harass the followers of Ibn Rasheed and, if possible, to recapture ar-Riyadh.

As they traveled, they gathered volunteers among the Bedouins, who were inspired more by the love of plunder than by fealty; and, ultimately, their numbers had grown until they had an army of a thousand, and a cavalry of four hundred. They raided the Rasheed partisans wherever they found them.

This procedure annoyed Ibn Rasheed, and he complained to his allies, the Turks, about the vexations of this puny enemy. Thereupon, the Turks ordered their Governor of al-Hasa not to permit Abdul Aziz and his followers to replenish their provisions in his domain. Ibn Rasheed, on his own part, ordered the Governor of Qatar to take the field.

Thus blocked from provisions, and facing the coming of winter, the Bedu gathered up the loot which they had collected, and dispersed to their tribal pastures in time for the planting and grazing season.

Ibn Sa'ud was left with his original forty companions, but his determination to do or die was unaltered.

The King has described those discouraging days in his own words, which were taken down by His Excellency, Sheikh Fuad Hamzah:

"Our provisions were meager," he related, "and we were

poorly armed. I had been advised by my father and Ibn Sabah (Mubarak) to return to Kuwait and save ourselves lest we perish. But we were determined to succeed, with the help of Allah, or perish if it were so ordained.

"Fearing that the spies of Ibn Rasheed might carry the news of our whereabouts, we traveled into the Empty Quarter, where we spent the whole month of Sha'ban and until the twentieth of Ramadhan.*

"Suffering from poverty and ill-nourishment, with very poor mounts and arms not of the best, we wended our way northward without being discovered until we neared ar-Riyadh, hoping that luck would continue to favor us and allow us to take the citadel by surprise. Of course, we knew that the Sa'udi capital and its environs harbored many of our partisans and well-wishers.

"Ibn Rasheed had torn down the walls protecting the city, and placed his governor, 'Ajlan, in the Mismack, the fort built by Imam Abdullah. Since our previous raid of Riyadh, the garrison had become wary, and at night 'Ajlan would enter the citadel and close its massive gate as a precaution against surprise. After sunrise, he and his guards would go back to their families in the town and neighborhood.

"When we were within two hours' walk of the city, we left the few men who had joined us in that section, and started at midnight with the forty original companions toward the city, with whose inhabitants we had no contact or understanding, not knowing what might be our kismet (fate).

* The Muslim calendar is based upon a year of twelve lunar months: Muharram, Safar, Rabi' al Awwal, Rab' ath Thani, Jumada al Akhirah, Rajab, Sha'ban, Ramadhan, Shawwal, Dhul Qa'dah, and Dhi-l-hijjah. Since a lunar month, or the time between successive new moons, is about 29½ days, the basic year is 354 days. An additional day is therefore added eleven times during each thirty-year cycle.

[78]

"Arriving at the gardens of Shamsiyah, at the edge of the town, I left my brother with thirty-three of our men, while seven of us proceeded: myself, my three cousins, Jlewis, Nasir ibn Sa'ud, and our two servants, Ma'Shouq and Sab'an.

"Near the citadel lived a gray-haired man named Jwayser (still living when Abdul Aziz recounted the tale), who traded in cattle. I also knew that a certain Ibn Mutriff was in the service of the guard in the citadel. Proceeding to the home of Jwayser, I knocked at his gate. A daughter came forth and asked from behind the bolted gate: 'Who are you?'

" 'I am Ibn Mutriff. Amir 'Ajlan sent me to buy two cows from your father and I wish to see him.'

" 'May you be reviled, O son of cursed woman! Does anyone who knocks at the door of a woman at night seek but impiety? Away and be gone!'

" 'I shall inform the Amir in the morning, and he will slay your father.'

"When the father heard this, he came out, terrified, and opened the gate. I then seized him and said: 'Silence, O cunning one!'

"The woman then recognized me, saying: 'Ammana—Ammana,' meaning 'our uncle—our uncle' [used here to signify "master"], for the girls had known me from the previous raid of Riyadh.

" 'Hush, hush!' I said.

"We entered the yard and locked the women within the house, while the father, unbeknown to us, sneaked into the groves beyond the city and hid himself.

"From this house, we found it impossible to reach directly the home occupied by 'Ajlan and his wife, where he was in the habit of coming to breakfast with her, and

[79]

sometimes sleeping there. We found ourselves separated by another house, so we jumped from the house of Jwayser to the next, and found the owner and his wife asleep.

"We rolled them in their bedding and locked them in a room, threatening them with death if they made the least noise or uttered a word. At this juncture, we sent Abdul Aziz and Fahd, sons of Jlewi, who brought my brother, Muhammad, and his Khwayah (sworn brothers) from outside the city.

"After resting awhile, and assuring ourselves that our affairs had not been discovered, we left my brother Muhammad and his Khwayah in the house, and, mounting on each other's shoulders, we reached the house of 'Ajlan and dropped into the interior.

"As we had a candle, we searched from room to room until we reached 'Ajlan's chamber, gathering the servants together and locking them in a room. At 'Ajlan's door, we posted five of our number, and, with one carrying the candle, I entered the chamber.

"I had a cartridge in the magazine of my gun, and, when I found the bed, I lifted the coverlet. To my great disappointment, I found that the bed contained 'Ajlan's wife and her sister, asleep together. I then took out the cartridge and poked the wife with the gun. Sitting upright and seeing me, she cried out: 'Who are you?'

" 'Hush, I am Abdul Aziz!'

"She knew me immediately, for her father and uncle had been in our service.

" 'What do you wish?'

" 'I am looking for your man, O wanton woman who married into Shammar.'

" 'I am not wanton; I did not marry into Shammar until you ignored me. Why are you here?'

[80]

" 'I am looking for your man to kill him.'

" 'I do not wish you to kill my husband. As to Ibn Rasheed and Shammar, you may kill them for all I care. But how could you overpower my husband while he is in the citadel with eighty men? Should he find you, I fear that you and your men could never save yourselves and leave the country.'

" "When does your husband come out of the citadel?'

" 'He does not come out until the sun rises three lances in the sky.'

"We thereupon locked the women with the servants and opened a passage in the wall between us and the house where my brother, Muhammad, was; and joined forces.

"This was about half past three in the morning, and dawn would break at five o'clock, so we sipped our coffee, partook of the dates we had, and slept a short while. Refreshed, we prayed, and commenced to plan our course of action. We inquired of the women: 'Who opens the house door for 'Ajlan when he comes in the morning?'

" 'This one,' they said.

"So, we chose a man of her height and dressed him in her garments, posting him near the gate that he might open the door for 'Ajlan when he knocked. Then we mounted to a room on the next floor, which had a small window overlooking the gate of the citadel (about two hundred feet away).

"After sunrise, the Fatha, a small door within the gate, three feet above the ground, was opened, and the servants, as was their custom, started for their homes, for, since our previous invasion of Riyadh, they had become cautious.

"Then the larger gate of the citadel was opened, and the grooms brought out the horses and tethered them in the spacious front. Seeing this, we descended, intending to rush

[81]

through and enter the citadel. We had posted four of our number with guns in the upper room and instructed them, should they see us run toward the gate, to fire on those near it.

" 'Ajlan was standing by the horses, and, when he and his companions saw us, the retinue fled into the citadel, while he stood alone.

"I had no side arms but the gun, and 'Ajlan had his sword pointed in my direction, and to face the sword is not pleasant.*

"I raised my left hand before my face, rushed at 'Ajlan, and the gun went off. I heard the sword clatter to the ground. It seemed that the bullet hit 'Ajlan, but did not cripple him, and he headed for the Fatha, or vent in the door.

"By then, the garrison were firing from all vantage points, and shots and rocks rained down upon us. My cousin, Abdullah ibn Jlewi, racing toward the gate oblivious of the bullets, sped his javelin at 'Ajlan, who was entering the vent, and missed him by four inches. The head of the spear was embedded in the solid door, where it broke and is still to be seen.

"I caught 'Ajlan by the feet as he drew himself through the vent, but he held onto the inside with his hands and kicked me in the side. I must have fainted from the blow and let go of his feet. I wished to follow him, but the Khwayah prevented me from doing so.

"However, none could stop Abdullah ibn Jlewi from following, catching up with 'Ajlan, and killing him. The rest of the ten [with Abdul Aziz] entered and opened the gate wide, while [the rest of] our men followed.

"We killed forty in the fight, plus four who were thrown

* A Najdi without a sword considers himself unarmed.

[82]

over the parapets, and the rest were taken prisoner. Two
of our companions were killed and four wounded.

"The affair took but a short time. The hardest struggle
was in a hall on the second floor; and the blood, seeping
through the thick flooring, is still visible on the ceiling of
the hall below."

In a short time the criers were out in the city, announcing to the people: " 'Ajlan is killed, and the rule belongs to
Allah first and to Abdul Aziz ibn Sa'ud next."

The victorious young leader immediately sent Nasir ibn
Sa'ud to carry the news to his father and Ibn Sabah in
Kuwait. The father, delighted, sent him a hundred soldiers
and ammunition under the leadership of Sa'd ibn Abdul
Ruhman; and a thousand volunteers poured in from the
district.

This was January 15, 1902. *This* was the real start of
the climb of Abdul Aziz to supremacy in Arabia: the start
of a climb that was to require thirty-two years.

CHAPTER TEN

The Rasheeds:
Battle of Giants

Southeast of the Great Nufud and west of the Dahna Ribbons in northern Najd lies Jebel Shammar. The "Jebel" is undoubtedly a Bedu corruption of "Jibal" (mountains), for the name is now applied to the basin and plains situated between the Aja and Salma mountain ranges, and inhabited by the agrarians of the Shammar tribe.

The district has an elevation of more than 2,000 feet, with its capital city of Haiel standing at 2,800 feet, while some of the granite peaks of its mountains reach an altitude of nearly a mile. Its climate is dry: cold at night and temperate in the daytime.

Throughout the small valley, springs of water are plentiful. In the flat, broad plains, water is tapped at thirty to seventy-five feet, and is drawn from the wells by the ancient method of skin buckets and camel power. In summer, camels and buckets are kept busy, for irrigation during that season is urgently needed.

Date palms thrive and are extensively cultivated, forming, as in the province of al-Hasa, the most important product. Grown also are grapes, figs, pomegranates, apples, pears, plums, and citrus fruits, along with wheat and some rice. Yet, the district does not produce enough for its own consumption.

Haiel is strategically located on the Hajj * Road from

* Pilgrimage.

[84]

Iraq and Kuwait to Medina and Mecca, being 280 miles northeast of Medina and 355 miles northwest of Riyadh.

Here in this valley, the tribe of Shammar established itself, reaching the height of its power in those days at the turn of the century when the youthful Abdul Aziz ibn Sa'ud was serving his apprenticeship in the desert struggle. They were one of the great tribes, rivals of the 'Anaza, with whom they were continually engaged in the universal sport of ghazu. For the ruhhal, it was ever thus: "If you have not, go and get it; if you have it, try to keep it, or it will be gone tomorrow; for life is a game of give and take, and nothing is permanent or certain but death."

The game was an open one: "Laba'as, ye akha al Arab" (Never mind, O brother of the Arabs). One day for you; the next against you.

Although the nineteenth century was to end with the Sa'uds and the Rasheeds in virtually continuous battle, it had started with the two families on the warmest terms.

At that time, Sheikh Ali ar-Rasheed, the chief of Shammar and Amir of Haiel, had two sons, 'Abdullah and 'Ubaid. While Imam Turki al-Sa'ud and his son, Faisal, were fighting to oust the Turks and Egyptians from Najd, many of the Shammar and Mutair, two of the strongest tribes, were assisting the Turks to fight the Imam and Faisal.

But, 'Abdullah, the elder son of Sheikh Ali ar-Rasheed, went over to the Imam, who had begun to build Riyadh as his capital, and joined him. Thus a fast friendship was established between the two families.

'Ubaid, the second son, was a devout Wahabi, and gave himself to the spread of the Reform among the people of northern Najd.

When Imam Turki was assassinated, in 1930, by Mushari al-Sa'ud, who coveted the leadership, it was 'Abdullah ibn Rasheed who attacked the fort, scaled the tower with his men, and killed Mushari, thus avenging his friend, the Imam.

The grateful Imam Faisal promptly appointed 'Abdullah as Amir of Haiel. He ruled for twelve years, dying in 1847-48,* leaving three sons.

Tallal succeeded his father, and ruled wisely. He encouraged trades and crafts, and, in general, endeavored to improve the condition of the people. In 1853, he added Wadi Sirhan and the oasis of Jauf to his domain; and forced the Turks out of Khaybar and Tayma. He also built, of stone masonry, the magnificent "Barzan" palace, the loveliest edifice in all Najd.

After a rule of nineteen years, he died in 1866 from the effect of a wound received in war. Rumor had it that the wound was suicidal, although this is a rare act among the Arabs, especially those who enjoy life in the open. He left six sons: Bandar, Badr, Mussallit, Nahar, Abdullah, and Naief, none of whom died a natural death.

Mut'ib ibn Abdullah, brother of Tallal, succeeded him, but shortly thereafter, in 1868, he was assassinated in front of the palace by Tallal's sons, one of whom, Bandar, usurped his place. This marked the beginning of an unholy orgy of murder in the Rasheed family: Bandar, himself, was to be the next victim, in 1871.

His uncle, Muhammad ibn Abdullah, had been commissioned by the Turkish Government as Amir al-Hajj, to act as guide and guarantor of the safety of the Muslim pilgrims on their journey from Baghdad to Medina, thence to Mecca, and back. These included Persians, Afghans, Kurds, Caucasians, Tartars, Turks, Syrians, and others.

* Because the Muslim calendar is based upon lunar months, there is sometimes an overlap in comparison with years of the Gregorian calendar.

In 1871, while returning from Iraq, after safely escorting the pilgrims, he brought with him to Haiel some men of the Zafir tribe, whose entry had been forbidden by Bandar. Learning of this, Bandar rode outside the city walls to reprimand his uncle for defying his wishes. In the ensuing argument, the uncle struck Bandar from his horse and killed him; then killed two of his brothers, Badr and Mussallit.

During the next two years, Muhammad, the uncle, also disposed of the three remaining nephews: Nahar, Abdullah, and Naief. The last was killed by an arrow, darted by an unidentified hand, during a tournament, in the uncle's presence.

Whatever may be said of his manner of achieving power, there is no doubt that Muhammad ibn Abdullah brought the prestige of the Rasheeds to a new zenith, extending their rule far over Najd, including al-'Aridh, the home domain of the Sa'uds.

Energetic, able, and progressive, he made his rule effective from Tudmor (Palmyra), sixty miles northeast of Damascus, including Hauran; from Tayma and Khaybar in the west to the approaches to the Persian Gulf in the east; and Wadi ad-Dwaser in the south.

He was greatly helped, of course, by the dissension among the sons of Faisal in their fight over the succession, but this does not detract from his accomplishments.

The only noteworthy effort by the Sa'uds to stop him was that made by Imam Abdul Ruhman, the father of King Abdul Aziz, when, in 1890, he rallied the people of al-Qasim, 'Unaiza, and Buraidah, to fight the Battle of Milaidah.

However, before reaching the battleground, he learned of the crushing defeat suffered by his allies of 'Unaiza and

Buraidah, who lost 3,500 killed, while the forces of Ar-Rasheed lost 400.

After a rule of twenty-six years, Muhammad ibn Abdullah died childless in 1897, and there came into the succession the most spectacular fighting man whom the Rasheeds had yet produced: Muhammad's nephew, Abdul Aziz ibn Mut'ib, son of Muhammad's murdered brother, Mut'ib ibn Abdullah. It was this battle-loving Rasheed who was to fight against the other Abdul Aziz—Ibn Sa'ud—for the lordship of Arabia. These of the same given name were to stage the Battle of the Giants.

In pre-Islamic days, Arabia produced some phenomenal warriors, whose skill and courage matched those of the legendary heroes of Greece. Such were 'Omar ibnul-Tafil, Antarah al-'Absi, 'Amru ibn Ma'dy Karab; and, in the days of Islam, Khalid ibnul-Walid. Of their timber were built these two modern antagonists.

Abdul Aziz ibn Mut'ib was a rare specimen of physical manhood: of medium height, he possessed terrific strength, great agility and skill, and a heart which knew no fear.

Many a story is told of his contemptuousness of pain and danger. One of them has it that he was engaged in a council of war when he felt a severe sting between his shoulder blades. Disdaining to show concern, he awaited the dispersal of his councillors; then went into his tent and ordered his slave to pull down his garment.

The slave was terrified to find a large scorpion, and uttered a yell. Abdul Aziz reached with his own hand, took hold of the scorpion, and threw it out of the tent; then, as though nothing had happened, ordered the slave to bring hot ashes and place them over the stings.

A well-known Amir told the writer of another episode, which occurred during a dinner. One of Abdul Aziz's men

[88]

entered and whispered to his master, who thereupon excused himself, requesting his guests to continue with their meal.

He left the tent, and returned in four hours, driving thirty zaluls ahead of him. These mounts represented thirty raiders who had been harassing his people, the inference being that he had sallied forth, disregarding numbers, and overcome the thirty, single-handed.

For all of this, his bravery had a streak of madness in it, as will be shown, in striking contrast with that other Abdul Aziz, with whom he was to wage a life-and-death struggle.

Abdul Aziz ibn Sa'ud, the Man with a Purpose, had proven his bravery and prowess in many a battle. Like his antagonist, he was oblivious to pain and fatigue, unmindful of defeat, and undistracted by anything that could swerve him from pursuit of his goal: restoration of the position of the Sa'uds.

Never did he stoop to the cruel retaliation of his foe, but won the admiration, friendship, and love of the Najdis by his mercy, forgiveness, and generosity to his foes in victory. His eyes were not on the moment, alone; he took the farsighted view, with a perceptive estimate of cause and effect.

From that day, January 2, 1901, when Abdul Aziz al Sa'ud recaptured Riyadh, he and his adversary, Ar-Rasheed, were in continued action: raids and battles, strategic moves and counter moves, victories and reverses for both, and always a return to the fight. The ruhhal changed fealty often, and were cajoled or coerced to take sides. Some tribes were divided in their allegiance, although, by 1904, Ibn Sa'ud had been able to consolidate the south, and had made inroads in the middle section: the Qasim.

[89]

It was in 1904 that the Turks sent eleven regiments, with high-ranking officers and fourteen cannon, to assist Ar-Rasheed; and it was in this same year that the twin battles of Bakriyah and Shananah had a decisive effect upon the fortunes of the two warring factions. They heralded the termination of Turkish suzerainty and influence in Arabia Deserta.

The twin battles were actually one continuous action, beginning with the Battle of Bakriyah, followed by a series of lesser engagements over a three-month period, and ending with the Battle of Shananah. The Arabs call the entire protracted struggle the Battle of Wadi-Irrumah, after the valley in which it was fought.

Wadi-Irrumah is the longest valley in Najd, stretching from the Harrah (volcanic oasis) of Khaybar eastward to al-Rass, then northerly to Basra. The valley runs through al-Qasim between 'Unaiza and Buraidah, dividing this fertile area of Najd into northwesterly and southeasterly sections. Bakriyah lies between al-Rass and Buraidah, and Shananah is an hour's travel south of al-Rass.

Here it was that Ibn Sa'ud and his partisans, including the people of Qasim, pitted their strength, their wits, and their staying power against Abdul Aziz ar-Rasheed and his partisans, supported by the eleven Turkish regiments.

The Battle of Bakriyah was fought at eventide at close quarters. It ended indecisively, with Ibn Sa'ud losing nine hundred killed, including 650 from Riyadh and its environs. The Turkish regulars lost one thousand, among whom were four high-ranking officers; and the deaths among the people of Haiel numbered three hundred, including two of the Rasheeds.

Ibn Sa'ud was wounded by shrapnel, and Ibn Rasheed

fell under his mare during the battle, suffering severe injury, but this did not stop him from resuming the fight.

During this action, some of Ibn Sa'ud's forces from al-Qasim and Muttair, led by Abdul Aziz ibn Jlewi, raided the Shammar wing and scattered them, winning their spoils. Meanwhile, the Shammar horsemen broke over the opposite wing of Ibn Sa'ud and won *his* spoils.

After the battle, as Ibn Jlewi was returning to his base, he and his men encountered three hundred of the Turkish regulars with their cannon; attacked and destroyed them, and gained their arms and ammunition—except the cannon: Not knowing what to do with these weapons, they left them on the battlefield.

After this bloody engagement had ended in something of a draw, the hostilities continued in different sectors of the fifty-mile valley for three months, wearing down both armies physically and taxing their strategy and maneuverability.

The decision finally came at the Battle of Shananah on September 29, 1904, at which Ar-Rasheed and his allies were utterly routed. The booty taken from the Turks, when distributed among the warriors of Ibn Sa'ud, amounted to 150 gold sovereigns and twenty camels per man. It was the custom of Ibn Sa'ud never to accept anything for himself or his relatives, but to divide all spoils among his soldiers.

In 1905, a few months after the Battle of Bakriyah, Abdul Aziz ar-Rasheed camped near Buraidah in the "Meadows of Mhanna," a grassy depression where camels and sheep were pastured, and where the poor of the district came to mow and glean grass for sale in the village, thereby earning a meager mouthful.

Ar-Rasheed, by this time, had begun to realize that his
[91]

grip was being loosened by his losses in men, allies, and materials; that he had been repeatedly outwitted, and was gradually being defeated, by one whom he had considered an upstart. All of these considerations made him morose. He developed an uncontrollable temper.

One day, there in the Meadows of Mhanna, he found about forty old men of the poor, accompanied by small children, the oldest about ten. These people, as was their custom, were peacefully and harmlessly gathering grass for sale. But, were these not of the Qasim district? And, had not the Qasim gone over to Ibn Sa'ud?

Ar-Rasheed ordered his men to round up the gleaners, and to place them in a row at equi-distance. Then, as they stood there bewildered, holding their jute bags and their sickles, the tyrant strode down the line and, laughing in stark madness, beheaded them, one after another.

One gray-haired elder, who realized his fate, held the hand of his grandchild and looked up at Ibn Mut'ib, pleading: "O, Amir, do with me as you wish, but please spare this child, for he will remain the only support of our women."

The answer was a stroke of the sword, and the child fell at the feet of the grandfather.

The news of this barbarity spread swiftly throughout desert and town, and many men of Shammar, Ibn Mut'ib's own tribe, left him and went over to Ibn Sa'ud, for this was not the act of an Arab nor a Muslim.

"Kill not a child, a woman, or an old man," the Muslim warriors had been admonished twelve centuries earlier by Abu-Bakr, successor of the Prophet. So, the massacre of the gleaners of Mhanna re-echoed through the land, and it is said that the murderer never enjoyed restful sleep for a full

[92]

year, until fate, or the avenging angel, led him back to the very spot where he had enacted his crime.

It was in the spring of 1906, while Ibn Sa'ud was seeking his enemy, when he learned that Ar-Rasheed had again reached the Meadows of Mhanna. Since it was late on a stormy afternoon with heavy rain, during which Arabs (like other people) do not like either to travel or fight, Ibn Sa'ud ordered his army to advance on foot in order to surprise the enemy.

But some of the Rasheeds learned of the advance. Ar-Rasheed decided not to attempt to move out into the stormy night, but, rather, to place his men in the most advantageous positions possible for meeting the assault.

Soon, the Sa'uds moved in to the attack, and some of the Rasheeds were driven back. Their leader, on horseback, moved from place to place, directing and encouraging his followers, and engaging whomever he encountered.

His standard bearer, Al-Fraikh, one of Shammar's best warriors, had set up a defense position with a small group, but the onrush of the Sa'uds had forced them to evacuate; and the position was taken over by a detachment of the attackers, led by Ibn Mutriff, standard bearer of Ibn Sa'ud.

Ar-Rasheed did not know of this change. Making his rounds in the darkness of the driving storm, he galloped toward Ibn Mutriff's standard, thinking it was his own. He called: "Minhan, yal Fraikh!" ("From here, O Fraikh!") "Yal Fraikh!"

The Sa'udi group recognized the voice, and among them the eager whisper passed: "Ibnul Rasheed! . . . Ibnul Rasheed! . . . Ibnul Rasheed! . . ."

Then their guns spoke. The wandering Amir fell from his mount with twenty bullets in his body. They

[93]

brought his head, with his sword and his signet ring to Ibn Sa'ud, who said soberly: "The innocents of the Meadows of Mhanna are avenged, for Allah never sleeps, and has his ways."

The Battle of the Giants was over. Abdul Aziz al Sa'ud was on his way. The date: April 14, 1906.

CHAPTER ELEVEN

Of Wars, Women, and Treachery

For the next half-dozen years, Ibn Sa'ud was given little worry by the Rasheeds; they were too busy quarreling among themselves, and killing each other.

Nevertheless, there was a battle now and then; and sometimes added color and drama was provided by the introduction of that opera-like institution which may well be called the cult of the Lady of Victory.

A classic example of this is "The Day of Jerab," January 24, 1915, as related by an eye witness to my late good friend, Ameen Rihani. The episode is given added color by the presence of a young British officer, Capt. W. H. C. Shakespeare, who had been sent to Arabia by his Government during World War I to counter the Turks in their efforts to woo Ibn Sa'ud.

He had met Ibn Sa'ud at 'Uqair with Sir Percy Cox, when the latter persuaded Abdul Aziz to conclude a treaty of friendship. This, of course, gave Ibn Sa'ud nothing except empty recognition, with all the advantages going to the English. Nevertheless, Abdul Aziz adhered to the spirit of the treaty, in spite of many contrary machinations by the party of the other part.

Captain Shakespeare had returned to Ibn Sa'ud as the latter prepared to move into action against the Rasheeds, although, as Ameen Rihani relates the episode, Ibn Sa'ud did not want the Captain to take the needless risks of battle.

"It is my advice," Abdul Aziz told him, "that you await us in Zalfa, where we will meet you on our return, Allah willing."

Shakespeare replied: "It must not be said that an Englishman neared the battlefield and returned from fear or cowardice."

The more Abdul Aziz counseled the gallant Englishman to refrain from joining the expected battle, the more he insisted, until, at last, Ibn Sa'ud consented.

This young officer was a true Englishman, holding fast to the customs and traditions of his people wherever he happened to be, "and I believe," Rihani wrote, "he was the only European who ever traveled in Arabia wearing a hat instead of the native head-dress; and the only change he affected in his appearance was to wear a mashlah over his European garments.

"But, the hat!" And the writer can see the amazement on Ameen's face, and hear him chuckle. "But, the hat."

He rode with the men of Ibn Sa'ud, wearing his hat and carrying his camera case, there amidst the Ikhwan who were proudly repeating their battle cry:

"Ahl al-'Auja, wat-tawhid!"
("We of 'Auja, people of unity!")

Shammar had brought forward its 'Amariyat: open hawdage frames, decorated with ostrich feathers in all colors, carried atop caparisoned camels, where stood one or more of their beautiful virgins, faces unveiled and hair unbraided, to encourage the fighters while they sang the famous Shammar cry:

"Senna 'eess—Senna 'eess,*
Senna 'eess—Senna 'eess."

This was a challenge to the enemy, and yet more so
to their own men of Shammar, for no warrior would value
his life and permit the capture of these maidens. And, so
the two armies met in battle, and nothing could be heard
from the Shammar side but the cry:

"Senna 'eess, senna 'eess."

The Sa'uds were also encouraging one another:

"The winds of paradise are blowing;
Who are ye who al-Janat seek?"

To be answered by the Shammar maidens:

"Senna 'eess, senna 'eess!"

Thanks to the Turks and the British, this engagement
was marked by the plentiful use of bullets † by the Arab
adversaries. Bullets sang past and fell near the 'Amariyat,
but the maidens paid no heed to them, and kept on sing-
ing, and the Shammar crowded around them and forged
ahead of them.

The 'Ujman cavalry of Ibn Sa'ud bolted and left the
field, a bullet killed the wearer of the hat, and the Bedu of
Ar-Rasheed attacked the left wing of the Sa'uds, looted
its possessions, and scattered with the booty; while, on the

* This is an expression meaning "indomitable" or "unconquerable."
† It was during the siege of Algeciras by the Spaniards, in 1344, that some
Englishmen, among them the Earl of Derby, first learned from the Arabs the
use of gunpowder, of which they first took advantage and used at the Battle of
Crecy. The development of this agency by the Europeans eventually gave them
mastery of Africa and Asia. It is interesting to note that Almansour Ath-Thahabi,
great monarch of the Maghrib, did not permit the export of sugar and saltpeter
(basis of gunpowder) except to England; and that he had entered into an agreement with Queen Elizabeth to attack the Spanish peninsula from the south while
the British attacked it from the west. The Queen's death, followed shortly by
that of Ath-Thahabi, cancelled the project.

other hand, the Bedu of Ibn Sa'ud, mostly of the tribe of Mutair, attacked the army of Ar-Rasheed and looted his camp and possessions, running away with the spoils.

Thus, the melee which took place at Jerab on that January day of 1915 was a stalemate: a bad day for Sa'uds and Shammar, alike; and the only gainers were the Bedouins of both sides, for they took the spoils and made away with them.

Poor Shakespeare, he belonged to a fine breed of individualists who builded an empire; and, like that other individualist, the swordsman of Najd, they are fighting a narrowing horizon.

The cult of the Lady of Victory is admirably described by Prof. Nabia Abbott.* She recalls that: "The custom had its origin back in pre-Islamic days, when the Queens of ancient Arabia led their armies, or accompanied their husbands on their campaigns. And, what a queen does, other women yearn to do.

"So, in addition to playing the role of women everywhere since time immemorial: being sometimes the cause and often the prize of intertribal warfare, and performing the spy service for which women have so frequently shown a penchant, the women of Arabia frequently went to battle with their men—husbands, brothers, sons—to inspire them to heroic action.

"Gradually, it was seen that it was important business: this function of urging men to heroism, even unto death; and so, on major occasions, it was not left to the inclination or patriotism of the individual women. It became established, instead, as a well-organized institution.

"A woman of outstanding social position would be

* *American Journal of Semitic Languages and Literatures,* Vol. LVIII, No. 3, July, 1941.

placed within, or associated with the probable qubbah, or sacred pavilion, of the tribal local deity. Other women, varying in number, would accompany her. The sacred group, within sight and hearing of the soldiers, if not in the actual fight from the start, would urge on and incite the men with stirring war songs, sung to the accompaniment of their lutes.

"The leader of the group was the Lady of Victory, herself, who, with hair flowing and body partly exposed, embodied a sensuous appeal to valor, honor, and romantic passion. Around her and her women, the battle raged until the day was lost or won.

"The practice, no doubt, had its derivation in some forgotten religious significance. In any event, its complex psychological influence upon the armies is not to be underestimated. For, according to their code, the capture of the Lady of Victory meant the loss of the battle to her side, and the consequent disdain of the women for the vanquished fighters. For the captured women, themselves, it meant slavery and dishonor.

"On desperate occasions, as, for example, in the Battle of Dhu Qar, the Arabs either hamstrung the camels carrying the women, or severed the saddles and litters so that the women fell to the earth. This device, of thus incapacitating the women at a time when they were exposed to extreme danger, was meant to banish from the minds of the men any thought of retreat or surrender, it was fight or die."

In any event, with or without Ladies of Victory, the battle-seasoned Ibn Sa'ud had been having no serious challenge from the Rasheeds from the time of Abdul Aziz ar-Rasheed's death until World War I.

Ar-Rasheed had left four sons—Mut'ib, Mish'il, Muhammad, and Sa'ud. The succession went to the eldest, Mut'ib, but only for ten months: He and his brothers, Mish'il and Muhammad, were murdered the same year by their cousins, Sultan, Faisal, and Sa'ud, children of Hamoud ibn 'Ubaid. The remaining brother, eight-year-old Sa'ud ibn Abdul Aziz, was carried away to Medina by his maternal uncles, the Sibhans, and so he was able to live to take the rule later, and be assassinated by another.

Meanwhile, with Mut'ib's assassination, one of the slayers, Sultan ibn Hamoud, was installed as Amir. He ruled for seven months before he was killed by his brother, Sa'ud ibn Hamoud. This brother did better: He lasted for fourteen months, before he was murdered in a palace conspiracy.

The third brother-assassin, Faisal, who had become Amir of Jauf, was the only one of the trio to escape violent death: He made his way south and surrendered to Ibn Sa'ud.

The Rasheed affairs then remained in a state of utter confusion, until about 1908, when the Sibhans brought out the boy they had rescued: Sa'ud ibn Abdul Aziz, and made him Amir of Haiel, with his uncles and his grandmother, Lady Fatima, directing his affairs.

One understands, then, that the Rasheeds, over this period, were in no position to cause major problems for Abdul Aziz ibn Sa'ud. But, a challenge was developing in another direction: The Turks were building up for trouble.

Although the defeat inflicted upon them by Ibn Sa'ud, in 1904, had doomed Turkish influence or interference in the affairs of Najd, they still held the province of al-Hasa. Within its fortifications, they maintained strong garrisons, and continued to claim that Najd was a Turkish province. They took the view that Ibn Sa'ud was just

[100]

another temporarily troublesome desert chieftain, with whom they would settle their accounts sooner or later.

In 1913, the Young Turks appointed, as military governor at Baghdad, the later-notorious Jamal Pasha, whom the Arabs were ultimately to know as "Jamal the Butcher," because of his atrocities in Syria. He sent a message to Ibn Sa'ud, saying that he would like to confer with him.

Ibn Sa'ud assigned Ahmad ibn Thinyan to go to Baghdad and find out what Jamal Pasha wanted. But, by the time Ibn Thinyan arrived, Jamal had begun to hear that the youthful Sa'ud ibn Rasheed was possessed of considerable ability; and he had decided to assist Ar-Rasheed in defeating Ibn Sa'ud.

Therefore, when Ibn Thinyan presented himself to inquire the reason for Jamal Pasha's call, he was ushered into the presence of the overbearing militarist and was told with sneering arrogance that Ibn Sa'ud had been mistaken about his real position. Jamal declared that the Turkish Government wanted to warn Ibn Sa'ud that, unless he conformed to its order, Jamal, himself, with two regiments, and two regiments only, could run through Najd from north to south, and teach Ibn Sa'ud a never-to-be-forgotten lesson.

Ibn Thinyan returned to inform Ibn Sa'ud of the message, and the latter promptly wrote Jamal a letter, in which he said: "As you say that you could penetrate Najd with two regiments, my answer is that, Allah willing, I shall soon shorten the route for you."

Now, al-Hasa, fertile coast of the Persian Gulf, blessed with abundant water springs, was the most lawless province of Arabia. Safety, indeed, was unknown. Trade had been paralyzed by this very lawlessness, and productivity had waned. It was hinted that the Turkish officials, who had no control whatever over the brigandage, shared at times in the ill-gotten spoils.

Abdul Aziz prepared his army for its invasion, including a substantial number of Ikhwan (religious zealots, of whom more later); and made arrangements with the various warring units to make their rendezvous near Hofuf, the capital, which was occupied by the main Turkish Army. The city was well-fortified by high walls, and the citadel had especially good protection from smooth, high walls which should defy any Arab army.

Before it was time to strike, Ibn Sa'ud returned to Riyadh, and made sure that the Turks learned of his presence there. His purpose: to make certain of accomplishing the element of surprise. His ruse accomplished, he slipped back to his fighting men in al-Hasa.

On April 13, 1913, he struck. He had divided his army into three sections, and they crept by night from three directions, equipped with improvised ladders, and under orders to scale the walls, make no noise, and refrain from answering any challenge or returning any salutation until they were within the city walls. After that, they were to fight those who wanted to fight them, and to refrain from molesting the inhabitants, or entering their doors, or speaking to their womenfolk.

The job was well accomplished. At early dawn, Ibn Sa'ud's Ikhwan commenced to assail the Turkish soldiers, who hastened within their fortification for protection. In contrast, the city's inhabitants joyously welcomed Ibn Sa'ud as a deliverer.

By the end of the day, the garrison surrendered. Out of respect for the Turkish soldiers, Abdul Aziz permitted them to take all of their belongings, including their guns and ammunition, as well as their families. He had them escorted to the port of Qatif, and shipped them by sailing vessels to Bahrein Island, from which they were supposed to sail for Basra, to rejoin the Turks in Iraq.

Instead, when these soldiers reached Bahrein, they were told, for some obscure reason, that their surrender was unnecessary, and that they could return with their arms and ammunition and defeat Ibn Sa'ud and his Ikhwan. They thereupon sailed back to Qatif and attacked the small garrison there, but ran into unexpected resistance.

Hearing of this development, Ibn Sa'ud hastened to the rescue of his supporters, defeated the Turks again, and took all of them prisoner except thirty who were killed. Then, instead of punishing them for their treachery, he sent them back to Bahrein with a letter to the British agent and the Government of Bahrein, blaming them for the double-dealing, and asking them to state frankly whether they were the friends they claimed to be, or his enemies. In response, he received the incredible excuse that, when they shipped the Turkish soldiers, they were not aware of their intent.

It mattered not. What was important was that Abdul Aziz had now added to his Sultanate the province of al-Hasa, which stretches eight hundred miles along the Persian Gulf, from Kuwait to 'Omam, and westward a great distance into the Empty Quarter.

He *knew* that he had made major progress. He had assured himself an outlet to the sea, and possession of a number of ports. What he could not know was that he had gained a region which, a quarter-century later, was to become the major source of the revenue that was to enable him to remake his country.

But, all of that was still for the future. He was still busy with the present, and doing very well at it: In the south, he had become the dominant figure. In the north, his relatives, the ruala of 'Anaza, were pressing against Shammar, while Ibn Sabah was working his machinations against them from Kuwait.

So it was not long after the Battle of Hofuf before Zamil Sibhan, aware of the seriousness of the situation, acknowledged the Sultanate of Ibn Sa'ud, and made a treaty with him for his nephew, Sa'ud ibn Abdul Aziz ibn Rasheed.

The treaty was almost broken before the ink was dry, for, at this point, Sherif Hussein of the Hijaz offered the young Ibn Rasheed support in war against Riyadh; and Ar-Rasheed fell into the scheme. But, the people of Haiel told him plainly that they did not care to dig their own graves; that Ibn Sa'ud had always kept his word to friend and foe.

The affair ended with an apology from Sa'ud ar-Rasheed and his clique, which was accepted by Ibn Sa'ud; and the treaty was renewed. For, the Holy Writ admonishes: "Should they seek peace, seek ye peace, also, and trust in Allah."

It was not long thereafter that World War I began. It found Imam ibn Sa'ud thirty-five years of age, a successful and purposeful chieftain. Though isolated in the heart of Arabia Deserta, he was already farsighted and constructive enough that he wrote to all of the Amirs, friend and enemy alike, saying: "You have undoubtedly learned of the war. I, therefore, suggest that we hold a meeting and confer on uniting and saving the Arabs from its calamities, allying ourselves with one power to protect our rights and strengthen our interests."

As might be supposed, nothing came of his efforts. The only clear and direct answer came from Ibn Rasheed, who replied: "I am of the men of the Turkish Government, and shall fight on its side if it wars, and hold my peace if it so desires."

The Turks, who once had tried to destroy Ibn Sa'ud, now tried to court him. They were rebuffed. The British, we recall, succeeded, through Sir Percy Cox. Ibn Sa'ud aided the British throughout World War I by harassing the Turks' allies, the Rasheeds. With arms and ammunition supplied by the British, he successfully blocked all efforts by the Rasheeds to give any effective aid to Turkey, or to harass Al-Hussein, who was then fighting on the Allies' side.

When world peace came in November, 1918, the Man With the Purpose was ready to set about accomplishing his basic original ambition: recovery, for the Sa'uds, of full control of Najd.

[105]

CHAPTER TWELVE

Murder and Triumph

The whole world gave a grateful welcome to the year 1919: It was the first peaceful one since the slaying of the Archduke Ferdinand had precipitated World War I, in 1914.

Thanks to the truce with Ibn Sa'ud, it was even a year of peace for Sa'ud ibn Abdul Aziz ar-Rasheed. It was a year, as well, in which he could have another basis of satisfaction: Having been Amir of Haiel since 1908, he had ruled longer than anyone since the Amirate of his celebrated father, Abdul Aziz ibn Mut'ib, was ended at the Meadows of Mhanna.

So it is understandable if he had no sense of imminent danger when he started out on the last afternoon of the fasting month of Ramadhan to break his fast with a picnic and hunting trip at the suburban garden called Ghubran. With him were seven of his freedmen, and his small nephew, Abdullah, son of his assassinated brother, Mut'ib ibn Abdul Aziz.

On the way, they were joined by Abdullah ibn Tallal ar-Rasheed and his slave. Most of the party were equipped with fowling pieces.

Arriving at the garden, Amir Sa'ud stationed himself on a rock below a hillcrest, while one of the freedmen, Al-Anber, sat close by to the right, with the child, Abdullah, leaning on his knee. Slightly to the left and behind Amir Sa'ud stood Ibn Tallal and his slave.

Another of Amir Sa'ud's freedmen, Ath-Tha'ite, went a

distance to place the target, and to attend it when it was hit. The rest of the party scattered to gather firewood in preparation for the sunset meal.

Amir Sa'ud took aim first, and fired. He scored a center hit, and Al-Anber, looking through the binoculars, shouted: "Long may you live!"

Ibn Tallal then asked permission of Sa'ud to try for it, and this was readily granted. He also scored, and Al-Anber exclaimed in admiration: "Long may you live!"

Then, Amir Sa'ud aimed again, while Al-Anber held the binoculars to his eyes to watch the target. Simultaneously, Ibn Tallal took aim.

Amir Sa'ud again hit his target. So did Ibn Tallal: His target was Amir Sa'ud.

The victim fell into the lap of Al-Anber, who, thinking merely that the rifle had recoiled, raised his Amir's head, comforting: "Khayr, khayr" ("No harm, no harm"). But, as he lifted Sa'ud's head, the blood spurted forth: He had been shot through the neck at the base of the skull.

Ibn Tallal did not give the freedman and the small boy a moment's chance: he shot the freedman, and the faithful servant purposely fell over young Abdullah, covering him with his own body. Ibn Tallal emptied six bullets at the twain at close range. Three of them went through Al-Anber's sides, and three through his legs, but the boy was unharmed.

The assassin and his slave hastily mounted their horses and galloped away toward the town. Ath-Tha'ite, attending the target from a sheltered spot, heard the shooting and was puzzled to see the target untouched. He stood up to see Sa'ud and Al-Anber on the ground, and the latter raised his head and cried: "They've killed your master! Hasten after Ibn Tallal and kill him! I am wounded, hurry!"

Ath-Tha'ite jumped onto his horse and raced toward the fugitives, shooting as he rode, but his fire missed. The brave Al-Anber rose painfully to his feet and, seeing Mahdi, the old slave of Abdul Aziz ar-Rasheed, he called: "Race after Ibn Tallal and his slave! They have killed Sa'ud!"

The old war horse, Mahdi, who had fought through many a battle beside Abdul Aziz ar-Rasheed, did not even stir from his place, but merely took aim at the hurrying Ibn Tallal and, with the first shot, hit him in the leg, causing him to tumble from his horse. He then fired once at the slave, who went down also.

By this time, Ath-Tha'ite had reached them, and he quickly dispatched them.

The faithful slaves and freedmen gathered around Sa'ud to weep and bemoan his death, but Al-Anber told them to cease their useless crying: "We have avenged them by killing the criminal assassins," he told them. "Now let us look to the future of Haiel and ourselves."

"What shall we do?" he was asked.

"I fear that behind this action there is a conspiracy to seize power in Haiel. Muhammad ibn Tallal, the assassin's brother, is in town. By now, he may have taken the palace and the Government.

"Let one of you go secretly to the city and find out what is the true situation. If the Tallals have seized the reins of government, we will depart with Abdullah until we can gather enough strength to regain the principality."

Ath-Tha'ite was chosen for this mission. The rest waited beside their murdered Amir. It was only a short time later that Ath-Tha'ite returned to report that he had found the town unaware of the assassination. They, therefore, took their dead master back to Haiel, and established the boy, Abdullah, as their Amir.

This tragic episode was destined to bring to a head the long-indecisive relationships between the Rasheeds and the Sa'uds. Abdullah was obviously too young to make any attempt at leadership; and, moreover, he lacked the characteristic ferocity of the family. Realizing the weakness of the Rasheed position, his advisers asked Abdul Aziz al Sa'ud for a renewal of the peace treaty which he had granted to Abdullah's uncle, the late Amir Sa'ud.

Ibn Sa'ud, however, had learned that, even while the advisers were asking for renewal of the treaty, they were in contact with the Sherif Hussein, who had promised them assistance; and they had also been trying to arrange for arms and ammunition from the Turks.

The Man With a Purpose realized, therefore, that a renewal of the truce would serve only to give Haiel time for preparation to resume their fight against Riyadh. Besides, Abdul Aziz had struggled for twenty years to attain his objective of a united Najd; and, now that he saw final success on the horizon, he decided to put an end to the interminable warrings with the House of Rasheed.

Accordingly, he proposed the following conditions:
1. Continuation of the rule of the Rasheeds at Haiel.
2. Autonomy for Haiel and Shammar in their internal affairs.
3. All foreign relations to be referred to Ar-Riyadh for handling; no treaty or other dealing with an outside power to be undertaken by the Rasheeds.
4. The Government of Riyadh to guarantee the safety and defense of Shammar and Haiel in case of attack.

Although these terms would have brought the people of Haiel and Shammar a welcome end to destructive wars, the palace clique saw humiliation in the terms, and so rejected them.

Abdul Aziz was not bluffing: He marched forth with ten thousand warriors; and, upon reaching the Qasim, divided his forces into two armies, one of them under the command of his brother, Muhammad, and the other under that of his eldest son, Sa'ud,* the present Crown Prince, who had not yet reached his twentieth year. Abdul Aziz, himself, remained to direct the handling of supplies, and to receive and dispatch the forthcoming reserve troops.

Then, while Amir Muhammad began laying siege to Haiel, the Crown Prince began raiding Shammar and harassing its allies, so as to prevent reinforcements and provisions from reaching the city.

The partisans of Abdullah ibn Mut'ib had determined to defend his capital, and displayed unexpected ability in doing so. Ultimately, however, scarcity and hunger began to plague the city; and, to aggravate the situation, there arrived an unwelcome guest in the person of Muhammad ibn Tallal, who had come from Jauf to join his cousins in the conflict. He, be it remembered, was the brother of Amir Sa'ud's assassin, Abdullah ibn Tallal.

On the basis of his record as a soldier, Muhammad should have been a welcome addition to the defense, but Abdullah feared him more than he did the chivalrous Ibn Sa'ud: the erstwhile little boy, who had once so narrowly escaped the bullets of Abdullah ibn Tallal, was stricken with shattering dread by the presence of the assassin's doughty brother.

He went to the same faithful Sulayman al-Anber, the one who had saved his life before, and said to him: "O, Sulayman, our enemy within the gates is more dangerous and ruthless than Ibn Sa'ud."

"What is your wish, O long of years?"

* The two older brothers, Turki and Khalid, were deceased.

[110]

Crown Prince
Sa'ud al Sa'ud

"People are communicating with Ibn Sa'ud, and I fear Ibn Tallal."

"By Allah, O uncle (O master), should you wish me to wade the sea with you, I would not hesitate; therefore, speak plainly and I will obey."

"I suggest that we go to Ibn Sa'ud and surrender."

"As you see fit."

"Prepare yourself, then, for we shall leave the city before dawn, and meet outside."

The loyal freedman then went home, preoccupied, and called for his son, Ghati, saying: "My boy, tomorrow we shall go to Ibn Sa'ud."

"Are you seeking my advice, O father?"

"No, just informing you. Get ready."

"And the Amir?"

"He will accompany us."

Ghati went away, muttering to himself: "As Allah willeth."

Before dawn, the Amir slipped forth, accompanied by four of his freedmen, including the same Ath-Tha'ite, the target tender who had pursued and put the final avenging bullets into Ibn Tallal and his slave. Outside the walls, they met Al-Anber and his son, and marched until they reached a Bedouin encampment, and found its Amir.

Word was promptly sent to the Crown Prince, who ordered that all hospitality and consideration be extended to them; and that they should be mounted and escorted to his headquarters. Here, he received them, and took them in his retinue to Riyadh, where his father settled them in comfort.

Thus, whatever motive had prompted Muhammad ibn Tallal to come to Haiel, he was now to become its leader: when the people of the city learned of Abdullah's flight, they called Ibn Tallal and installed him as their Amir.

This last of the Rasheeds was a strong, courageous fighting man of exceptional ability. Of all of the Rasheeds, he most resembled Abdul Aziz ibn Mut'ib in military prowess and fearlessness. Unlike his predecessor, he showed keen discernment in the conduct of his campaigns, and lacked the other's cruelty.

Those who have read the story of "Revolt in the Desert," as told by Lawrence of Arabia, may recollect Audi Abu Tayeh, chief of the Hwaytat tribe and hero of that campaign: a true Knight of the Jahiliyah.

Audi once told how the Hwaytat joined with the Ruala in a battle against Shammar, and how he noticed an irresistible warrior who charged right and left, inflicting havoc in the ranks of the Ruala warriors. Audi inquired who the warrior might be, and, when he was informed that it was Ibn Tallal (he related), "I turned the head of my mare in the opposite direction and made away as fast as it could fly."

Had Muhammad ibn Tallal come into the leadership of Shammar before the disintegration had set in, he might have stayed the collapse of the Rasheeds. As it was, he tried with diligence and wisdom, but it was too late, even for a valiant soldier and intelligent administrator.

He appealed to Sir Percy Cox to mediate, and the Englishman, wanting to keep a balance of power in Arabia, tried to prevail upon Ibn Sa'ud to make peace. The effort was futile.

Ibn Sa'ud had passed the point of being willing to make further concessions. He insisted on unconditional surrender, and the termination of the tribal wars: Najd had given its best blood in this internecine struggle, and the time had come to give Najd and the Najdis the opportunity to

[114]

heal their wounds, and to march forth along the road of peace and progress.

But, terms of unconditional surrender are not the kind that are accepted by men of Ibn Tallal's calibre. He remained adamant in the face of the pleas of his people that they could no longer bear the loss of life, the hunger, and the destruction of property which interminable warfare was imposing upon them.

At this impasse, there entered Abdul Aziz ibn Ibrahim, who later was to become an invaluable aid to Ibn Sa'ud. He was a partisan of the Rasheeds and was highly respected by the people of Haiel. He went to Ibn Tallal alone and forcefully pointed out to him the futility of his stubbornness, and the stupidity of his refusal to recognize the inevitable.

Ibn Tallal capitulated to Ibn Ibrahim. He gave the latter his signet ring as a token of his acceptance of the terms which he would arrange with Ibn Sa'ud.

Thereupon, Ibn Ibrahim went to the Sa'udi camp and surrendered the city. Abdul Aziz ibn Sa'ud, on his part, granted full amnesty to warriors and civilians, alike. He agreed to forget the past, and called on all to look to the future interest of all of the Najdis.

The conqueror entered Haiel amidst the welcoming cheers of its people, who at last saw the dawning of peace. They requested Ibn Sa'ud to appoint one of his sons or relatives as ruler of Haiel, but he answered, out of that wisdom which he had so often displayed:

"Under no circumstances. The old wounds have not fully healed. Choose one of your own to rule Haiel."

The one whom they chose was Ibrahim as-Sibhan, a relative of the Rasheeds by marriage, and a former minister.

As for Ibn Tallal and the families of the Rasheeds, they were settled in Riyadh as guests of their conqueror, who gave them homes and monthly stipends, according to them the same comforts which he gave to his own children.

It had taken twenty years, but the Man With a Purpose had attained his first and dearest objective: he had united Najd. The date: 1921.

THE RASHEEDS OF HAIEL

Abdullah ibn Ali ibn Rasheed. Died, 1848.

Tallal ibn Abdullah. Committed suicide, 1866.

Mut'ib, brother of Tallal. Murdered by his nephews, Bandar and Badr, 1868.

Bandar ibn Tallal. Killed by his uncle, Muhammad, 1871.

Muhammad ibn Abdullah. Ruled from 1871. Died childless, 1897.

Abdul Aziz ibn Mut'ib ibn Abdullah. Killed in battle, 1906.

Mut'ib ibn Abdul Aziz. After ruling ten months, he and his brothers, Mich'il and Muhammad, were murdered by the sons of Hamoud ibn 'Ubaid ar-Rasheed, 1906.

Sultan ibn Hamoud. After seven months was murdered by his brother, Sa'ud.

Sa'ud ibn Hamoud. Ruled fourteen months, murdered in the palace by conspiracy, 1907-1908.

Sa'ud ibn Abdul Aziz. Assassinated by Abdullah ibn Tallal, who was killed by the freedman of the murdered Sa'ud, 1919.

Abdullah ibn Mut'ib ibn Abdul Aziz. Surrendered to Ibn Sa'ud, 1920.

Muhammad ibn Tallal. Surrendered to Ibn Sa'ud, 1921.

CHAPTER THIRTEEN

Al-Hussein:
Accepted Challenge

East of Najd lies the seven-hundred-mile strip of coastal plain and volcanic mountains that borders the Red Sea From its topography, it derives its name: The Hijaz, or "Barrier." It is the Holy Land of Arabia, for it is the seat of Mecca. It is the land of commerce, too, for on its shore stands the busy port of Jiddah.

Toward its southern end, Mount Hadhan stands as a lofty sentry, looking down onto the key city of Tayif, 5,200 feet above sea level; and proclaiming to travelers from Najd that they are now at the edge of the Hijaz.

Fifty miles east of the mountain is the town of Khurma; seventy-five miles south is Turbah. Both towns derived their importance from their strategic location on the route to Tayif, and so they became trading centers for merchants traveling between Najd and the Hijaz.

The reason why the towns became important to this narrative is not that they were population centers: the total inhabitants of Khurma and Turbah, and of the surrounding country, did not exceed 25,000.* But, Mount Hadhan, by long tradition, had become regarded as part of Najd, and the people of the region had been partisans of the Sa'uds, and under the nominal protection, since the days of Sa'ud the Great.

* Khurma, 3,650 feet above sea level, had a population of 5,000; Turbah had about half that many inhabitants.

The people had adopted Wahhabism in the early days of the Reform. Their district was ruled by the Sherifs of the Luwi branch of the "Abadillahs," the Hussein family, but had long been staunch Wahhabis.

Here, the test of power between Al-Hussein, ruler of al-Hijaz, and Ibn Sa'ud, master of Najd, was to come to decision.

Al-Hussein, it will be recalled, made two unsuccessful attempts to intrude himself into the quarrels between Ibn Sa'ud and the Rasheeds: once, in 1919, through Sa'ud ar-Rasheed; and again, in 1920, through Sa'ud ar-Rasheed's nephew and successor, Abdullah ar-Rasheed.

But these were not the first efforts of Al-Hussein to undermine the man of Najd, whom he considered only an upstart, undeserving of really serious attention.

His first gesture was in 1912, when he equipped an army and, with his sons, Ali and Faisal, marched against Turbah and Khurma. His purpose was treble: to bolster his standing with the Turks, to discipline the people for their fealty to the Sa'uds, and to lower the prestige of Najd and its ruler.

He accomplished all three. Despite valiant resistance, the tribes were beaten, and submitted to the Hijaz Government. Ibn Sa'ud had sent his seventeen-year-old brother, Sa'd, with forty horsemen, to rally the 'Utaibah tribe, but, through their treachery, he was taken prisoner.

To free his brother, Abdul Aziz was forced to accept the terms of the Sherif, who had sent word: "If you attack us, we shall move on, but wherever we go we will take Sa'd along." Abdul Aziz yielded, and agreed to recognize the nominal sovereignty of the Turks. This was accomplished through the advice and mediation of Khalid ibn Luwi, a staunch friend of Ibn Sa'ud, albeit a Sherif of the Hussein family.

[118]

The situation between the antagonists remained relatively static for the next two years, and then both became largely preoccupied with the developments of World War I. Dazzled by extravagant promises from the British, Al-Hussein and his son, Faisal, undertook to battle the same Turks whom they previously had wooed. Ibn Sa'ud, on his part, was harassing the pro-Turkish Rasheeds, pacifying al-Hasa, taming the refractory tribes, and generally consolidating his sultanate.

Nevertheless, even during World War I, the Sa'ud and Hussein interests were brought into a series of clashes by one of those completely unpredictable and trivial happenings which have so often led to conflict.

It happened toward the end of 1917, at Medina, where Hussein's son, Abdullah, was engrossed in the three-and-a-half-year siege against the Turks. He had been joined by Sherif Khalid ibn Luwi, ruler of Khurma and Turbah, who had been on excellent terms with his kinsman, Al-Hussein.

But, one day Ibn Luwi had an altercation with a Bedouin chief, who slapped his face. Abdullah imprisoned the offender for only a few days, and this enraged Ibn Luwi, who considered that favoritism had been shown to the one who had insulted him so grievously.

He asked leave to return home, but Abdullah ordered him to report, instead, to his father in Mecca. Defying this order, Ibn Luwi went directly to Turbah, told his people what had happened, refused to heed the many summonses from Al-Hussein, and went instead to Riyadh.

There, he acquainted Ibn Sa'ud with what had happened and warned him to beware of Hussein and Abdullah. Ibn Sa'ud promised him assistance, and Ibn Luwi returned to Turbah and prepared for eventualities.

He did not have to wait long, for, in 1918, Al-Hussein

sent out five hundred soldiers to punish the defecting sherif. But, Ibn Luwi's spies saw them coming. He awaited them near Khurma; destroyed them, and won their equipment.

Next, Hussein sent a thousand men. Again, the Ibn Luwi forces ambushed and defeated them, and took their arms and ammunition. This caused the tribes of the neighboring country to flock to Ibn Luwi's banner, and so, when Hussein made his third try with a well-equipped force of 2,500 men, they were scattered to the winds by those whom they had come to vanquish.

Hussein had learned his lesson, he decided. Burning with rage, he equipped four thousand men, and ordered them to camp at the foot of Mount Hadhan and await his orders. They camped. They waited. They were not attacked, nor did they attack. Finally, weakened by sickness, they simply degenerated. It was Hussein's turn to wait. But, his waiting was soon to be ended.

World War I ended with Al-Hussein glowing in the optimistic belief that the British would keep their promise to make him King of all Arabia. Not long after the armistice in Europe, he was able to glow additionally, for the Turks finally yielded Medina, and all of their large store of arms, ammunition, and equipment went to the Hijaz Government.

This acquisition strengthened Al-Hussein's hand greatly, and he calculated that now was the time to chastise the people of Turbah, and to put an end, once and for all, to the pretensions of Ibn Sa'ud.

By way of putting Ibn Sa'ud off guard, Hussein's son, Sherif Abdullah, began a correspondence with the Najd ruler, pretending that he was returning with his army to Mecca. But Ibn Sa'ud's partisans sent word of what was really happening, so he promptly set his spies to watching every movement.

[120]

Abdullah camped with his army at Ashira, a point at which the road branches: one way to Mecca, the other to Khurma. There, with Al-Hussein presiding, a council of war was held. While it was in progress, the British agent at Jiddah, having learned of developments, sent his secretary, Hussein Ruhi, to advise against the move.

In a loud voice, heard not only by the councillors, but by the soldiers outside, Al-Hussein told the emissary:

"Go and tell them (the British) that we do not permit anyone to interfere with our affairs as we have the right to do what we please!"

The army began to move shortly thereafter: eight thousand Bedu, two thousand regulars, twenty mounted cannon and howitzers, twenty-five machine guns, and a full complement of small arms and ammunition. They camped at the foot of Mount Hadhan, and commenced a series of raids of harassment; meanwhile, pressing the tribal chieftains to join them.

Even as they had started for Mount Hadhan, Ibn Sa'ud had sent Sultan ibn Bajad, chief of the Ghat-Ghat Ikhwan, with twelve hundred cameleers to help Ibn Luwi and the people of Turbah to defend themselves. Their instructions were to take defensive action only until Ibn Sa'ud could arrive with a substantial army.

Ibn Bajad met Ibn Luwi, and they traveled together toward Turbah. Since it was an open city, they camped on the alert about twenty miles away, which was about a four-hour journey.

In the meantime, Abdullah had remained in his encampment about a month; and, during that time, he had enticed some of the tribesmen, whose people dwelt in Turbah, to set up a fifth column within the city. So, when Abdullah arrived (May 24, 1919), these men opened the forts and permitted him to enter, and he killed whoever opposed him. He then set up camp outside the city.

With this easy victory, his attitude became that of an arrogant conqueror, and he began summoning the tribes and settlements of the region to present themselves obediently, or take the consequences.

Ibn Sa'ud, meanwhile, had sent two messengers, pressing Al-Hussein for a settlement of boundary questions; and they had delivered the message to Abdullah, who had forwarded them to his father by courier. Abdullah detained one of the messengers to await the answer; and, when it arrived, he handed it to him, along with the following verbal message:

"Go and speak to your lord of what you saw, and say to Ibn Luwi and the handful of rebels who follow him: let them stay where they are, and not trouble themselves to come to Turbah. We shall go to them for we are not satisfied with taking Khurma; for, while we may fast Ramadhan in Khurma, we shall celebrate the Feast of Adha in the citadel of al-Hasa, after giving these reviled ones a taste of their deserts, and bring them death and destruction: a small part of what they deserve."

The dismissal of the messenger had been stoutly opposed by Hilmi Pasha and Subri Pasha, who were the leaders of the regular army; as well as by Hamid Pasha Alwadi and Ibrahim Bey Arrawie, who were military men with training and experience in the Turkish Army. These and others had advised Abdullah not to permit the messenger to depart, for they feared that, during his stay, he had learned the secrets of the army and its disposition. But, Abdullah, in his imperious way, gave no heed to their warnings.

Abdullah's aides had been correct in their judgment:

The messenger went directly to Ibn Luwi and Ibn Bajad with his report, and they then realized the great strength of the enemy, and his excellent equipment. They were puzzled as to how to proceed, and inclined to delay any action. But, the Ikhwan, who always considered martyrdom a privilege, uttered their war cry: "It is Thou (Allah) we worship, and of Thee we seek aid!"

So, on this evening of May 25, 1919, the leaders decided to attack immediately; and the march was begun . . .

"The winds of Paradise are blowing. Where are ye who Al-Janat seek?"

As they moved toward the city under cover of darkness, a Bedouin ran into Abdullah's camp to tell him that Ibn Luwi and Ibn Bajad were going to attack that night. Angered, Abdullah took him for a spy, sent to deceive them, and ordered him beaten, and it is said he was killed.

Then came a disagreement on strategy. General Hilmi urged Abdullah to move the army to Turbah, instead of camping outside; to station cannon and machine guns, and be alert for any assault. Abdullah overruled him: It was folly, he exclaimed, for anyone to believe that the scorned opposition would venture to attack so formidable a force. So he and his army went to sleep for the night.

Ibn Luwi, who had learned from the detained messenger the disposition of Abdullah's army, divided his forces into three sections. It was shortly after midnight when they silently struck. Ibn Bajad attacked the regular army with his Ghat-Ghat Ikhwan and, in the ensuing battle, destroyed them. Ibn Luwi stormed the camp of Abdullah with such violence that immediate confusion and disorganization beset the erstwhile sleepers: None knew enemy from friend or ally.

Abdullah, himself, rudely roused from his slumber,

found that his position was hopeless; and so, with twenty of his men, he made a break for safety (in his nightgown, it is said). His mare was shot from under him as he fled, but he hastily found a zalul, and continued his exit.

When morning came, Ibn Luwi found that the remnants of Abdullah's army had taken refuge in a palace, which he and the Ikhwan immediately attacked, destroying those within.

None of the regular army of two thousand survived except six officers and twelve soldiers. Altogether, five thousand of Abdullah's men died in the battle. The killed among the attackers were five hundred Ikhwan, four hundred of the Ghat-Ghat, and one hundred of the people of Turbah and Khurma. All of the arms, ammunition, and equipment which Al-Hussein had taken so gleefully from the Turks at Medina, had now become the spoils of Ibn Sa'ud.

Abdul Aziz, himself, arrived five days later with twelve thousand warriors, ready for the battle, which none had expected to start so soon. When he witnessed the holocaust, he shed tears of pity; and, when the soldiers asked permission to proceed to Tayif, he restrained them, saying: "Sufficient unto the aggressor is his punishment."

Ten days later, Ibn Sa'ud received from the British the request that he proceed no further into the Hijaz. This was at the prompting of Al-Hussein, who had lost not only his army, but his prestige among the tribes of Arabia and in the eyes of the Muslim world.

Abdul Aziz acceded to the British. He ordered his army to withdraw. The time to take the Hijaz had not arrived . . . yet.

CHAPTER FOURTEEN

For Hussein, Exit; for Ibn Sa'ud, the Hijaz

Abdul Aziz ibn Sa'ud did not waste his time brooding over the British ban against his advance into the Hijaz, although he well knew that his Ikhwan could have stormed across it handily. Although the Hijaz had been, for a time, a part of the Sa'udi domain, he had given no particular thought to the idea of invading it. Even had he so desired, he knew that the time would not be propitious, with the British supporting Hussein, and with his own forces well occupied with the establishment of order in his existing sultanate.

Pressing him for attention, for example, was the situation in that province south of the Hijaz, well-named "Asir," meaning "difficult," where rugged mountains make travel or campaigning extremely arduous.

Asir, like the Hijaz, had been a part of the early Sa'udi Amirate, but, during the family decline, it had fallen under the influence of the Turks, and had suffered years of misgovernment. Finally, the people appealed to Ibn Sa'ud to deliver them from their plight, and to take over their protection, so that they might live in peace according to the laws of the Koran.

So, in May, 1921, Abdul Aziz assigned a force to go to Asir under the leadership of his cousin, Abdul Aziz ibn Musa'id ibn Jlewi, admonishing him not to resort to fighting unless so obliged.

[125]

He *was* so obliged: the governor, one Ibn 'Aidh, opposed Ibn Jlewi bitterly, but the latter conquered him and occupied the country. After the surrender, Ibn 'Aidh was sent to Riyadh, where he was received kindly, and was reinstated to his former position on the condition that he would improve the condition of his people. Ibn Sa'ud's largesse even included a gift of 65,000 riyals (6,500 gold pounds).

But, instead of reforming his government, Ibn 'Aidh utilized the money and the opportunity to re-equip an army of his partisans, and to revolt against the Sa'uds.

This was enough for Ibn Sa'ud. So, in 1922, after the surrender of Haiel, he equipped an army of six thousand Najdis and four thousand Bedouin of the Quhtan tribe, under the command of his second son, Faisal, then a youth of seventeen. Tutored in the same school of hardship and warfare which Abdul Aziz had obliged all of his children to follow, Faisal proved himself well equal to the difficult task, and conducted the campaign like a veteran.

His defeat of the dissidents included the storming of Harmalah, the all-but-impregnable city atop a steep mountainside, which had defied the best efforts of Turkish regulars and Turkish cannon.

Of particular satisfaction to his father was the strategy by which Faisal waylaid and routed an army, well-equipped with mountain artillery and rapid-firing guns, which had been sent by that old foe, Sherif Al-Hussein, to assist the rebels. Young as he was, Faisal did not make the mistake of being satisfied with this victory, but followed the remnants of Hussein's defeated army well beyond the borders of the Hijaz.

During a year's campaigning, Faisal pacified the country, reorganized civil and military affairs, and, on January 8, 1923, this now eighteen-year-old veteran returned to

Amir Faisal

Riyadh, where his father, his grandfather, and the people
of Najd gave him a welcome such as befitted a victor.

Among the prisoners whom Faisal brought back with
him was the rebelling governor, Ibn 'Aidh, and his family.
Characteristically, Ibn Sa'ud pardoned them, domiciled
them in Riyadh, and provided for their support.

Asir acquired a new Amir, the intrepid Ibn Ibrahim:
the same former partisan of the Rasheeds who had persuaded Ibn Tallal to surrender to Ibn Sa'ud back in 1920.
This man of steel had become the invaluable aide of Ibn

Sa'ud, second only to Abdullah ibn Jlewi, the co-hero of the Sa'udi wars. When he took charge in 'Asir, its deserts and mountains were infested with revolts, raids, and brigandage; general turmoil prevailed. By his energy and his iron hand, he so pacified the entire country that the mere mention of his name was sufficient to frighten evil-doers.

He was a man of extraordinary administrative capacity, and unfailing loyalty. Digressing briefly for a glimpse into the future, we find Ibn Sa'ud, in 1927, removing him from the governorship of Tayif, and calling him to Mecca to tell him: "We did not remove you for a fault in your trusteeship or laxity in religion, but for your severity, as we desire leniency for the people."

To which Ibn Ibrahim answered: "Praised be Allah who appointed you over the Muslims, as you are better aware of their needs. While I am deprived of this position (the governorship), I am happiest to be near you morning and eve, and this is the dearest desire of my heart."

A few months later, he was made Amir of Medina, where he pacified the country and made the Mecca road safe for pilgrims. The Bedu, especially the banu Harb, had been in the habit of robbing the pilgrims, with the tacit forbearance of the former Government. But, Ibn Ibrahim taught them a lesson which they have never forgotten. Sa'udi Arabia, indeed, found that it had acquired two poles of discipline: Ibn Ibrahim in the north and Ibn Jlewi in the south, and woe unto the Bedouin who reverted to transgression!

But, to return to 1922 . . .

After losing the Battle of Turbah to Ibn Sa'ud's leaders, Ibn Luwi and Ibn Bajad, Al-Hussein began having troubles from other directions. Among other things, his relations with Egypt became strained. During 1922, the

Mahmal (procession) left for the Hijaz, bearing the annual kiswa, or cover, for the Ka'ba,* the furnishing of which had become the Egyptian's prerogative for seven hundred years. The Egyptians returned from Jiddah without having reached Mecca.

Moreover, Hussein had gained the ill will of the Indian Muslims because of taking up arms against the Turkish Khalifah, and because of the ill treatment meted out to the pilgrims of that country, and the Sherif's inability to guard them against banditry, especially on the road between Mecca and Medina. For these reasons, a substantial proportion of the Indian Muslims had resented Al-Hussein's claim to the Khilafah.

Indeed, Muslims everywhere were complaining of conditions existing in the Holy Land, and of the dangers to which pilgrims were exposed.

At this point, Ibn Sa'ud began to communicate with leaders of the Muslim world, establishing friendly contact with King Fuad of Egypt, and making known, through his son, Faisal, his position on important questions affecting the Faith, including his stand on the Khilafah: that it was a question for the Muslims at large to decide.

Through British offices, a number of conferences were held, aimed at peaceful resolution of the disputes among the Arabs, and of the various other differences which World War I had left in its wake.

Ibn Sa'ud went into these conferences with serious worries on his mind. He had seen Al-Hussein's son, Faisal, made King of Iraq to his right, and Al-Hussein's other son, Abdullah, made Amir of Transjordan on his left; and, with the Hussein controlling the Hijaz, he saw himself sur-

---

* The small rectangular building which is the center of the Pilgrimage ceremonies.

rounded in such wise that the independence which he had won with the blood of his people was being threatened by the sherifs.

Therefore, the Sa'uds issued a Green Paper, giving a full account of the conferences, and of the demands made by both sides. This, they distributed widely through the Muslim world, where it gained Ibn Sa'ud immeasurable good will.

King Hussein had already forbidden the Najdis to make the Pilgrimage; and the Ikhwan, who were thus prevented from performing one of the Great Pillars of Islam, were furious with Abdul Aziz for counselling them to hold their peace, and await a peaceable solution.

All deliberations of Ibn Sa'ud's Court were public, and the Ikhwan leaders were outspoken in their protests: "O, Abdul Aziz, we have given you the reins of our affairs as Muslims, and the Hajj (Pilgrimage) is incumbent upon Muslims; therefore, why do you prevent us from performing our devotions?"

Or: "We are able to make the Hajj in spite of Al-Hussein. Why delay us? Why prevent us from the Jihad (endeavor, or holy war) to cleanse the Holy House of Allah? Why stand between us and martyrdom?"

Yet, with all of these pressures and concerns, Ibn Sa'ud's demands and his attitude at the British-sponsored conferences were extremely modest. On the contrary, the conditions put forth by some of the opposing delegates could hardly have been more arbitrary if they had been the result of a victorious war.

Thus, Ibn Sa'ud bided his time, but his patience was unrewarded. Finally, it became apparent that something had to be done. In 1924, when the chiefs of the Ikhwan came to felicitate Ibn Sa'ud on the occasion of the Adha Feast, he consulted them as to their attitude toward invading the Hijaz. One need not guess their answer! They were delighted! At long last, they could re-establish the True Faith in the Sacred Precinct.

Home they went, to prepare for the long-yearned-for Jihad, and this part of their task was easy: all that they wanted was a zalul, a gun, a belt of cartridges, a sword, and a bag of dried dates. They were ready to move.

The Sa'udi army mobilized at Turbah. Its three thousand-man strength was made up of sixteen units from different localities, each with its Amir and banner; and it marched away to its mission under command of those two stalwart veterans of 1919, Khalid ibn Luwi and Sultan ibn Bajad. No one in Tayif or Mecca was aware of their movements until, in September, 1924, they reached the town of Huwayyah, about fifteen miles from Tayif.

At Tayif, General Sabri Pasha received orders from the Hijaz Government to defend the city. He had four hundred regulars, with a complement of mountain artillery and machine guns; and, with them, he moved out from Tayif to meet the Sa'udis. In the ensuing battle, he inflicted heavy casualties upon the attackers, but was finally forced to retreat to the city.

But this was to be only a beginning. Al-Hussein sent his son, Ali, with his cavalry and cameleers, to relieve the garrison. And *then* the struggle *really* began.

There is no need to go into detail. In fact, it is difficult to evaluate in the ordinary way the movements and valor of the opposing armies. The men from Najd were not ordinary soldiers: they were fired with a religious zeal that had reached fanaticism, and they courted martyrdom.

[131]

Under such inspiration and impetus, human beings are filled with an exaltation that places them beyond reasonable analysis.

Suffice it to say that the battle lasted for four days, and ended, after a valiant defense, in the capture of Tayif on September 7, 1924. The Bedu of Hijaz, who had volunteered with the sherifian army, had deserted to the attackers, and with them they entered Tayif at night to break into stores and houses, and to steal whatever they could lay their hands upon. Some three hundred civilians were killed unnecessarily, and in some cases the inhabitants, firing from their windows or housetops, provoked the attackers to break in.

Still being told is a story of a religious elder from Mecca, Sheikh Abdul-Kadir Ash-Sheebi, a trustee of the Ka'ba and, therefore, a man of very high position, who had been summering in Tayif and was unable to escape. One of the Ikhwan, with his sword ready to strike, asked him: "Why are you crying, ya Kafir (o infidel)?"

The elder answered: "I cry of joy, O Ikhwan, because I realize that I have spent all my life in infidelity, and now Allah has graciously decreed that I die as a true Unitarian believer, for I bear witness that God only is great, and that there is no God but One God."

This confession of faith so affected the would-be slayer that he threw down the sword, and he and the Ikhwan with him shed tears with the Sheikh, and kissed and congratulated him on his true faith.

In the morning, Sultan ibn Bajad arrived to put an end to all depredations.

Meantime, Amir Ali had reached 'Arafat, twenty miles from Mecca, only to find that his father, the King, had hastily gathered together about two thousand warriors, and ordered the son to return to battle. The gesture was futile. On September 26, the two armies met again, and this time the defeat of the Hijazis was completed.

The people of the Hijaz were in a panic. In response to their entreaties, Al-Hussein abdicated in favor of Ali; and then, with his family and a great many people from Mecca, he hastened to the seaport of Jiddah and sailed away.

As far as the people, themselves, were concerned, the panic was unnecessary: Ibn Sa'ud had sent orders to the Ikhwan not to enter Mecca as warriors, but as pilgrims. Obeying his instructions, they did so, and engaged in no killing, although they could not resist looting the palaces of the sherifs.

So, those Meccans who had not fled the city were re-assured, and Mecca returned to its peaceful pursuits under the governorship of Sherif Khalid ibn Luwi. Ibn Sa'ud followed to Mecca on October 18, 1924, and soon the armies had fresh orders: besiege Medina and Jiddah.

During the siege of the two cities, there were attempts to initiate mediation, but Ibn Sa'ud disposed of them with the acumen of a seasoned diplomat, emerging from all discussions with the good will of those whose proposals he rejected.

The British, to whom Ali appealed for help, refrained from complying. They reminded Ali that, when they had proffered their services once before (just before the Battle of Turbah), they had been told quite firmly that it was a Muslim affair and that their offices were not required.

H. St. John Philby, the eminent British Arabist and explorer; and Ameen Rihani, the Lebanese scholar, came to Jiddah to offer their aid in mediation, but were politely told that the dispute concerned the Muslims, alone. When

[133]

Egypt sent a delegation, headed by the rector of al-Azhar, they were informed that, since England's offer of good offices had been declined, it might be considered a slight to accept those of another government; but Ibn Sa'ud would be most happy to have King Fuad call a Muslim conference, to be held in Egypt under King Fuad's leadership.

All of these maneuvers appeased the sensitiveness of the various groups, but there was one point on which Abdul Aziz took an adamant and immovable stand: The absence of protection for the pilgrims, during their visits to the Holy Land; and the fact that other Muslims, like those of Najd, had been forbidden to make the pilgrimage, and had demonstrated the unfitness of the sherifs to administer the Hijaz. Therefore, Abdul Aziz insisted, Al-Hussein and his children must leave the country.

The siege of the cities went on unabated. Medina, isolated and cut off from supplies, suffered a great deal, lulled by the never-materializing promises of relief from the sherifs. After ten months, it surrendered to Amir Muhammad, the fourteen-year-old son of Ibn Sa'ud, on December 5, 1925.

Entering the city at the head of his troops, Muhammad received a great ovation; then went directly to the Prophet's mosque, where he asked for mercy for the living and the dead. After prayer, he visited the tomb of the Prophet and those of his two companions, Abu Bakr and Omar.

To Jiddah, meanwhile, Abdullah had sent Syrians and Palestinians to help Sherif Ali; and the defense became a stout one. The port was protected on the land side by a crescent-like wall, fortified by towers, trenches, and land mines.

Made restless by the inactivity of siege warfare, the Ikhwan continually asked for the opportunity to attack and force surrender. Continually, also, the soldiers who manned the artillery, taken from the army of the sherif, begged for the chance to use it against the city. Ibn Sa'ud, however, did not want to see any needless depredations, or any avoidable shedding of Arab blood. He refused his permission, and kept his men within bounds.

The besieged garrison attempted a few sorties, but they fizzled out pitiably, and the condition of Jiddah went from bad to worse. At last, after a siege of one year, King Ali saw the hopelessness of the situation. Acceding to the entreaties of the people of Jiddah, he sailed away from the port, never to return.

On December 22, 1925, Jiddah capitulated to Ibn Sa'ud. The rout of the Husseins had been consummated.

The next step had to be establishment of a new government. Having declared firmly and repeatedly that the Holy Land and its future belonged to all Muslims, Ibn Sa'ud's actions were in harmony with his words: He had issued an invitation to all Muslim countries, and to prominent Muslim dignitaries, to meet at a general conference and decide the fate of the Hijaz. He received no response.

So, with his triumph over the Husseins, he called the people of the Hijaz to a public meeting, and told them to choose their own form of government. The only conditions which he imposed were that the Koran should become the law of the Holy Land, and that the government should be under the guidance of a consultative body: "Shawra."

The Hijazis acted promptly: by universal acclaim, the man whom they chose to be their King was Ibn Sa'ud, the same man of Najd whom Hussein had once regarded with disdain.

Poor Hussein had not been without admirable qualities. He was a man of integrity and high purpose, possessed of great courage and determination. But he was impatient of the counsel of any other person. One of his basic mistakes, of course, was his unflagging faith in the British promise (when they were at the nadir of their World War I fortunes) that they would make him king of an independent Arab kingdom, embracing all of the Arab lands then included in the Ottoman Empire.

Through the turbulent postwar years, he tenaciously refused to compromise on behalf of the Arabs and their aspirations, and he went into final eclipse and exile declaring: "I will not give in one inch, but shall hold fast to my obligations, no matter what the English do with theirs. I am now the prisoner of their power, and they may blow me to Mars, but shall not humble my spirit!"

Hussein's greatest error of all, of course, was his appraisal of his adversary, Ibn Sa'ud. He insisted upon thinking of him as a Bedouin chieftain, never realizing the Najdi's enormous ability, his inspiring leadership, his heroism and his wisdom. Nor did he gauge the religious impetus which the Reformation gave to the Ikhwan.

By these defects, by his maladministration of the Hijaz, by his neglect of the pilgrims and his inability to guarantee their safety, he demonstrated that he did not have the stature to rule the Holy Land of Islam, but, on the other hand, he raised a moral standard for the Arabs to emulate by refusing to barter Syria, Lebanon, and Palestine to the secret designs of the English and French, whose secret covenants had been secretly arrived at.

CHAPTER FIFTEEN

One More Barrier

With the conquest of the Hijaz, the one-time Youth With a Purpose, whose greatest ambition was to regain Najd for his family, was now, at forty-four, ruler of a broad domain, reaching from the Persian Gulf to the Red Sea, and from Iraq and Transjordan to the borders of the mite-sized coastal states of the southeast and south—Qatar, 'Oman, Hadrumut, and Yemen.

He was *ruler* of this broad domain, but not yet its *master*. There was one more barrier to be hurdled: the recalcitrance of the Ikhwan, who would fight beside their Sultan one day, and fight against him the next. The taming of these wild zealots was a problem that Ibn Sa'ud had faced from that day of his first great victory at Riyadh: January 15, 1902. It was a task that took him thirty years.

The rise of the Ikhwan had its origin in the Reformation of Muhammad ibn Abdul-Wahhab and his ally, Muhammad ibn Sa'ud. After the initial opposition and subsequent enforcement, the Reformation spread to the Ruhhal; and, true to the dictum of Ibn Khaldun ("It is only by religious issue that the Arab is aroused"), the Wahhabi teachings sank deeply into their consciousness. . . .

We are the people of Allah,
Brothers of those who obey Him.

The impetus of the Reform carried Hadhar (town dwellers) and Ruhhal, alike, sweeping like a flame to the Jihad,

[137]

in order to force the Mushrekine (non-Unitarians) to join the movement or be proscribed; and ultimately the Ikhwan (brothers) became fired with the zeal to reform all of Arabia, or else to cleanse it of those who did not conform. Their battle cry:

> The winds of Paradise are blowing;
> Where are ye who Al-Janat seek?

Uncouth but fearless warriors that they were, they had always raided and fought for gain; now, after embracing the Reformation, they had a double incentive for the Jihad: the worldly goods of the Mushrekine; or, failing this, Paradise in the hereafter, "where rivers of sweet waters flow."

The teachings of the Prophet Muhammad had united them; the Khalifahs had directed their energies to the Jihad for Islam; and Sa'ud the Great had enlisted them to consolidate the Reformation launched by his grandfather and Ibn Abdul-Wahhab.

In fact, it was the ferocity of the Ikhwan in battle which enabled Sa'ud the Great to extend his rule over the greatest territory ever controlled by the Sa'uds; and he might have taken in Syria and Iraq had it not been for his severity with the pilgrims, and his destruction of what he looked upon as innovations. As it was, the reaction to his harshness, plus exaggerated rumors of the fanaticism of the Ikhwan, brought about the Turko-Egyptian war against Arabia, with its consequent legacy of misery.

It remained for Abdul Aziz, a hundred years later, to whip the Ikhwan into orderliness, and to unite them in his efforts to bring a saner life to all of his people; but the task required all of his vast store of wisdom, patience, understanding, and firmness.

Individuals, groups, and whole tribes, after receiving

his clemency and pledging him their fealty, repeatedly re-
scinded their pledges and fought against him anew. When
he defeated them again, he forgave them, and accepted their
word once more, for he was a true teacher and reformer.
He knew their fickle nature, as he knew their potentiality
as fighters. As he commented on one occasion, after a typ-
ical defection: "These are our children and we must bear
with them. It takes time to remake men and their habits. I
have always appreciated the good in them, and hope for
their eventual enlightenment."

His cousin, Abdullah ibn Jlewi, co-disciplinarian (with
Ibn Ibrahim) of modern Arabia, took sharp issue with
Abdul Aziz over his lenience; and it must be conceded that
Ibn Jlewi could point to results in support of his advocacy
of sternness.

As governor of al-Hasa, Ibn Jlewi had under him a
province where lawlessness had reigned without restraint
under the Turks. He had to deal with the proud warriors
of banu Khalid, the doughty 'Ujman and Dawasirs, and
the untamed banu Murrah. But, Ibn Jlewi's iron hand was
quite equal to the challenge, and he administered undiluted
justice in full measure whenever an infraction occurred.

The contrast between conditions during his regime,
and that of the Turks, was striking: During the Turkish
regime, banditry made travel unsafe for merchant or wayfarer; indeed, an 'Ujman might steal a soldier's horse, ride
it audaciously into the capital city of Hofuf to have it shod,
and then ride away again without fear of the authorities.

Under Ibn Jlewi, when one of the Ikhwan entered
Hofuf, he removed his distinctive white headdress, went
quietly about his errand, and departed. For the thief lost his
hand, and the murderer, his head. "To the square with him!"
had but one meaning, for all executions took place in public,

and the news was quickly carried far into Empty Quarter, where it struck terror into the hearts of the Bedu. Brigandage lost its zest.

Abdul Aziz, while acknowledging that severity and swift punishment were deterrents to crime, did not believe that they effected *cures*. At the same time, he conceded that laxity and generosity alone were not always successful. He understood fully that the elusive Bedu were, in actuality, orphans of the desert; that it was difficult for them to forego the immemorial game of appropriating whatever they could, especially while "folding the desert" beyond the reach of Abdul Aziz.

With his clear vision, he saw the anachronism of former methods; he determined to try a new one: to tether these nomads to a home and a hearth, and thus gradually to settle them on the soil.

In 1911, he established his first settlement: the Irtawiyah of Mutair and Harb settlers. This was followed by the Ghat-Ghat of 'Utaibah, Daknna of Harb, and Ajar of Shammar.

The land was chosen for its fertility and the availability of water. The settlers were given farming implements, seeds, and shoots of date palm, and were taught to build sod houses. They sold their surplus livestock to the Government at a good price, and began to lead a productive life instead of one of precarious wandering.

They were told that their migration (Hijr) resembled that of the early followers of the Prophet, who disdained not to labor and trade and accumulate wealth; and that their former life was like that of the Jahiliyah.

Thus, weaned from their former banditry, they came to feel that it was incumbent upon them to guard the peace and protect the wayfarer; they had some of the exultation of a revival; and, in emulation of the early Muslims, the Ruhhal filtered in to join the settlers. At present, the number of these settlements is about four hundred.

In spite of this turn to a useful existence, it is probably not too surprising that their inherent zeal started them off on another tangent: so imbued did they become with self-righteousness that some of them commenced to look upon those who followed any other mode of life as out-of-bounds, and as unbelievers.

Ibn Jlewi quickly noticed this attitude and he sternly told them that their arrogance, intolerance, and general behavior as Ikhwan made their moral condition much worse than their former irreligious state of ignorance.

When Ibn Sa'ud observed this spirit of intolerance creeping through the migration, he took prompt action. In 1916, he uprooted every religious teacher from their midst and replaced them with men better instructed in the Faith, with its simple tenets and day-to-day application.

These murshidine (instructors) led them back into the straight path; men began to study anew; and the elementary schools were crowded with both children and adults. The people of the Hijr became, ultimately, the faithful and reliable soldiers of Ibn Sa'ud, ready at all times to answer the call of their Imam.

But, this harmonious condition was not achieved without some dangerous defections; and, ironically enough, the most serious trouble was started by two of Ibn Sa'ud's most intrepid and trusted warriors—Faisal ibn Dwaysh and Sultan ibn Bajad.

Ad-Dwaysh had been placed in charge of the first settlement: that of the Irtawiyah, inhabited mostly by Mutair. Ibn Bajad had been made leader of the second settlement, occupied by a section of 'Utaibah.

Ad-Dwaysh, however, had become disgruntled when he was sent back from the Hijaz by Ibn Sa'ud, and not permitted to join in the siege of Medina. He began to play upon the intolerance of the reactionaries in his settlement, and he enlisted the support of Ibn Bajad. Together, they began accusing Abdul Aziz of straying from the correct path of the Faith.

It was during the brewing of this discontent that a large group of chiefs was gathered at the Majlis, when Ad-Dwaysh arose and spoke in open court: "O, Abdul Aziz, we have placed you where you are by our swords . . ."

"True, O Ikhwan. By the grace of Allah and your swords, we have attained unity," was the reply of Abdul Aziz, the patient.

But, unfortunately for Ad-Dwaysh, Ibn Jlewi was on the dais, and he was on his feet immediately, cane in hand and striding toward Ad-Dwaysh.

"O, dog of the Arabs!" he shouted. "Who are you that you dare to speak in our presence?"

The story is that he thereupon set upon Ad-Dwaysh with his cane, at which the sheikhs rushed between them, and the Majlis adjourned in confusion.

As to Abdul Aziz, he had slipped out by the side door, and immediately sent for Ad-Dwaysh. When the latter came complaining of the berating and the caning, Abdul Aziz told him:

"O, Faisal, you should know Ibn Jlewi! Did you see me leave by the side door? Ay, Wallah! I feared that he was going after me with his cane, and it would not have been the first time, for you know that Abdullah is my elder, and I could never gainsay him."

Abdul Aziz then overwhelmed Ad-Dwaysh with largesse, and sent him away pacified.

[142]

However, this was not to be the end of the revolt of the Ikhwan. In 1926, the dissidents held a meeting at which they decided to rescue the Faith from the corruption and innovations which they fancied had been developing. They censured Abdul Aziz for the following:

1. For sending his son, Sa'ud, to Egypt, a country of innovations.
2. For sending his son, Faisal, to London, the capital of the Mushrikine.
3. For his use of automobiles, and for installing the telegraph and telephone.
4. For the imposition of taxes in the Hijaz and Najd.
5. For permitting the Bedouins of Iraq and Transjordan to graze the lands of the Muslims.
6. For forbidding trade with Kuwait, "for, if the people of Kuwait are infidels, they should be fought, and, if not, they should not be boycotted."
7. For not forcing the people of al-Hasa and Qatif, who belonged to the Shia', to follow the Sunna.

There were assorted other allegations. Hearing of this open rebellion, Abdul Aziz realized the great danger of it, for he saw in it the potential destruction of the accomplishments of his lifetime.

At first, he decided to try patience; then, he realized that this would not suffice; the situation called for boldness. So he returned to Najd; and, in 1927, called for a general meeting of the Ikhwan. More than eight hundred delegates responded.

Ibn Sa'ud arose and faced them. He told them he was ready to resign his leadership to whomever they wanted to nominate to manage their affairs; that he stood before them, not as King or Imam, but as a man in court to be judged by them for any remission in his policy and conduct; that he was only one of them, and he entreated them to speak openly and frankly, for his desire was to clear his conscience before God and the people.

The reaction to this was the unanimous assurance of support, and readiness to discipline the dissidents, who, understandably enough, had refrained from attending the meeting.

Abdul Aziz, with forty thousand men, marched to Buraidah and sent word to his opponents to surrender to the judgment of the 'Ulama (religious leaders) in all disputed matters or prepare to fight. Needless to say, Ad-Dwaysh, who was the principal instigator, decided to fight.

On March 30, 1929, the Battle of Sabla was waged, with Abdul Aziz charging at the head of his troops, and defeating the dissident Ikhwan. Ibn Bajad escaped, but Ad-Dwaysh, who was grievously wounded, was carried to Abdul Aziz, with wife and children in tears. The King was greatly affected; forgave him again; and sent him back, with his own physician, Dr. Medhet Sheikh ul-Ardh, to attend him.

Three days later, Ibn Bajad offered to surrender, but the King sent word not to come to him, because he feared that harm would befall him at the hands of the soldiers; but, to give himself up in Shaqra or Riyadh. This he did, and was imprisoned.

The King returned to the Hijaz to attend to the administrative reorganization of that province, and ordered Ibn Jlewi to quell the depredations of the 'Ujman in the region between al-Hasa and Kuwait.

But, it seemed that there was no hope of redemption in Ad-Dwaysh, who had pledged obedience and fealty. A few months after the defeat of the Ikhwan at the Battle of Sabla,

this man of the meaningless oath had recovered from his wounds; so, while Abdul Aziz was busy in the Hijaz, he commenced his rebellion anew.

He joined the 'Ujman in raiding north and south, killing, robbing, and raiding into the territory of Iraq, thus causing the British to retaliate by bombing the border tribes of Najd; and causing added concern to the King, who wanted to maintain good relations with the British.

The King determined to act swiftly and forcefully. Using new armored cars and automobiles, he surprised the rebels so effectively as to scatter Ad-Dwaysh's followers thoroughly, and to inflict such severe punishment upon the dissidents of 'Utaibah and Mutair that they had no power for resistance thereafter.

Ad-Dwaysh took refuge in Iraq, where he surrendered to the British on January 9, 1930. But, on the twenty-eighth, upon Ibn Sa'ud's insistence, the British turned him over, and he was imprisoned in Riyadh, where he died.

The revolt of the Ikhwan had finally been put down permanently, after having brought death, suffering, and hardship to many thousands of people. A dramatic story of this uprising was told to the writer, during his visit to Amir Sa'ud ibn Jlewi in al-Hasa, by an official who had witnessed a spectacular march under the command of Ibn Jlewi's son, Fahd.

The youthful Fahd, his father's pride, had set forth from Hofuf to seek the 'Ujman, leading three hundred horsemen who were generally considered the finest crack troop in all Arabia. Their horses, caparisoned in superb tooled leather, were of the premier blood of the land.

Upon making contact with the rebels, Fahd sent word to the chiefs to present themselves. Dhidan, chief of As-Siqhan, and three others came to Fahd's camp in the evening, contrary to the advice of their own warriors. Dhidan told Fahd that, if they did not return to their people that evening, the tribesmen would attack the camp in the morning.

The son of Jlewi would not be intimidated. If he had permitted them to return after that threat, he would have lost face in the eyes of the 'Ujman, and, more important still, in the eyes of his own father. He, therefore, ordered them to be detained in an adjoining tent, and set up a guard over them.

Early the following morning, the plains were alive with warriors, who formed a ring around the camp. A woman, with face unveiled, was riding around among them, urging them to attack and free their chiefs.

Fahd saw the hopelessness of the situation. He knew the type of warriors surrounding him. He knew, also, that a Jlewi would never capitulate. He, therefore, ordered his men to behead the detained chiefs, and immediately to hamstring the tethered thoroughbreds. . . .

When the bodies were found later, Fahd's lay atop that of Dhidan and his companions.

It was on January 10, 1930, when Ibn Sa'ud was pressing against the warring tribes on the borders of Iraq, that the scouts brought word of a large encampment ahead. It proved to be that of the tribe of Siqhan: the beheaded Dhidan's people.

This news reached Ibn Sa'ud's eighteen-year-old son, Muhammad, nephew of Abdullah ibn Jlewi; and he begged his father to let him lead the attack. The King refused. Not to be denied, young Muhammad vowed that he would either lead the charge or take his own life.

"All right!" Abdul Aziz retorted. "Go and get killed!"

Muhammad went. After a while, the worrying King-father followed. And at length he found his son—returning with the women and children of the tribe of Siqhan. The men had all gone down fighting.

Muhammad had avenged his first cousin, Fahd ibn Abdullah ibn Jlewi.

There was to be one interruption of the peaceful days which the conquest of the Ikhwan had brought to Arabia, but this was not sufficient to retard the progress which Ibn Sa'ud had inaugurated.

In 1933, relations between the Kingdom of Sa'udi Arabia and the Imamah of Yemen had become strained as the result of a drawn-out dispute over boundaries. The delegates of the two countries, meeting in an effort to effect a settlement, gradually found tempers rising and attitudes stiffening.

At last, in spite of the better intents and wishes of both King ibn Sa'ud and Imam Yahya of the Yemen, they drifted into war.

The King appointed the Crown Prince to command his Najdi troops, and Amir Faisal, Viceroy of the Hijaz, to lead the Hijazis.

Faisal, then twenty-seven years of age, was a seasoned veteran. He advanced along the shore of the Red Sea and through Tihamah with mountain batteries, armored cars, and machine guns.

A companion, close to Faisal, described this campaign to the writer:

"We were exhausted from the heat and strain of marching; and, whenever the order came to stop and rest, were it night or day, everyone threw himself down and fell asleep —all except one person: Faisal. He was ever moving, in-

[149]

specting the men, the equipment, the guards, the outposts; or accompanying the scouts in advance of the army. When or where he got his energy or rest, I do not know."

One thing was certain: his progress was too rapid for the Yemenites, and he pushed irresistibly through, to occupy Hodaidah and to organize its administration. The victorious and ambitious warrior then set up a radio station, and communicated to his father his confidence of reaching and occupying San'a, the Yemen capital, in one or two weeks. He asked permission to continue the invasion. Back came the reply: "Stay where you are."

"I need neither men nor supplies to take it," Faisal persisted.

"Do not move farther," the King repeated.

Chafing under this restraint, and certain of his calculations, Faisal turned for support to Abdullah Sulayman, the Finance Minister, knowing that he enjoyed the King's full confidence. The latter, who had accompanied the expedition, and who was charged with provisioning the army, joined Faisal in his plea, assuring the King by radio:

"Neither supplies nor additional men are needed for the venture."

To their chagrin, the answer came: "I know what is best for the Muslims; stay where you are."

So, the campaign was halted, and the King ordered his sons to vacate the occupied Yemen cities and territory. The conferees reassembled at Tayif, with Prince Khalid ibn Abdul Aziz as the Sa'udi negotiator. He acquitted himself with credit. The boundaries were settled; Najran and the Yam district were retained by the Sa'uds; and amity was re-established.

When the subject of Prince Faisal's frustrated invasion plans was recalled, the King patiently explained: "We at

His Majesty King Abdul Aziz Ibn Abdur Rahman Al Faisal Al Sa'ud, founder of the Kingdom of Sa'udi Arabia.

School children chat with th[e]
teacher on the porch of t[he]
gleaming white school at Hof[uf,]
Sa'udi Arabia.

Street scene in Jiddah, Red [Sea]
port of entry into Sa'udi Ara[bia.]
Jiddah is the location of all f[or-]
eign legations and embassies [in]
Sa'udi Arabia and is the ma[in]
port of entry for Moslem [pil-]
grims en route to Mecca fr[om]
all parts of the world.

Wide World Photos

His Royal Highness, Amir Faisal, at the time of his return from the conquest of 'Asir in 1922. As Minister of Foreign Affairs, Amir Faisal is probably the most widely known of all the King's sons, having represented his country at the United Nations organization conference in San Francisco, and in subsequent UN meetings.

The determined spirit of the "Youth With a Purpose" is evident in this early photograph of King Ibn Sa'ud, taken at the time when he had become Sultan of Najd, and was about to embark on his conquest and unification of the rest of the Arabian peninsula.

Camel caravans still plod the Sa'udi Arabian desert despite the vehicular traffic now part of Sa'udi Arabian life. This caravan heads into the desert from Jiddah in western Sa'udi Arabia.

His Majesty, Kir Ibn Sa'ud of Sa'u Arabia with h son, the Crow Prince, look at t golden spike us on the last tie the recently con pleted Sa'udi Go ernment Railroa the only operatir rail carrier in t country. The lir runs from the Pe sian Gulf port Dammam 350 mil inland to the capit city of Riyad Built by the Ar bian American C Company, the e tire cost of t project, estimat at more than $50 000.000, is beir paid for out of royalties. The line expected to brir vast economic be efits to Sa'udi Ar bia in the for of regular low-cc transportation in the interior.

Sons of Abdul-Aziz Ibn Sa'ud.

ajesty and
King Ab-
of Trans-
In the back-
is H. E.
ey Hamza,
his Maj-
visors.

H.R.H. Amir Khalid, negotiator o
the Yemeni peace treaty.

Date palms thriving in a garden a
Al Kharj in Sa'udi Arabia. Amer
can farm experts, brought int
Sa'udi Arabia at the request of th
Sa'udi Government, have helpe
Arab farmers to learn the techniqu
of modern, scientific farming.

H. E. Sheikh Muhammad ibn Isa al-Khalifa, elder of the family, who enjoyed two visits to the U.S. in 1939 and 1949.

An Arabian American Oil Company drilling rig atop a crescent-shaped sand dune on the desert near Abqaiq, Sa'udi Arabia.

Amir Abdul-Muhsim ibn Abdullah b. Jlewi, Vice-Governor of al-Hasa.

H.R.H. Sa'ud al Sa'ud is greeted by Speaker of the House Joseph W. Martin, during the Crown Prince's visit to the U.S. in 1947 at the invition of President Truman.

H.R.H. Amir Faisal with Secretary of State Acheson and (right) H. E. Asad al Faqih, Sa'udi Arabian Ambassador to the U.S.; and (left) H. E. Sheikh Ali Abdullah Alireza, Minister Plenipotentiary.

The Crown Prince with his little daughter.

H.R.H. Amir Mansour with Admiral Cunningham when Prince Mansour visited Egypt to stimulate the Muslim World War II fighters from India. H.R.H. died in 1951.

In recognition of the support given to the United States and its allies in World War II, President Truman presents to H.R.H. Amir Sa'ud the medal of the Legion of Merit, Degree of Commander, in a ceremony at the White House.

Amir Sa'ud, Crown Prince of Sa'ud Arabia, is actively interested in administrative affairs of the kingdom His full title is: His Royal Highness Amir Saud ibn Abdul Aziz ibn Abdul Rahman Al Faisal Al Sa'ud Crown Prince of Sa'udi Arabia.

Crown Prince Sa'ud watches interestedly as a young Sa'udi Arab mechanic adjusts a carburetor in a machine shop in Dhahran.

The Crown Prince and his brother, Muhammad, Prince of Medina, on their first visit to London, 1938.

At Ras Tanura, in strange contrast, stand the symbols of the very old and the very new. A Bedouin and camel against a background made up of the Arabian American Oil Company's ultra-modern refinery indicate in part the change that has come over present-day Sa'udi Arabia.

H.R.H. Prince Faisal at the
Second Assembly of the UN
chatting with Sir Alexander
Cadogan, head of the United
Kingdom's Delegation, and
Faris Bey El-Khoury of Syria

Prince Sultân, Governor of
Riyadh.

Amir Masha'al, Min-
Defense of the Sa'udi
n Government, visit-
h Maj. Gen. Leland S.
during a visit to the
early in 1952. Amir
'al succeeded to the
post in 1951 upon
th of his brother, Amir
ur.

Abdullah Al-Faisal,
appointed Minister
ior and Health.

The Dammam port in
ation, showing part o
trestle and causeway
extends almost seven
into the Persian Gulf.

A master carpenter
structing a tool shack f
Arabian American Oil
pany at Ras Tanura,
Arabia.

ran Cub Scouts, young-
of Arabian American
Company employees,
as a Sa'udi Arab Bed-
spins yarns of desert
ture on the desert near
ran, Sa'udi Arabia.

a'udi Arab Bedouin
s for the camera. Many
e Arabian American Oil
pany's 14,000 Sa'udi em-
es were desert wander-
st a few years ago.

Th:rsty journeyers. A camel caravan drinks at one of the desert way stations where newly drilled wells have provided adequate supplies of water. Though the airplane, the motor vehicle, and the railroad train have now become part of Sa'udi Arabian life, camel transportation across the caravan trails of the desert is still a familiar sight in Sa'udi Arabia.

present lack sufficient men to staff our administration properly; what could we have done under the added responsibility of administering al-Yemen?"

Besides, Abdul Aziz ibn Sa'ud, the Man With a Purpose, was not seeking conquest; he was seeking peace. After he had completed the thirty-year task of taming the Ikhwan, he was determined that this should mark the end of the old life and the beginning of a new one for Arabia.

As he had told his counsellors at that time, in words that have proved to be truly prophetic:

"From now on, we will, Insha Allah, lead a new life and go forward."

A new Arabia was coming into being.

OUT OF CONTINUAL WAR FOR THIRTY-FIVE YEARS THE FOLLOWING ARE THE MAJOR EVENTS

Battle of As-Sarif . . . . February 16, 1901
Occupation of Riyadh and al-'Arid and named
    Amir of Najd and Imam of Wahabis . . . . January 15, 1902
Annexation of Karj, Mahmal and Washm 1902-1903
Conquest of Qasim 1903-1906
Occupation of 'Unaizah . . . . March 23, 1904
Battle of Bakriyah . . . . May 16, 1904
Battle of Shananah . . . . September 29, 1904
Meadows of Mahanna—Death of Ar-Rasheed . . . . . . April 14, 1906
Pacification of Tribal Revolts 1906-1909
Battle of Tarfiyah . . . . September 14, 1907
Occupation of Buraidah . . . . May 23, 1908
Battle of Hadiyah (The Gift) . . . . January 10, 1910
Conquest of al-Hasa . . . . April 13, 1913
Battle of Jerab . . . . January 24, 1915
Battle of Turbah . . . . May 25, 1919
Abdul Aziz Elected Sultan of Najd 1921
Repossession of Asir Province . . . . January 1921-1923

Battle of Homs 1919
Battle of Jahra.............................October 11, 1921
Surrender of Haiel, Jauf, and Wadi Sirhan......November 2, 1921
Battle and Occupation of Tayif...............September 7, 1924
Occupation of Mecca (without fighting).........October 18, 1924
Surrender of Medina after ten-month siege.......December 5, 1925
Surrender of Jiddah after one-year siege........December 22, 1925
Abdul Aziz Elected King of Hijaz..............January 19, 1926
Protectorate of Tihamah.............................1926
Abdul Aziz Elected King of Najd and its
    Dependencies ....January 19, 1927
Battle of Sabla..........................March 30, 1929
    and Crushing of Ikhwan Rebellion...............1928-1930
Unification of Country as Sa'udi Arabian
    Kingdom ....September 22, 1932
Annexation of Najran and District of Yam—
    Settlement of Sa'udi Yemeni Boundaries.................1934

[152]

CHAPTER SIXTEEN

Every Inch a King

It had been thirty years since those days when the Old Fox of Kuwait, Mubarak ibn Sabah, had enticed the Sa'uds into joining him in a campaign against the Sa'douns, Amirs of the Muntafiq tribes of Iraq, strongest northeast of Najd, and renowned for their valor and chivalry. The Sa'douns were commanded by 'Ujaymi as-Sa'doun, an intrepid horseman who repeatedly led the charges, and thoroughly defeated his foes, among them Abdul Aziz ibn Sa'ud.

Now, the word had come to King Abdul Aziz that this one-time gallant adversary was coming to make the pilgrimage. No sooner had he learned of this than he dispatched two automobiles to meet him en route, and to escort him on his journey. Then, when the old antagonists finally met, Abdul Aziz greeted him with warm enthusiasm: "Hla 'Ujaymi! . . . Hla 'Ujaymi! . . . Hla 'Ujaymi!" (Welcome 'Ujaymi!)

Embracing the Sa'doun heartily, he held him away at arm's length and, beaming at him, asked: "Were you the wearer of the red gutra, mounting the sorrel mare that day?"

"By Allah, O long of years, those were the days of Jahiliyah!"

"I can still see you as you charged that day on the sorrel mare, and this I well remember."

"It was Jahiliyah time for us—glad it is over, O long of years."

Thus, the two knights were united in friendship. No

[153]

one who knows Abdul Aziz could be surprised by this showing of appreciation of valor in a foe, for valor is an integral part of his own character, as he has well shown on many a battlefield. At the battle of Shananah, he led, in person, the attack on the Turkish cannon; and, after reaching the age of fifty, he headed the charge at Sabla, sword in hand, in open view of both armies, for, like all Najdis, he preferred to wield the sword at close quarters.

Fortunate for him that he had had that early training among the banu Murrah, whose life was the hardest in a hard land, for he was to need all of the endurance and battle wisdom which he acquired there. Once, for example, when the mounts were tiring and his exhausted companions were lagging in pursuit of the enemy, he slipped from his zalul, put his sandals in the saddlebag, and, in his bare feet, hastened ahead of his followers to spur the chase. Again, after seven sleepless nights and days, his zalul fell from exhaustion, and the following cameleer and his mount fell over him; after a good rub with oil and salt, and a few hours' sleep, he was ready for action again.

He still carries the scars of combat: shrapnel in the knee and left hand from a Turkish cannon, a soft-nosed bullet in the hip from an 'Ujman gun, sword wounds in arms and body, and a broken shoulder from a fall in action.

Many a Western reader, conscious of the huge casualties in the two world wars, and remembering that a single bomb killed 210,000 people at Hiroshima, may be inclined to look with disdain upon the hundred-odd battles fought by Ibn Sa'ud, but the philosophic historian, Ibn Khaldun, has admonished us not to judge historic events by contemporary standards, but, rather, to project them against their own background.

Thus, to maintain a sense of proportion, one may profitably remember that the Battle of Gettysburg, greatest in the Civil War, lasted for three days, from the morning of July 1 to the evening of July 3; that General Meade reported the killed of the Northern Army to have been 2,834 men; and that, if one assumes General Lee's losses to have been equal, the total killed would not greatly exceed the combined dead at the Battle of Turbah: 5,500.

Like all successful military leaders, Abdul Aziz repeatedly demonstrated that he had, not only courage, but a natural gift for strategy. An early example was his procedure after that first significant victory: his capture of Riyadh on January 15, 1902.

First, he set about, with strict secrecy, to fortify the city. Then he caused word to be spread to the Rasheeds that he had fled to the south. This misinformation prompted the powerful foe to march upon Riyadh, only to be dealt a surprise attack on the road, and to be forced to return to Haiel without having accomplished their proclaimed purpose. This cost them much loss of prestige in the eyes of their tribes.

The element of humor pervades another instance: The armies of Haiel and Shammar, with superior forces of Bedouins, were seeking battle with Ibn Sa'ud, who had captured great flocks of their camels. Camels, as we know, represented wealth to the Bedouins.

So, Abdul Aziz ordered his men to keep the flocks in camp, unhobbled and untethered. Then he moved his fighting force into ambush. When the enemy forces appeared, and saw the camp with its wealth of camels, they charged eagerly, firing their guns as they advanced.

The camels, hearing the firing and being unhobbled, scattered and ran for the desert, and what happened next was just what Ibn Sa'ud had expected: The Bedouins, unable to resist the tempting prizes, broke ranks and chased after the camels. Ibn Sa'ud then attacked the army of Haiel and Shammar, and won his battle.

Yet, with all of his courage and strategy, Ibn Sa'ud did not, as this narrative has shown, have an unbroken series of victories. His saving virtue, in time of setback, was his capacity to appraise results with realism and a sense of humor. By way of illustration, he was asked by a friend on one occasion why he had retired with his warriors from a certain action.

Abdul Aziz laughed. "You are mistaken," he assured the friend. "We did not retire—we ran away and flew as fast as we could to escape!"

Never a man to pretend to virtue where none existed, he was once praised by another friend for his generosity in agreeing to a peace treaty with Sa'ud ibn Abdul Aziz ibn Mut'ib ar-Rasheed. But Ibn Sa'ud quickly corrected him: "Your brother (meaning himself) is no hero. I had other pressing matters to attend to, and felt unable to carry on on all fronts."

Ordinarily, Ibn Sa'ud is a man of vast patience in negotiation: he has had to be even more so in his dealings with the sheikhs and chiefs of the Arab tribes than he has with foreign powers. But, on many an occasion he has flared in anger at negotiators who have dared to overstep the boundaries of honor.

One such episode occurred back in 1907, a few months after Ibn Sa'ud had defeated the mighty Abdul Aziz ar-Rasheed at the Meadows of Mhanna. In command of the Turkish forces at Medina at that time was one of the Government's most competent generals and diplomats, Sami Pasha Farouki. He had marched to Haiel, the Rasheed capital, at his Government's instructions; and had asked Ibn Sa'ud for a conference. It was arranged.

Sami Pasha told Ibn Sa'ud that the people of al-Qasim wanted the Turkish Government to rule their country, because "you, as well as Ibn Rasheed, are unable to protect them."

"And," Ibn Sa'ud responded, "did the Turkish Government protect them? Their leaders are present at this gathering. Ask them and they will answer you."

"We did not come here," Sami Pasha retorted, "to ask your permission, nor to lure you. We came only to give you a lesson in fealty and obedience to our exalted Government, and we have no other teacher but the sword!"

"I very much regret what you have stated, and that a government should entrust its affairs to a person like you. Know you, O Sami, that the Arabs have never humbly obeyed any except Allah, and were it not that you are our guest, we would never have permitted you to leave your seat!"

Frustrated and annoyed, Sami Pasha returned to his camp. Later, he sent a messenger to Ibn Sa'ud, saying: "The Pasha sends his regards to you, and says that the Government is ready to pay you twenty thousand gold pounds and an annuity to acknowledge its suzerainty over the Qasim."

Ibn Sa'ud went white with rage, and his words were searing as he told the messenger: "Dare you, O cunning one, to carry such a message to us? Are you bereft of Arab honor? Since when did Ibn Sa'ud sell his country and subjects to those who wished to enslave them? I shall not degrade my sword with your blood, O cunning one, but I shall not prevent the sword of another from doing so!"

[157]

The messenger flew from the tent and kept right on going until he got to Medina, not bothering to stop to deliver Ibn Sa'ud's answer. As to Sami Pasha, he thought better of his intention of taking over al-Qasim, and returned with his army to Medina.

But, if Ibn Sa'ud is sometimes given to anger on occasions when it is justified, he is quick to repent and to make amends if he finds that he is wrong. A case in point occurred in the summer of 1940, when Abdul Aziz, having finished holding court and judging disputes, was preparing to leave for home. Then, he remembered that he had overlooked a certain matter, so he picked up the telephone.

Despite repeated efforts, he could not get any response from the "central" (Merkaz). Highly irritated, he ordered the jailing of Mahssoun, the Director of the Wireless. Told of the order, Mahssoun presented himself to the jailer and had himself locked up.

When the King reached his palace, Prince Faisal said to him: "You have imprisoned Mahssoun; he is the Director of the Wireless, and has no connection with the telephone."

His Majesty, who by then had calmed down, replied: "I meant he who is responsible for the telephone system, for if the service of the palace is bad, what becomes of the service in the rest of the kingdom? Bring me Mahssoun forthwith!"

He dispatched two of his sons, Mansur and Nasir, who brought Mahssoun from jail, after twenty-five minutes of imprisonment, and replaced him with the director of the telephone system. The King asked Mahssoun:

"Who imprisoned you?"

"You did, may Allah prolong your years, and I demand my rights from you."

With a twinkle, the King countered: "I did not imprison

you, Nasir did. (Nasir being the governor of Riyadh.) Demand your rights from him."

But Mahssoun was unabashed: "You did, my lord, and I demand my rights of none other but you."

"What do you wish?"

"I want the house in which I live, and it is your property. Are you giving it to me?"

"It is yours."

"And I ask from Your Majesty something else."

"What is it?"

"I beg you, O long of days, to forgive the Director of Central."

"And that is granted also."

The house given to Mahssoun had a value of two thousand pounds. The episode is indicative of the fact, not realized by many in the West, that democracy is a living, actually-practiced reality in this land governed by a paternal autocrat, instead of just a word to be given lip service.

The humblest Bedouin addresses the King by his first name: "O Abdul Aziz," or "O father of Turki" (his first-born, deceased in 1918). When they speak of him, they say "Imam" or "Sheyoukh" (plural of Sheikh).

The King, himself, dislikes titles, especially those designed to glorify, such as "Your Majesty," et cetera; but, unfortunately, the protocol that goes with international relations has become generally accepted. Concerning this, the King once remarked: "People speak of someone who is honored by being received by the King. The truth is that, by the Grace of Islam, I do not value what they call 'Kingship,' or care to be surrounded by grandeur and might.

"Rather, it is a boon of Islam that I am privileged to sit with you, and you with me, to converse and pleasantly exchange views. It is a boon expressing the liberty that reigns in Islam that my door is open to all who wish to enter, without the formality of permission, guard, or scrutiny.

"At one time, a dignitary said to me: 'Why do you not place guards at your door, that none may enter without your permission?' I answered that no guard or barrier should stand between me and my people. My conscience and my nature would not tolerate this."

At mealtime, the King, Amir, Sheikh, and servant, as well as any guest present, regardless of station, sit down to partake as equals. (The Wedgewood Room of the Waldorf Astoria had its first black guest when the Amir Faisal brought to his table his freedman, Marsuq, whom he deems a gentleman in his own right.)

The sedentary Arabs of other countries, who have learned to conform to form and ceremony, idealize Ibn Sa'ud for these Bedouin virtues. In the Hijaz, as a carry-over from Turkish influence, the people entering the Majlis kiss his hand, although he prefers a handshake. In Najd, no one presents himself abjectly, nor kisses the hand. What the Najdi may do is implant a kiss of fealty and respect between the eyes of an elder, or kiss his head or shoulder.

The King's contempt for pomp is accompanied, logically enough, by a distaste for sycophants. Faithful to Muslim injunction, he has established a High Council (Shawra) to advise him on all matters of importance. A story is told that, on one occasion, he struck the carpet sharply with his cane, and angrily rebuked the councillors: "What sort of councillors are you? I come to you seeking your views, and all I get are nods of assent to everything I say! There is no profit to me or the country to see you nod your heads in chorus! Begone, I do not need you!"

He practices frankness, and demands it of those about

him, for, as he once put it: "Every man should say what he thinks, with complete candor, without fear of blame for being truthful. Every individual should boldly state what he believes to be of benefit, for research, examination, free discussion, and adjustment lead to the best results. Men should endeavor, and fulfillment is in the hands of Allah."

In addition to seeking the advice of his High Council, the King believes in decentralization of governmental functions, within limitations. While he keeps in close touch by radio and telephone with all parts of his kingdom, he permits his governors to conform with the traditions and customs of the various widespread localities, so long as they do not conflict with Koranic law, and so long as they do their jobs well. He simply will not tolerate incompetence.

No qualities in a man win him higher regard from Ibn Sa'ud than kindness, generosity, and hospitality; and this, too, is to be expected, for the endearment in which he is held by his people derives in great measure from those same qualities in the King. In battle and in peace, to friend and foe, he has manifested these qualities repeatedly.

Around the capital, Ar-Riyadh, from one to ten thousand Bedouins may camp, awaiting the opportunity to tell the King of their problems or their wants, for, in a paternal government such as this, the ruler considers himself the responsible father of his subjects, and they come to him to make their wants known.

They may stay for a week, or a month, or until they please to move; but, as long as they are there, they camp as guests of the King, and he supplies them with food from the public kitchens. Then, their problems disposed, and provisions supplied to them, they move away again to their pasture lands or homes.

[161]

In 1911, some of his relatives in the south had declared a revolt against Ibn Sa'ud, and were having a measure of success with the assistance of the 'Ujman, their maternal uncles, who were intrepid fighters. While this was in progress, still more trouble developed:

First, as we will remember (Chapter 13), Sa'd, the younger brother of Abdul Aziz, went on a mission to the tribe of 'Utaiba in 1912, as a boy of seventeen, and was treacherously taken prisoner and turned over by the 'Utaiba to Sherif Hussein, who exacted a treaty of truce as ransom for the youth.

Then, on top of all of this, as we will also remember, Zamil as-Sabhan, who was directing the affairs of his nephew, Sa'ud ar-Rasheed, repudiated the truce which he had entered into with Ibn Sa'ud.

Thus, Ibn Sa'ud, who had theretofore been adding victory to victory, found himself hemmed in by enemies, without resources, and at nearly the nadir of his career. In such circumstances, he moved into al-Hasa to quell the revolt led by his relative, Salman ibn Muhammad ibn Sa'ud, and his allies, the 'Ujman.

Salman had sent a delegation of three to seek assistance, including arms and ammunition, from the sheikhs of Qatar, Bahrein, 'Oman, and Musqat. This trio sailed across the Gulf and received one hundred muskets and four thousand rupees from Sultan al-Hamadh on the Persian shore; Sheikh 'Aisa of Bahrein gave them one hundred muskets and twelve thousand rupees; and the rulers of 'Oman supplied them with an even greater amount.

While they were sailing back to the port of 'Uqair, which was in possession of the 'Ujman, Ibn Suaylim, the ruler of Qatif, dispatched his fighters in sailing vessels, surrounded the boat of their foe, and brought the men and

[162]

their newly-acquired arms and money to al-Hasa, where Abdul Aziz was camping.

Ibn Sa'ud ordered that their chains be struck, and that they be immediately taken to the guest tent, where they were treated with full hospitality. After the third day, Ibn Sa'ud ordered them brought before him, where they expected to be executed. He addressed them as follows:

"O, my people, we do not wish to avenge ourselves or anyone. He of you who wishes to return to his chief may do so, and he who wishes to stay with us is welcome."

One of the three men answered: "O, long of years, I prefer your hell-fire to Salman's paradise."

Ibn Sa'ud ordered that the man be given garments (kiswas) and arms, and entered him as one of his fighting men.

One of the other two, speaking for both, declared: "We prefer to go to our chief to support him and be killed in his cause."

Thereupon, Ibn Sa'ud ordered kiswas, zaluls, and gifts of money given to them and released them.

In view of the straits in which Ibn Sa'ud found himself at this period, this magnanimity is well indicative of the character of the King.

It was just before the oil concession was granted that a friend and subject of Ibn Sa'ud visited him from Kuwait. In the course of their visit, the King realized that his visitor's circumstances were straitened.

When the guest was ready to depart, after a visit of several days, the King ordered a gift for him, consisting of wearing apparel, and a sum of money, for which he penned the order. The visitor presented this to the King's personal secretary, who, at that time, was none other than the present Minister of Finance, Sheikh Abdullah Sulayman.

[163]

Knowing the full details of the Kingdom's financial position in those pre-oil days, Sulayman quickly realized that the amount was more than could be afforded. He also questioned whether the King had actually intended to make it so large. So, he went to him and asked whether he intended the final dot (which is the Arabic zero), pointing out that the order called for fifteen thousand riyals. Abdul Aziz answered: "I had meant fifteen hundred, but let it remain thus. We shall not let the pen outdo us in generosity."

Whenever he is traveling by automobile, he carries along purses of silver and gold. One day, as he sped across the desert, a Bedouin ran toward him, waving his hand. In greeting, Abdul Aziz tossed him a purse, which delighted him.

The chauffeur drew the King's attention to the fact that this purse contained, not silver coins, but one hundred gold pounds (the gold pound today is worth $14, U. S.) and fifty-four Sa'udi riyals.

Abdul Aziz called to the man, and he returned dejectedly sensing that he would have to return the money. Instead, Abdul Aziz told him: "You thanked me for the purse I gave you. I had intended to give you a purse of silver, but Allah in his mercy gave you the gold purse, instead. Therefore, you do not owe me any thanks, but thank Allah, the Great Giver, for the gift. My advice to you is to choose a fertile spot, settle down, plant some palms, and better your condition, and that of your family, through the gift of God."

It is said that the man has, in fact, profited, not only by the gift of gold, but by the advice which Abdul Aziz gave him.

It was the King's habit for years to hold court on the doorstep of the palace, where anyone with a grievance might

[164]

come forth and state his case. During his sojourns in the country, this court was held at the door of his tent.

He disposes of all matters of right and wrong according to Koranic law. Litigation concerning differences over property are turned over to arbitrators for study and recommendation.

In his paternal government he very often compromises, not at the expense of a litigant, but with the justice of a father. We find this illustrated in one of the delectable tales related by Murdum Bey, then Prime Minister of Syria, during a visit to King Ibn Sa'ud in 1946:

"While we were at court, a Bedouin came in and addressed the King by his first name, saying: 'O Abdul Aziz, our confidence in you prompts us to come to you as the administrator of justice who gives each his due.' "

The King listened patiently and attentively and ordered the judges to look into the matter carefully, for the complaint related to a land dispute. Murdum continued:

"The Bedouin had hardly left when the representatives of two disputing tribes presented themselves so the King might judge their differences.

"He took up the subject with a great deal of ability and mellow wisdom, and called upon the chiefs to embrace each other, ordering that the damage and indemnities claimed by the two tribes be paid to each from his own treasury.

"It so happened that Sir Abdullah Philby, the well-known Englishman, was present with us. When Philby saw this he turned to the King and said: 'By Allah, Your Majesty, what you did just now is the greatest manifestation of democracy, which cannot be found today in America or in my own country, England.' "

In his personal and private life, Abdul Aziz maintains

[165]

the same simplicity which marks his appearances in public.

He rises an hour before dawn, and reads a portion of the Koran, awaiting the call to dawn prayer. Then he has breakfast, mostly of cultured milk, dates, bread, and honey; at noon, a vegetable soup, meat and rice; and, for supper, the same fare, with the addition of a light dessert. He rarely takes tea, but drinks camel's milk, and is very fond of coffee.

His clothing is simple, made of white cotton and linen; and, in these later years, he also uses woolen garments. He dislikes silk, and never wears it, or anything embroidered. His ghutra, or headdress, is of plain cotton or cashmere, and is held in place by an 'iqal (twin cords, holding the ghutra, or head scarf, in place) spun with gold thread. He uses sandals in summer and oxfords in winter.

In performing his five daily prayers, he leads his retinue as Imam. Although he uses glasses, he often reads without them if the writing is clear and legible; otherwise, communications are read to him by secretaries.

Perhaps mindful of the hard desert days, when niceties were all but impossible, he is very fond of bathing. Yet, in contrast, it is apparently the habit established by those same desert days which causes him never to use a bedstead, but to prefer having his bed made up, Arab style, on the floor. He sleeps lightly, and only six hours daily; but, at the same time, he can sleep in almost any circumstances, for his life has accustomed him to doze in an automobile, on camel's back, or wherever he rests his head on a pillow.

He prides himself on his stable of thoroughbred Arab horses, whose pedigrees he knows by heart; and his other hobby is his collection of ancient swords, especially those of his forbears. Although he carried a Mauser rifle during his wars, his preference, like all Najdis, has always been the sword.

[166]

He always spends his evenings in the family circle, surrounded by his children and grandchildren; and these he describes as the happiest moments of his busy life.

In the East, the harem, protected household, has never been the subject of inquiry by anyone outside the family. The ladies of the house are never the subject of discussion with acquaintances, and the desire to ferret out its inner secrets has never been a part of Arab curiosity.

It is only on serious occasions such as sickness, when a friend may inquire about the health of the wife, designating her as "bint Ammak" (the daughter of your paternal uncle). One ventures upon this tabooed subject only because of the oft-repeated interest in the household of Ibn Sa'ud.

The King has strictly conformed to the Muslim law by limiting his marriages to four at a time. Many of them were to establish relations with the principal tribes of Arabia, so as to weld them as much as possible into close ties with his family.

The Man With a Purpose built a kingdom and rebuilt a family whose manpower had been decimated by interminable wars, and anyone seeing his sons cannot help but say: "May Allah increase his tribe."

In Sa'udi Arabia, no stigma attaches to divorce, nor is it considered wrong for a divorced wife to remarry. If she prefers to remain unmarried and to look after her children, she has the choice of being maintained in proper style, or of receiving a dower commensurate with her husband's position, thus assuring herself of independence.

If the code of the West is different from that of the East in the matter of marriage, that is not important to this narrative. The important consideration is that Abdul Aziz ibn Sa'ud has been *faithful* to his code: a code that demands courage, steadfastness, chivalry, patience, justice, generos-

[167]

ity, and honor; that has made his word inviolate when others have forgotten theirs; that has made him recognize his own limitations, and respect the talents of others; the code, in brief, that marks him every inch a King.

CHAPTER SEVENTEEN

From the West: A Partner

When Abdul Aziz ibn Sa'ud drove the Husseins out of the Hijaz, he had completed his conquest of Arabia Deserta. When he quelled the years-long revolt of the Ikhwan, he had accomplished the other phase of his task: unity.

One recalls, however, that Ibn Sa'ud had other dreams for his people: He wanted to bring some substance into their lives, and at least a bit of lustre.

But, how? The arid, barren land had never yielded enough of life's necessities to provide more than the minimum essentials to the Bedu who roamed its wastes with their camels and goats, and to those who managed to exist in its scattered towns and villages. There was no industry, except of the most rudimentary sort, and it offered only a bare subsistence to those who engaged in it.

Consequently, agriculture and industry together were impotent to support the Government, or to provide the exports with which to pay for the things which Arabia must import: rice, flour, tea, dry goods and other necessary manufactured products.

The country's chief source of direct and indirect revenue was the annual pilgrim traffic, but this was never enough to pay for anything beyond the most routine requirements. Nor did customs duties yield anything of real consequence.

The net result was that the Government had never been able to build up any reserves, whether of taxable income sources, savings, or credit; and, in times of stringency, was hard-put to find ways of operating at all. This was the case despite the simplicity and compactness of the Government, requiring no large outlay of cash beyond the support of the officials, the Royal Family, and the large number of dependent subjects.

Two forms of expenditures the King insisted upon, and still does, as absolutely essential: (1) a bounty in the form of money and food for many of the Bedu tribes, who otherwise would be likely to cause trouble; and (2) support and equipment for an adequate army.

So, as Ibn Sa'ud pondered his problems in those early days of his rule of a united Arabia, the essential question was: *Where* might one look for the wherewithal of progress?

Ultimately, the time came when Ibn Sa'ud thought that he could see the answer, if only he could devise the formula: Perhaps beneath those vast sweeps of inhospitable sand, there *might* be oil.

The King's speculation had been stimulated by the activities of an energetic New Zealander named Major Frank Holmes, who had been brought to Bahrein in the early 1920's to assist in developing water resources. In 1922, he crossed over to Sa'udi Arabia and, the following year, persuaded the then-Sultan Ibn Sa'ud to grant him a mineral concession covering thirty thousand square miles in al-Hasa. He followed up this accomplishment by getting a concession in Bahrein two years later.

Holmes took these concessions in the name of a British group known as the Eastern and General Syndicate, which hoped to dispose of them to British oil companies. This effort was unsuccessful. The al-Hasa concession was allowed to lapse. Then, in the hope of salvaging something out of the venture, the Syndicate turned to the United States.

The Gulf Oil Corporation was interested. It took an op-

[170]

tion in November, 1927, and sent a geologist to examine and map Bahrein. But, Gulf was doomed to frustration: As a participant in the Iraq Petroleum Company, it had signed the famous "Red Line Agreement," by which all signatories agreed not to act independently within an area roughly constituting the old Ottoman Empire. When Gulf referred the question to IPC, the Board of Directors ruled that it could not take the concession.

It was then that Gulf approached the Standard Oil Company of California, which had been experiencing very poor fortune, indeed, in its enterprise abroad, having drilled more than thirty wells in a half-dozen foreign countries, and carried out exploration in a dozen others, with no substantial oil production to show for its efforts.

But the company decided that it would try again, and, in December, 1928, Gulf assigned its option to California Standard. This, it turned out, was only the beginning of two years of disputation with the British, because Bahrein was a British protectorate. It was not until 1930 that it was possible to elicit acceptable terms from London, and it was in June of that year when an agreement was signed with the Sheikh of Bahrein.

To operate the concession, California Standard established the Bahrein Petroleum Company, Ltd., incorporated in Canada as demanded by the British. Exactly two years later, oil was discovered.

This discovery very naturally stimulated the company's interest in other Persian Gulf areas. The British, by dint of earlier treaties with the Persian Gulf sheikhs, were able to block their American rivals from Qatar and Trucial Oman. But, there remained Sa'udi Arabia: a completely independent kingdom.

At this point, Major Holmes' Eastern and General Syndicate reappeared on the scene. Although it had allowed its al-Hasa concession to lapse, it managed to persuade California Standard that its contacts and experience would make it very helpful in any Sa'udi Arabian negotiations.

Whether it *could* have been helpful or not was never established: The Syndicate continued to postpone action so many times that California Standard finally served notice that it intended to go ahead on its own—and did.

As events turned out, it now appears that the delays were not without their value. The company was unknown to the King when the Bahrein venture started. But, as time passed, he had the opportunity to observe how the Americans conducted themselves, and had learned that they had earned an excellent reputation. They had demonstrated that they operated efficiently, paid their obligations promptly, kept their word, got along well with the people and the Government, and, perhaps most important of all, their interest was confined strictly to oil, unaffected by any political entanglements or ambitions.

It was early in November, 1932, when the first approach to the Sa'udi Government was made. It was in the form of a telegram from H. St. John B. Philby, the distinguished British author and explorer, who was then in Jiddah, asking permission for California Standard to make a preliminary geological examination of al-Hasa, with the purpose of negotiating a concession if the results seemed to justify it. The Government, however, wanted to put the concession discussions first.

Three months thereafter, in mid-February, 1933, Lloyd N. Hamilton arrived in Jiddah to represent the company. Accompanying him was Karl S. Twitchell, the engineer, who was favorably known to the King. He had made an extensive

survey of mining and water resources in Sa'udi Arabia at the King's request.

Hamilton found himself not without competition: The Iraq Petroleum Company had sent an agent to dicker. Even Major Holmes had reappeared. The King, himself, participated in the negotiations part of the time, so important did he consider the project; but, most of the time, his ministers represented him, keeping him constantly posted.

At the end of May, the decision was made: Hamilton won the concession, and signed it with Sheikh Abdullah Sulayman, the Finance Minister, on May 29, 1933.

In essence, the concession gave the Company the right, for sixty years, to explore for, produce, transport, and manufacture petroleum in an area covering the eastern part of Sa'udi Arabia up to the western edge of that vast ribbon of sand known as Dahna, with a line extending north and south from the limits of Dahna to the borders of Sa'udi Arabia. The Company was to make certain advance payments and loans, and to pay rental until oil was produced in commercial quantities. Thereafter, royalty was to be paid at a rate of four gold shillings per ton, or a comparable amount in dollars. The area of the concession was originally expected to cover about 160,000 square miles, but the promising surface indications extended so far south that the area finally agreed upon covered roughly 320,000 square miles. Six years later, by supplemental agreement, the area was enlarged to about 440,000 square miles; and, still later, the Arabian American Oil Company's right to operate in the submerged lands of the Persian Gulf was officially affirmed.

Then, moving ahead for a moment, we find another revision of the agreement, concluded at Jiddah on December 30, 1950, which marked an additional forward step in the harmonious relationships between Company and Government.

By the terms of this new agreement, the Sa'udi Arab Government became equal partner in all profits made in the oil operation, and, at the same time, was assured a return even if there were *no* profits. Specifically, what the new accord provides is that, after deduction of operating, exploration and development expense, depreciation, and foreign government taxes, including U. S. income taxes, half of all operating revenue goes to the Sa'udi Arab Government.

The payments are made by paying the SAG royalties in the regular manner, and supplementary taxes to bring the share up to half of the profits. Thus, even if the Company operated at a loss, the SAG would receive its royalties on all oil produced; and, whatever the profits may be, it gets half of them.

At the same time, the Company benefits by stabilization of its financial arrangements with the Sa'udi Arabs. Thus, under the original concession, Aramco agreed to pay royalties of four gold shillings per ton. At the U. S. official price of about $8.24 per gold pound, this amounted to approximately 22 cents per barrel. However, for years the SAG argued that the royalty should be based upon the prevailing gold price in Sa'udi Arabia, usually above the U. S. price, and at one time up to $20 and $21 per gold pound.

Although holding that the official gold price should prevail, the Company agreed, in 1949, to pay royalty on the basis of $12 per gold pound, or about 32 cents per barrel; and agreed, also, to pay a premium for all local currency purchased for operating expenses in Sa'udi Arabia.

Under the new agreement, the Government accepts the

official exchange rates of the International Monetary Fund; permits the purchase of riyals without premium rates; and authorizes payment of SAG taxes in the currencies which Aramco receives for its sales.

The progressive nature of the new accord evoked widespread acclaim from the American press. Aramco's president, W. F. Moore, commented:

"The Jiddah agreement is a forward-looking arrangement which is expected to increase the income of Sa'udi Arabia, enabling the Government to go ahead with its economic growth and development at an increased pace . . . We believe that the best interests of the United States and Sa'udi Arab Governments, and of Aramco, have been served."

The leaders of Sa'udi Arabia apparently felt likewise, for, a little more than three months later, when Iran ordered the nationalization of its oil fields, Prince Faisal was quoted in Cairo as saying firmly that his country would not do likewise. The Iranian action, the Prince stated, "will not affect the Sa'udi Arabian oil fields in the least."

But, to return to that day of May 29, 1933, when the Finance Minister and Lloyd Hamilton signed a piece of paper at Kazam palace, on the outskirts of the same city of Jiddah. Both men knew that what they had signed was important, but neither could possibly have envisioned what it was to mean in the years ahead. Even the King could not have foretold that this was the act that was to enable him to remake his country.

*　　*　　*

It was March, 1938. The concession granted by the King to California Standard was now nearly five years old.

The Company had gained a name: The California Arabian Standard Oil Company.* It had acquired a new parent, too: The Texas Company had bought a half-interest in 1936. Otherwise, the only thing that either King or Company had gotten out of the concession was disappointment. The little oil that had been found was insufficient to be worth moving to market.

The start had been made less than four months after the signing of the concession, when two geologists drew up to the shore at Jubail in a native launch. Being the first men of the western world which most of the inhabitants had ever seen, they had grown beards, and wore Arab attire, to minimize their strange appearance.

They wasted no time. On the very day of their arrival, they made their first reconnaissance, and five days later they were delighted to find an oil-promising structure which they called "Dammam dome." When additional equipment arrived a month later, they completed their studies and began congratulating themselves because their work was to be so easy.

It took a while, of course, to transport engineers, construction men, drillers, and equipment, but the No. 1 well at Dammam dome was started on April 30, 1935, with practically everybody happily certain that it would be a producer . . .

By March, 1938, ten wells had been drilled. Three had yielded insignificant quantities of oil. One turned out to be a gas well (still in use, incidentally, for camp purposes). One yielded water. None gave commercial quantities of oil.

But, as most people know, oilmen are a strange breed: they never know when to quit. So, they took a look at Well

* The present name, Arabian American Oil Company, was adopted in 1944.

[178]

No. 7, and said: "Let's try it deeper." They did. And that is how it happened that March, 1938, was the month that established Sa'udi Arabia as an oil country.

It is unnecessary to go into detail here as to the lively activity that followed. Suffice it to say that plans that had long been in the blueprint stage were now transformed into reality: Gathering tanks were installed in the field, a six-inch pipeline was laid to Al-Khobar, a small shipping terminal was established, construction of housing was pushed rapidly, and every manner of facility was set up for the comfort of the increased personnel which would now be necessary.

Finding that there were no satisfactory hydrographic charts of the Persian Gulf waters off the coast of Arabia, the Company employed experts to make one so that ocean-going vessels could approach safely. On the basis of this and other information, they selected Ras Tanura as the deep water terminal, and started a ten-inch pipeline to link it with the field. By the spring of 1939, the essentials of production, transport, storage, and trans-shipment had been provided; a 45,000-barrel stabilization plant was nearing completion at Dhahran, and a 3,000-barrel refinery was under construction at Ras Tanura.

The time had come for a celebration, and the date was set for May 1, 1939. On that day, the first tanker was to be loaded at Ras Tanura: Standard of California's "D. G. Schofield."

His Majesty, the King, accepted the Company's invitation to participate, and the occasion turned out to be a memorable one. Seventeen members of the Royal Family accompanied the King, and so did four of the country's ministers. A military escort of four hundred soldiers, prominent officials and merchants, friends, attendants, and servants made up an assemblage of more than two thousand persons.

Considerable preparation had been necessary to transport this large number of guests across the desert, from Jiddah, Mecca, or Riyadh. Some four hundred automobiles were used. The visitors were established in a colorful camp of 350 tents, adjacent to Dhahran.

The ceremonies, lasting for several days, included the opening of the Ras Tanura terminal and an inspection of the Company's facilities there, at Dhahran, and elsewhere.

Everything was very heartening . . . or so it seemed: Three months later, Hitler was to invade Poland. . . .

During the first months of World War II, the so-called "phony war" stage when the French and German armies sat and looked at each other across the Maginot Line, oil operations in Sa'udi Arabia continued more or less normally, except for the cutting off of free, uncensored communication with the United States. Under the momentum of previously-laid plans, and with materials previously ordered, the Company went ahead with production, discovered two new fields (Abu Hadriya and Abqaiq) and started the little new refinery in operation.

But, it was not in the cards for this to continue. The demand for unrefined crude oil dried up. Most of the geological crews were pulled in from the desert. Wives and children were shipped home, and the number of employees shrank from its pre-war peak of 371 to less than 100. The refinery at Ras Tanura stopped operating, and the terminal closed down, its beacon lights no longer flashing through the night.

War had finally made itself felt, and the employees who remained were left in no doubt about it. To augment the dwindling food supply in the commissary, a stock farm had to be started. Scrawny sheep and cattle were bought in the local market and fed up to fair butchering size. Oilmen thus became farmers, stockmen, and butchers. One of the air-conditioned cottages was transformed into a chicken-breeding establishment, where home-made incubators coaxed chicks out of eggs.

Not that they were idle: the skeleton staff that remained was kept busy maintaining large shipments of oil to Bahrein, and assisting the Sa'udi Government in coping with its war-time difficulties. As a means of dealing with the very serious food situation, Company engineers surveyed the water and agricultural possibilities of the al-Kharj district, southeast of Riyadh. Their recommendations led to the installation of large new diesel-driven pumps and an eleven-mile canal, which made it possible to bring an extensive area under cultivation for the first time.

The Company also drilled a water well on the long, waterless stretch between Oqair and Riyadh, thus facilitating the inland movement of food. When drought placed such a load on the Government's food transport operations that camel transport became inadequate, the Company responded promptly to the King's request and placed a number of its specially-designed trucks in this service, although it was sorely in need of this equipment for its own work.

But, of course, peace ultimately came. And, even before it did, the Arabian oil venture saw a burst of activity such as it had not known before. For, the Allied military leadership knew that great increments of strategically available petroleum products would be needed if full-scale land and sea operations were to be conducted against the Japanese after the European phase had been concluded. One result of their planning: approval for construction of a

50,000-barrel refinery at Ras Tanura, to be financed and built by the company.

High priorities were assigned to the steel and other critical materials needed for the project, trucks and other equipment which could be spared from Army stocks were sold to the Company, and co-operation in the movement of men and materials by sea and air transport was readily given by the military.

Before long, the slumbering oil community was transformed into a scene of intense activity and monumental confusion. Men arrived before they could be properly housed. Both men and materials often arrived in the wrong order. A whole shipload of exceptionally important materials was lost by enemy action. Wartime shortages and Government controls caused delay after delay.

So, what happened? Nobody is quite sure even yet how it was accomplished, but the refinery, with its storage tanks, loading lines, and new pier for tankers, was *finished on time*.

It was early in September, 1945, when the refinery went into partial operation. Since V-J Day, to everybody's grateful surprise, had come the month before, the new plant was not called upon to do the war job for which it had been created. But, the by-then enormous United States Navy was no less grateful for its existence as a source of much-needed supply.

Moreover, the post-war requirements of the Navy provided only part of the reason why the Ras Tanura refinery has proved to be a wisely-conceived project. Almost all forecasters had expected petroleum consumption to fall off when military demand ceased. Instead, U. S. consumption showed an astonishing upturn, and oil from Arabia did its part to overcome the resulting shortage. When the Marshall Plan was launched, the oil of Arabia played a major role in the job of rebuilding western Europe. And, although 1950 produced knotty problems in the international petroleum trade, they were resolved, and it became plain that the future was full of rich promise for the oil of Ibn Sa'ud's Arabia.

Aramco's production had grown so greatly after the war's end that much more extensive marketing facilities were needed. To provide this deficiency, the Standard Oil Company (New Jersey) and Socony-Vacuum Oil Company were given the opportunity to participate in the ownership. Under the new arrangement, Standard of California, The Texas Company, and Standard Oil (New Jersey) each owns 30 per cent; and Socony-Vacuum owns 10 per cent.

Here was a venture that had started back in September, 1933, with two bearded geologists and a hope that there might be oil. Here was a venture which, nearly five years later, was still a failure. Let us look at the venture at mid-1951:

Eight oil fields had been discovered beneath the sands of Sa'udi Arabia, and, in July, the first field had been found offshore, beneath the Persian Gulf.

Crude oil production had reached a peak of more than 800,000 barrels daily, and had totalled 199,000,000 barrels for 1950.

The Ras Tanura refinery, designed to manufacture 50,000 barrels of products daily, was operating by mid-1951 at a rate of 177,000 barrels per calendar day.

The Company is operating 170 miles of pipelines (of 10-, 12-, and 14-inch diameter) and 61 miles of larger diameter lines (20, 22, and 30 inches) to move the crude oil from the fields to the stabilizer at Dhahran, the refinery and terminal at Ras Tanura, and the Bahrein Petroleum Company's refinery on Bahrein Island. In addition, of course, is the great 1,075-mile Trans-Arabian pipeline system (30- and 31-inch diameter), which is moving 300,000 barrels of oil daily from the Persian Gulf coast to the Mediterranean.

In 1949, the number of employees reached a peak of more than 20,000, of whom more than 12,000 were Arabs.

Three modern communities had been created where sixteen years before there was nothing but desert: Dhahran, the headquarters town; Ras Tanura, the refinery and terminal site; and Abqaiq, the production center. They present an impressive sight, with their acres upon acres of industrial installations, all manner of storehouses, workshops, and garages; their great clusters of homes, dormitories, office buildings, schools, hospitals, recreation buildings, commissaries, and dining halls; and their paved streets, electric lights, and taxicabs.

To service its far-spread operations, the Company was operating nearly eighteen hundred motor vehicles of all types, fifteen aircraft (including two four-engine craft for trans-Atlantic transport), and eighty-two launches, tugs, and barges.

The investment by mid-July, 1951, had exceeded $394,-000,000. In addition, the 1,075-mile Trans-Arabian pipeline system had been completed at a cost of $147,000,000.

In brief, eighteen years had given dramatic proof that Sa'udi Arabia was a land of great petroleum resources. They had given proof also that Ibn Sa'ud had been right in his belief that, beneath the vast sweeps of inhospitable sand there might lay fruition for his dream of bringing some substance into the lives of his people, and at least a bit of lustre.

CHAPTER EIGHTEEN

A Land Transformed

Back in 1925, we may recall, Ibn Sa'ud's Ikhwan became restless under the inactivity of the long siege of Jiddah, and nagged persistently at their leader for permission to use the captured cannon to blast down the walls of the city. Ibn Sa'ud said "No!"

But, the walls were blasted down, nonetheless—twenty-two years later—on orders of the King, himself.

The blasting was done, not with cannon, but with dynamite, by the American contractors, Bechtel International, Inc., with Arab co-workers joining in the demolition. Its usefulness a thing of the past, the ancient barrier was serving no purpose except to block the city's orderly growth, and to stand as an obstacle to commerce. Razed in the fall of 1947, its rubble served as fill for harbor development, and as base for new streets.

What happened that day in 1947 to the wall of Jiddah is just a small sample of what has been happening all over Sa'udi Arabia as Ibn Sa'ud utilizes his nation's expanding income to bring to his people the better life of which he had dreamed for so long, and for which he had struggled so earnestly.

The transformation which he is accomplishing has been telescoping centuries of advancement into a few decades: new buildings, new schools and hospitals, new roads and ports and piers, improved water supply, electrification, sanitation, and the great new port-railroad project, with its terminal at Dammam, just to mention a few highlights of a public works program which has involved expenditure of more than $20,000,000 with one American engineering firm in the four post-war years, alone.

The city of Jiddah, itself, offers a striking example. This port of entry for the Hijaz, through which the pilgrims from all over the world have poured each year for centuries, was considered, during the days before Ibn Sa'ud, to be one of the shabbiest spots of the tropics. Today, it is a boom city which bids fair to become "The Pearl of the Red Sea."

As the boat steams into the harbor, the azure sea forms an impressive foreground, with the distant town built of white coral rock, its quaint mashrabiyahs (screened balconies) and residential villas extending to the left, and piers and warehouses to the right; the beautiful Nuzla palace of the King, on an elevation beyond the city, forming the background; new buildings, new houses, paved streets spreading in every direction; for Jiddah today is the commercial heart and diplomatic seat of the Sa'udi kingdom.

The first of the great new projects to greet the traveler is, of course, the new deep-water pier and wharf, with its related harbor facilities. From the shoreline, about a mile south of the heart of the city, a 5,000-foot causeway extends seaward to the inner reef. From there, a steel-pile approach trestle carries onward for 1,300 feet to the pier-head, where the water is fifty feet deep.

The pier-head is 100 feet wide, and 560 feet long, and so arranged that two cargo or passenger ships can dock simultaneously on the sides, while a third moors at the end. The trestle is well-illuminated, and the pier-head has powerful floodlights mounted on towers.

Rising above the pier are office and storage buildings, while on deck are waterline outlets and a full assortment of cargo handling gear, including a great stiff-leg derrick which can unload fifty-ton pieces of cargo from the ships alongside.

At the base of the trestle, a rock-fill marginal wharf provides space for mooring and unloading of cargo and passenger craft of low draft. Along the causeway, about midway between the shoreline and the marginal wharf, is a man-made island of rock, which is being equipped to warehouse goods for customs examination, and to provide immigration services.

The new pier development is of prime significance to Arabia, for it will not only permit the handling of vastly increased shipping, but it will enable some 75,000 additional pilgrims to come and go by sea each year.

To the traveler arriving by air, the evidence of advancement is no less striking. Two beautifully paved runways, of 6,000 and 6,350 feet, permit smooth landings for the big aircraft of today. The airport is equipped with a modern administration building, large and well-equipped hangers and shops, and a lighting system which meets the latest international standards and specifications. Competent authorities have pronounced the Jiddah airport one of the best in the entire Middle East.

Within the city, rejuvenation moves at the same rapid pace. Streets have been paved, a new radio station has been built, the customs guard pier has been enlarged and extended, and a health clinic has been established. The power plant has been enlarged, and a distribution system is being set up to supply current to all parts of the city and its environs.

To residents and visitors, alike, there is occasion for gratitude in the change in water supply. Until recently, the city had no drinking water except that which was distilled

[187]

from the salty sea. To improve this situation, the merchants had planned to bring in drinking water from a distance, but the King called a halt to their project, and, himself, donated to the city the fresh waters of Wadi Fatima, which have given an abundant supply.

The water system has a capacity of 1,500,000 gallons daily, supported by a 1,000,000-gallon reservoir. Its cost was approximately $5,000,000.

In addition, over a good distance of the Pilgrim Road from Jiddah to Mecca, the King has established fountains and rest stations where the travelers can refresh themselves and perform their ablutions. Add to these improvements the paving of this forty-seven-mile road, and one can imagine the blessings which the pilgrims shower upon Abdul Aziz, who has assured their safety and relieved them of great hardships.

Besides all of these things already accomplished in and around Jiddah, others were ready to be undertaken: a new sixty-bed hospital, a sanitary sewage-disposal system for the whole city, enlargement of the power plant and distribution system to supply Mecca as well as Jiddah, and widening and reconstruction of the Jiddah-Mecca highway.

Preparations were also in progress for the erection of a twelve-acre Government warehouse; and negotiations were under way for the installation of a new, fully-automatic telephone system. In the planning stage was a beautiful boulevard, to run along the waterfront of the city, and to extend on past the villas of the crescent for miles.

All of these are, of course, Government projects. Meanwhile, the business and professional people of the city are rearing new commercial buildings and homes at an impressive pace.

Jiddah can still be greatly improved, but the foreigner

[188]

must realize that this is only the *dawn* of a new day, and so the communities of the Hijaz, including the Holy Cities of Mecca and Medina, are just now entering into their era of modern improvement. As we know from our old seaboard cities in the United States, it is much easier to build new structures than it is to revamp old ones. Nevertheless, I believe that anyone visiting Jiddah, and seeing its physical rejuvenation and its activity, cannot doubt my statement that it "bids fair to become the Pearl of the Red Sea."

But, let us leave this bustling seaport and move five hundred miles across the desert to the King's capital city: Riyadh, the one-time primitive community where the youthful Abdul Aziz won the battle which started his ascent to power.

Not a commercial city like Jiddah, nor as populous, Riyadh has nevertheless lagged no whit in the march of progress. As at the Red Sea metropolis, the air traveler finds here an excellent airport, with runways of 6,000 and 5,500 feet, a modern administration building, lighting that meets the highest standards, and a full complement of warehouses, repair shops, and living quarters for working personnel.

During my last visit to Riyadh, the impressive electrification system was nearing completion, including the municipal power plant, with four six-hundred-horsepower diesel engines operating four hundred-KVA generators to supply power and light. I was told that twenty-five miles of transmission lines were to be ready shortly after my departure; and that these units would be sufficient to supply three hundred homes, and to operate pumps for more than two hundred water wells, theretofore donkey-powered, to irrigate the gardens of Wadi Hanifah.

It may be of interest to note that the power units had

started their journey to Riyadh from San Francisco, twelve thousand miles away; had been brought ashore at Ras al Misha'ab in the northeast corner of Sa'udi Arabia, and then had been brought four hundred miles across the desert on the great trucks that one sees today carrying unbelievable loads over hitherto impassable sands.

Subsequently, I have learned that the power plant is being increased by 50 per cent by addition of an 1,140-horsepower diesel engine, connected to an 800-kilowatt generator. Distribution of current for house and street lighting, and for power for water pumps, was being rapidly expanded.

Construction of the spacious new academy, of which the Crown Prince is rightfully proud, was completed when I was there. It heralds the change from the old to the new concept of what a school should be.

Under way, also, was construction of a fifteen-mile road from Riyadh to al-Kharj, the building and improvement of other roads in and around the capital, construction of dykes against the flash floods which occur during the winter months, and remodeling of water and sanitation services in hospitals and other buildings.

Moving northeast about 250 miles, we come to the center of one of the most interesting projects which the King and his Government have so far undertaken: the Dammam port development, and the railroad from there to Riyadh by way of Dhahran, Abqaiq, and Hofuf. It represents the fulfillment of one of His Majesty's most cherished hopes.

To understand its importance, one must bear in mind that, even with the great advances which have been made, Sa'udi Arabia still produces very few things, and must therefore import a great many things. The problem of port facilities and inland transportation has consequently long been one of the country's greatest concerns; and, in fact, one which the Arabian American Oil Company has shared with the country as a whole.

The only port on the Persian Gulf coast which could accommodate ocean vessels had been that of Ras Tanura, constructed by Aramco and fully occupied with the handling of oil shipments. Accordingly, the Oil Company was compelled to lighter freight ashore in barges from the open roadstead at Ras Tanura: an economically impractical operation for the great quantities involved. The Government, on its part, had to bring in foodstuffs and other imports at Ojair, haul them inland by camel caravan to Hofuf, and then transship them by truck to Riyadh.

So, a few years ago, the Company initiated a plan to install deep-water port facilities at the town of Dammam, and a railroad from that point to Dhahran, ten miles away, and to the oil-producing center of Abqaiq, forty miles beyond. The work was planned for the two-fold purpose of alleviating the freight handling situation, and of making a start in the development of an improved Arab community accessible to the oil operations.

The King, however, had long been conscious of the need for solving the Government's own transportation problems, and he considered that an essential step would be a Government-owned railroad from the eastern seaboard to Riyadh. This would be an important start toward developing settled communities in the interior, wherever water will permit agriculture.

So, after the Company had told the King of its plans, he proposed that the project be made a part of the Government program. Aramco agreed, and construction has been proceeding on that basis.

The project includes a seven-mile causeway to deep

[191]

water, which was finished in 1950, and a large steel trestle and wharf which were sufficiently completed by the spring of 1950 to permit offloading of the first ship.

The railroad extends out to the end of the pier, from the warehouses, customs buildings, and other port facilities which are under construction on the Dammam waterfront.

The entire 350-mile line was scheduled for completion late in 1951. The first freight was hauled on February 23, 1949, between Dhahran and Abqaiq; and commuter passenger traffic between Dammam and Dhahran was started March 7, 1949. At the end of 1950, there were thirteen diesel electric locomotives and two hundred freight cars in operation. More equipment was on order.

Meanwhile, Aramco engineers have laid out a plan and survey for the development of Dammam townsite, which will probably become the principal Sa'udi Arab seaport on the Persian Gulf. The Company is assisting many Arab employees financially in building homes there.

*　　*　　*

We have had, then, a brief view of the accomplishments that are being wrought in Sa'udi Arabia in the huge job of enabling that great land to move forward. In all of the public works projects, the Government has assumed the cost, for payment out of either current or future royalties from oil production.

In line with its consistent policy of co-operating with the Sa'udi Arab Government in all feasible ways, Aramco has frequently furnished technical counsel and assistance without charge, and has performed such services as surveying for water sources, drilling water wells, maintaining Government motor equipment, making purchases in the United States, furnishing engineers for boundary surveys, et cetera.

But, as stated by a Company representative with long experience in the field: "As a matter of general policy, it is believed best, in the long run, to keep all relations with the Government not only on a co-operative basis, but also on a sound, equitable business basis."

His Royal Highness, the Crown Prince, expressed very much the same viewpoint when he said to me:

"The relation of the Sa'udi Kingdom with the Americans is built upon the friendliest exchanges for mutual benefit.

"It is founded on mutual profit, with both parties respecting the rights of the other. It is this understanding that underlies all efforts and continues to guide both sides.

"Besides perfect co-operation and good will, we pay our American friends the full cost and price of every service rendered, and they, in turn, pay us in full for our rights; therefore we feel that we are not under financial obligation to them nor are they under such obligation to us. It is on this foundation that our business and friendly relations will continue, Allah willing.

"Up to the present time, no problem has arisen in our relation with Aramco that we were unable to solve in a friendly way without the intervention of any third party."

CHAPTER NINETEEN

A People Reawakened

"At present, we are faced by three enemies of our country, whom we must bend all energies to conquer: poverty, ignorance, and disease."

—KING ABDUL AZIZ

*   *   *

Just for a moment, let us take a fanciful trip through time and space, and assume that we have made a rendezvous in the year 1933, on the vast, sandy, wind-swept desert of eastern Sa'udi Arabia. We are going to meet a youngster whose name (wholly fictitious) is Ahmad.

He belongs to a tribe of camel herders and shepherds who have known no life except endless wandering. He has never experienced anything but poverty and hardship. The camel is his main source of existence. It provides his transportation. Its milk and its flesh feed him. Its hair clothes him. And its skin makes the tent that shelters him.

Ahmad has no money. He has no education. He has no skill. You might almost say that Ahmad has *nothing,* but that would only be if you did not *know* Ahmad. He has two things that sustain him, the second perhaps deriving from the first: a deep-seated religious faith, and an abiding good nature.

This is Ahmad. And this is 1933.

Now, let us move forward sixteen years, but remain at the same place in the desert. It is still the same place, but we would never know it. Not only are there the new, modern cities which have risen out of the empty sand. There is something else every bit as dramatic: a new type of young Arab.

We'll find one of these young men in the refinery. He is neatly dressed, and alert looking; and he is not immediately aware of our entrance because he is concentrated upon his job of checking the control board. He is, I am happy to tell you, Ahmad.

Ahmad is working for the oil people. He has been for fifteen years. His wandering days are over, and his poverty, too. He doesn't spend much time with camels any more, for automobiles and airplanes have become his routine means of transportation. He finds the diet a good deal more varied at the dining hall; the commissary is a ready source of clothing; and a clean, modern dormitory has taken the place of a tent before his seniority entitled him to a spacious house with a group of other bachelors.

Ahmad has money, now. His wages have mounted as he has learned new skills, and he is banking part of them under the employee thrift plan instituted by the company at the suggestion of the King. Ahmad learned to read and write at the Oil Company school, and has made good progress with his arithmetic.

This is the youngster whom we met on the desert back in 1933. Perhaps we can agree that it is not stretching a point to say that there has been a certain transformation in the life of Ahmad. Perhaps we can agree, as well, that the transformation is all the more interesting because it was not performed, like those of Middle East fables, by superhuman geniis who transformed sand into gold, or stones into pearls, or carpets into flying machines. This transformation was performed by dint of the teamwork of a thoroughly human

[195]

king who wanted to better the lives of his people, and a thoroughly un-magic group of oil men who came to the Persian Gulf for the prosaic purpose of trying to make a profit.

We recall that Arabia was a very doleful land, indeed, when Abdul Aziz launched upon his seemingly hopeless task of revivifying it. We recall, also, that the wherewithal was notably absent. And then the decision was made to invite foreign capital to look for oil.

With oil, Ibn Sa'ud reasoned, there would be royalties with which he could bring to his people the better life of which he had dreamed. With oil, there would be wages for thousands of workers, and the spending of the wages would mean business for tradesmen, and new sources of taxes to support the program of progress. On all counts, his reasoning has been proven correct.

As we have noted, there were more than twelve thousand Arabs engaged in oil work at the high point of employment, and in 1950 there were still more than ten thousand so employed. Moreover, the writer has no doubt whatsoever, that the peak figure will not only be reached again, but will be far exceeded when present international monetary difficulties are overcome.

Continually increasing emphasis is being placed upon the training of Sa'udi Arabs so that they may qualify as quickly as possible for the highest jobs which their individual experience and capabilities will permit. The progress along these lines is seen in the fact that a total of 4,333 merit increases in pay, and 3,593 reclassifications to higher rated jobs were made during 1949. In the previous year, there were 1,953 merit increases and 3,636 reclassifications to higher ratings.

The training of employees has been carried forward from the very beginning, along both academic and vocational lines. Originally, it was necessary to spread these efforts rather thinly over a wide range of activities, beginning with elementary schooling for young Arabs. Now, however, His Majesty's Government has made such progress in establishing elementary schools in the vicinity of the oil operations that the Company can concentrate upon the industrial training of more mature employees.

The King and the Crown Prince have always shown a deep interest in developing education in their domain, and are pushing the advancement of the school system in all possible ways.

The province of al-Hasa offers an excellent example, with its progress under the direction of the governor, Amir Sa'ud ibn Abdullah ibn Jlewi, whose farsightedness, keen interest, and encouragement of youth has been an inspiration.

Ibn Jlewi was starting thirteen additional elementary schools as of the summer of 1950, and had given approval to plans for seven more. In Hofuf, the capital of the province, a new high school was soon to be started.

Two new elementary school buildings, under construction in the summer of 1950, at Dammam, in al-Hasa, and at Qatif, are as modern as any found in the United States. Each has facilities for 450 students. Yet the cost was only 80,000 riyals (about $20,000), the reason being that contractors and laborers, working for themselves on their *own* school, were willing to work at practically cost, just to get the building up.

To encourage students to attend high school, the Sa'udi Arab Government gives special benefits to students. Inasmuch as most of the youth must start earning money at that age, their enrollment in high school would be difficult otherwise. As an Aramco official commented:

"After all, when you and I were young, our families, even in the United States, thought several times before letting us go to high school. We were needed on the farm, to help produce for the family; or, if we lived in the city, the family needed our earning capacity. In fact, it was commonplace for ambitious lads who were forced to quit school to go to work, to be compelled to go to night school to finish their education. And, all of this was not more than twenty years ago."

So, to meet a similar situation, the Sa'udi Arab Government gives room and board to those who enroll in high school, and, in addition, allows 30 riyals monthly (about $10) for personal expenses. If the student is willing to work one hour a day in the office of the Minister of Finance of Hasa province, he will get 150 riyals a month (about $50) in addition to his room and board.

The Sa'udi Arabs are hungry for education—so much so that the school system is having difficulty in keeping pace with demands. For example, enrollment of Hofuf elementary schools four years ago was 75; now, it is 750.

By way of illustrating the avidity of the people for learning: Abdul Aziz ibn Turki, Director of Education, decided that Hasa Province should have a night school, so he started one at Hofuf in connection with the elementary school system. Immediately, 240 fathers enrolled to learn arithmetic, English, and other basic subjects, even though the classes were at night, after they had put in long, hard days of labor in the date groves and at other tasks.

The King issued a royal edict recently, requiring that English be introduced into the fifth grade of all schools. The

[198]

people of Sa'udi Arabia had asked him for such training, because the ambition of many of them is to work for Aramco or one of the other companies doing business in the country, or to start a business of their own.

All of this is tremendously heartening to the writer, for, in my opinion, the countries of the Middle East had fallen far behind in modern education.

The Sa'udi Government is unstintingly generous and eager in its current program. Besides what it is doing in the field of elementary schools, it is sending students to study in the schools of Egypt and elsewhere, including the United States.

It is paying a higher cost per student than any other Government: for tuition and laboratory fees, $700 per year; for books, $200; and clothing, $400; plus a monthly allowance of $225, and an additional $25 per month during vacation.

Thus, with the Government assuming responsibility for academic training, the Company was able to intensify its vocational activities.

In this respect, the year of 1949 was one of significant developments, bringing, among other things, the inauguration of a five-year program to increase the number of Sa'udi Arabs in training, and to increase the rate at which they acquire skills.

The outstanding feature of the new program is the intensification of on-the-job training for more than eight thousand Sa'udi Arab employees who are either unskilled, or who possess relatively limited skill.

At the same time, special training is being offered to semi-skilled Sa'udi Arab employees. From a group of approximately eighteen hundred of these, the best-qualified will be selected for advanced training to develop administrative and supervisory qualifications, as well as to perfect technical skills.

In consequence of the training program, men who, a few years ago, had never seen a wheelbarrow or a monkey wrench are now operating machine tools, automobiles, trucks, and construction machinery, and are doing metal working, plumbing, welding, and wood working. They have learned to do efficient work on drilling derricks, to handle complex instruments and machinery in the refinery, and to do laboratory work requiring a high degree of precision.

As the Arab employees have advanced in their skills and earnings, they have left their nomadic habits ever further behind them: a goal toward which the King had steadfastly tried to guide his subjects. At the end of 1949, there were 2,195 Arab employees who had been engaged in the oil operation for five years or more, and, of these, 520 were ten-year men and six had completed fifteen years of service.

In the early days of the concession, when all efforts had to be concentrated upon finding out whether oil existed in the country or not, and, during the war and immediate post-war years, when materials were all but impossible to obtain, the Arab employees lived in rather crude wood-and-grass shelters known as "barastis." But, as rapidly as possible, these have been replaced by modern, well-built dormitories.

As a further forward step, progress is now being made in the provision of semi-private housing for senior Arab employees. This type of house has four bedrooms, living room, baths, and kitchen, and affords comfortable quarters for eight bachelors in a house.

Beyond this program for individual workers, the Company is assisting in all reasonable ways in the development of Arab *family* communities in the areas of its operations.

[200]

Even as Abdul Aziz ibn Sa'ud had foreseen, the combination of increased earnings and permanence of domicile have spread their benefits as circles spread from a stone thrown upon the water. They are helping Sa'udi Arabia to move forward in an economic advance which is bringing steadily rising living standards for ever-increasing numbers of its people.

Royalties, local wage payments and purchases, and payments to Arab contractors have been large factors in Sa'udi Arabia's achievement of the largest dollar income of any Middle Eastern nation.

The expanding spending power has brought about a progressive development of Arab small business and service organizations, and has encouraged the establishment of Arab branches of United States enterprises, most of them utilizing local managerial talent.

Perhaps no development has been more noteworthy, from an economic and sociological viewpoint than the increase in the number and diversification of Arab contractors.

Just a few years ago, if you wanted to go from one place to another in a Sa'udi Arabian town or city, you either walked or rode a camel, except in the cosmopolitan seaport city of Jiddah. Today, if you happen to live in, say, Dhahran, you take a taxicab: a gleaming new model, made in the United States and kept in flawless running condition by skilled Arab mechanics.

The operator of the Dhahran taxicabs is just one of the steadily-growing number of his fellow-countrymen who are getting into business for themselves, many of them with the co-operation of the Oil Company, which maintains an Arab Industrial Development Department (the A.I.D.D.) for the sole purpose of encouraging local enterprise. Indeed, many

[201]

of the new contractors and merchants got their start as oil workers, and they learned the trades which they are now utilizing.

The A.I.D.D. staff relies upon the initiative of the individual for the launching of projects, always avoiding any suggestion of paternalism, or any word or act which could make it appear to be intruding. It will discreetly let it become known that some service is needed—say an ice plant, or a garage—and then leave it to some alert entrepreneur to act upon the hint.

Thereafter, it makes its services available, upon request, in many ways: helping in setting up office procedures, in locating sources of merchandise, materials, and machinery, or in placing orders and arranging shipment. Financial assistance is *not* given: the Company wants no basis for any allegation that it exerts any economic influence or pressure.

Many of the new contractors must start from the simplest rudiments in learning to operate a business. By way of illustration, there have been a number of occasions when the Oil Company has received bids for services, and has found that it would be impossible for the contractor to make a profit, or even, in some cases, to break even. So, the industrial development people have gone over the bids with the contractors and revised the figures so that they could make money.

Happily, they learn quickly, and the number of these businessmen has grown greatly. Thus, there was virtually no activity by local contractors in eastern Sa'udí Arabia when the oil development began in 1933. Today, there are approximately four hundred contractors, and the number of their employees reached a high of more than eight thousand in March, 1949.

They are doing virtually every manner of work: constructing all types of houses and buildings for both Americans and Arabs; doing all classes of excavation; operating ice plants, rock quarries, personnel carriers, dump trucks, and camp facilities for geophysical and geological parties; manufacturing bricks, concrete blocks, tents, juss, and lime; and supplying such services as camp cleaning and sanitation, painting, gardening and landscaping, and fence building.

They service airplanes, and automotive and marine equipment; install utilities, including electrical, water, sewage, and other systems; and operate equipment of all types.

On the 1,075-mile Trans-Arabian pipeline system, recently completed, Arab contractors with more than four thousand employees performed a major share of the job. One of them operated the big central garage at Ras al Misha'ab for the Bechtel International Corporation, prime contractor for the pipeline.

Another, who had charge of much of the welding, established his own school for welders, with Arab instructors and an American inspector. So insistent was he upon competent performance that, if one of his men did a certain number of defective welds, he was sent back to school for six weeks at reduced pay. It is probably not too suprising, then, that the X-ray tests of every pipe joint showed fewer defective welds by Arabs than by Americans.

Arab contractors also did the cleaning of the pipe before it was laid, the tarring and wrapping of the pipe, and almost all of the trucking and road maintenance. They have not only their own automotive equipment, but their own Arab-operated maintenance shops and garages.

On His Majesty's new railroad all of the track has been laid by Arab contractors, and they are doing all of the main-

[203]

tenance work. They have performed, also, a substantial share of the big job of rearing the new port and city at Dammam.

As we have noted, many of these contractors are former Bedouins, who knew only the roaming and rigorous life of the desert; and many are former Oil Company employees, now capitalizing upon the skills which they learned with the Company. One of these started for the Company as an interpreter back in 1936. Now, he employs an average of twelve to fifteen hundred men in his construction business. Aramco has been paying local contractors more than $4,-000,000 annually in fees.

But, contractual services are not the only form of business to enjoy an upward trend in Sa'udi Arabia. In the light of the Arabs' traditional talent as merchants and traders, it is only logical that small stores have been mushrooming and prospering in the wake of the country's increased spending power. Many of the new tradesmen have utilized the services of the A.I.D.D.

The growing use of motor vehicles and airplanes as substitutes for the traditional camel has naturally stimulated the use of petroleum products. The Oil Company's policy has been to assign this activity to Arab dealers insofar as practicable. To that end, dealer appointments have been made at Jiddah, Tayif, al-Khobar, Dammam, Qatif, Abqaiq, Hofuf, Ras Tanura, and Ras al Misha'ab. They are doing a brisk business.

Other Arab entrepreneurs have been encouraged to start various other kinds of small businesses, selling such commodities as clothing, food, automotive parts, and other items. In al-Khobar alone, the number of shops has increased since the war from about ten to more than two hundred.

A by-product of the increase in the number of ice plants has been the popularizing of ice cream and soft drinks. Using old-fashioned, hand-turned freezers, the ice cream dealers have had a thriving business, with long lines of customers waiting to be served. Soft drinks, made by local formulae, have been in lively demand.

In these ways, then, have the oil operations served as a valued instrument of the King in his unending effort to better the economic condition of his country. In other ways, also, has it contributed.

We recall that King Abdul Aziz had noted three enemies of his country: poverty, ignorance, and disease. Through his public works, his agricultural projects, and the direct and indirect wages and payments resulting from the oil development, he is conquering poverty. Through his steady expansion of school facilities, and the educational program of the Oil Company, he is attacking ignorance with great effectiveness. And, with the co-operation of his business partners from the west, he is making great progress against disease.

Consideration of the health of employees prompted the initiation of a medical program from the very beginning of operations by the Bahrein Petroleum Company, owned jointly by Standard Oil of California and the Texas Company.

When Aramco began operating on the Sa'udi Arab mainland in 1933, it instituted its own medical program, and it now has expanded this work to the point where, at the end of 1950, it had a staff of 35 doctors, 120 nurses, and 360 technicians and attendants.

It is operating modern American and Arab hospitals, fully appointed with the newest and finest instruments and equipment, at Ras Tanura and Dhahran. The facilities of the hospitals have always been made available, not only to employees, but to the public in the neighboring area.

In 1948, when I visited the newly completed Arab hospital at Dhahran, I was told by an official that it cost more than $1,000,000. I could not then understand how it was possible to expend this large sum on a one-story brick building. But, after going through its interior and visiting its operating and sterilization rooms, laboratories, X-ray and physiotherapy facilities, and other equipment equal to the best to be found anywhere in the United States, I marveled that this was accomplished at so low a cost.

Indicative of the scope of the medical activity, a total of 6,821 patients were hospitalized during 1950, and 310,-000 out-patient treatments were given (the figures covering both Americans and Sa'udi Arabs).

Under discussion with the Sa'udi Arab Government is a proposal for establishing traveling medical units which would go through the back country and carry greatly needed medical attention to the people living there. The project would be for the Government's account, with the Company providing the technical direction.

Meanwhile, a truly amazing record has been achieved in the reduction of the incidence of malaria, utilizing every modern technique, including fly and mosquito eradication. Through a DDT program, initiated in 1948, homes and garden houses in thirty towns and villages, from al-Khobar through Qatif to Jubail, were sprayed by local Arab contractors under the general guidance of Aramco's medical department. The spraying program is being continued and expanded.

In consequence, the reported malaria cases declined from 2,101 in 1947, to 1,318 in 1948, and clear down to 94 in 1949. Most of the cases reported in 1949 were from the untreated areas of Tarut Island and the Hofuf Oasis.

Spleen and parasite surveys among children in test villages of the Qatif Oasis showed a continued decrease in percentage of enlarged spleens (indicative of malaria infection), and an even more rapid decline in the number of children harboring malaria parasites.

The DDT project was still further enlarged in 1950, with increased participation by His Majesty's Government and by the local communities. The Company continued to make its medical and technical staff available for this work.

A continuation of the DDT house spraying, plus constant control and education, may well be expected to reduce malaria to a rare disease, along with the train of complications consequent to the infection.

It is natural that the excellent work done in Sa'udi Arabia and on Bahrein Island should have attracted the attention of others confronted with similar problems throughout the Persian Gulf area. Hence, when the Bahrein Island Medical Society sent out invitations for a Medical Congress on November 4, 1948, thirty-six doctors came to the meeting.

The first of its kind in this area, the meeting was of an experimental nature, but none the less successful in affording opportunity for exchange of ideas among American, European, and Middle Eastern doctors as to the etiology, diagnosis and treatment of diseases endemic to the area.

Presided over by Dr. Robert J. Bigger, chief medical officer of the Bahrein Petroleum Company, the gathering was attended by civilian, military, and governmental medical representatives from Middle Eastern countries.

So helpful were the sessions in stimulating the exchange of ideas and experiences in an area where there is little access to large medical centers that the result was the formation of the Persian Gulf Medical Society, with committees appointed to study the problems of the region, and sub-committees assigned to report on various phases for later correlation. The Society will meet semi-annually, and it is certain that continued improvement in the health of the Middle Eastern people will result.

It should not be difficult for Americans to appreciate the essential role being performed in the Middle East by the medical profession, when it is recollected that the building of the Panama Canal was made possible just as much by the medical and sanitary staff under Colonel Gorgas as by the engineers under Colonel Goethals; just as the failure of de Lesseps and the French was caused by the anopheles mosquito.

And so, even as Abdul Aziz ibn Sa'ud won the wars which he fought with his sword, we find him now winning his war against poverty, ignorance, and disease.

In working with His Majesty to help hasten his victory, Aramco often goes beyond its expressly stated concession obligations. In so doing, it is motivated partly, as the cynical fault-finder will assure you, by purely selfish motives.

"Aramco," these critics will explain, "*has* to behave itself in Arabia if it wants to stay there."

Well, certainly! In fact, as a Company veteran once stated to me: "Would anyone allow a guest in his house if he didn't behave himself? If Aramco cheated the Government, and underpaid its employees, and failed to show respect for the laws and customs of the country, then I tell you very frankly that I don't think that it *should* be allowed to stay there."

But, there are things which go beyond routine good behavior. Remember, Aramco didn't *have* to drill water wells out along the camel trails, or operate free schools in the

[208]

days before the King was able to build and staff his own, or supply electricity without profit, or give free medical, surgical, and hospital care, or help Arabs to start in business. There are, indeed, a great many things which it did not *have* to do. Why, then, did it do them?

I think that part of the answer lies in the fact that the people who have represented Aramco have been decent people with decent motivations. I think that the other part lies in the King, himself.

If Abdul Aziz ibn Sa'ud had been a tyrant, interested only in his own comforts and aggrandizement, I don't believe that he would have inspired much co-operation from any concession holder. Allah be praised, he is not that type of King.

Thus it was that, when the people of Aramco came into Sa'udi Arabia, they found a land which had had a proud history, which had ultimately been conquered, and which had fallen into centuries of social and economic darkness. They found a King who yearned to bring about better days for his people. He placed his trust in these strangers to help him to achieve that goal. As time passed, these men of the West learned to know this King, and his people; to like them and respect them.

For a moment, then, let me use again the words of the same Company veteran whom I quoted above. As he spoke them to me:

"What are you going to do in circumstances like this, when a King has given you his trust, and a people their faith? Are you going to put these considerations out of your mind, and think only of making an extra buck? You know very well you are not: You are going to keep that trust and justify that faith.

"You're going to do it by putting in a lot of time and
[209]

patience, and hard work and discouragement. You're going to wonder more than once whether it's all worth while.

"Then, some evening when you're, maybe, watching the Arab youngsters playing baseball with the American kids, one of the young employees that you've worked with passes on his way to night school. He gives you a friendly smile, and you know he means it when he waves and calls to you: 'Sala'am aleikum' (Peace be with you).

"Right then, a nice warm feeling comes over you, and that night you can look right back at that fellow you see in the mirror, because then you know that you did something in Sa'udi Arabia besides just make a buck."

This, then, is the partnership between East and West. This is the means by which Abdul Aziz chose to find the wherewithal of progress. Did he act wisely? I think that he did. So do many others—including Ahmad.

CHAPTER TWENTY

Bloom in the Desert

We had just crossed the hot, desolate ribbon which is the Dahna, and there it lay before us in all of its refreshing luxuriance: the sweep of lush green fields, with eastern Arabia's clear-blue, crystalline waters breaking from their outlets in hasty abundance in a seeming effort to make amends for past shortcomings.

We had just left, also, a group of camel herders, moving across the desert in the same fashion which unnumbered centuries had left unchanged, and there before us he rode: a red-haired Texan, plowing with a diesel-driven tractor.

For, this was al-Kharj, fifty-six miles south of Riyadh, the great three-thousand-acre agricultural project which is one of the happy symbols of the ceaseless campaign of Ibn Sa'ud and his Government to bring Sa'udi Arabia closer to self-sufficiency in the matter of food supply.

No easy task is this, for there is many a formidable obstacle to be overcome, both physical and psychological, but Ibn Sa'ud is determined that it shall be consummated. Far-sighted as always, he neither takes account of the cost nor expects to reach his goal overnight. His eyes are focused steadily down the long road, and he has full faith that intelligence, toil, and patience will ultimately bring dividends of food to his people many fold greater than the investment.

In considering the problems faced by this earnest King and his agents, we begin with the basic factor of water, for agriculture everywhere is more a matter of weather than of soil. Yet, in Sa'udi Arabia, the average annual rainfall is estimated at not more than four inches. The land is mostly barren of forests, and lacking in loamy soil.

In the face of these conditions, the population is steadily growing. The three great cities of the Hijaz, for example: Jiddah, Mecca, and Medina, as well as the smaller outlying towns, are teeming with a poor population which is annually increased by pilgrims who decide to make the Holy Land their home.

In view of the many improvements which are being made in these and other cities by the Sa'udi Arab Government, particularly in the fields of sanitation and health, ever increasing numbers of people are certain to be attracted there. Indeed, the prospect is that the population of the country will be doubled in the not far distant future.

How, then, will the Government be able to sustain these people? By way of seeking the answer, let us see what nature has provided . . .

The volcanic, stony soil of the steep mountains of Asir (nine thousand feet) and the Hijaz (six thousand feet) does not absorb and store the scanty rainfall, but permits it to flush away swiftly, so that the word, "sayl," meaning "torrent," is applied to river beds.

Where the valleys widen sufficiently to permit water storage, and where good silt soil exists, wells to a depth of twenty to seventy-five feet permit the development of excellent orchards and vegetable gardens, just as these valleys have done since pre-Islamic times.

There are some good valleys (wadis) in the Hijaz. One of them, Wadi Fatimah, situated between Jiddah and Mecca, is blessed with excellent springs, from which King Ibn Sa'ud has brought the sweet waters thirty-four miles to Jiddah to replace the distilled sea water, formerly used. Enterpris-

[212]

ing Hijazis have invaded Wadi Fatimah, purchasing neglected properties and planting mango and other tropical fruit trees there.

Another great valley is Wadi Hamdh, near Medina, where irrigation possibilities are the best in the Hijaz. At Khaybar, one hundred miles north of Medina, the water flowing from under the lava, forms, at present, a malaria-infested, soggy land which is a deterrent to proper settlement. Reclamation of this section will take time.

The possibilities for fruit-growing in the Hijaz, as in many other places, is very good.

In fact, wherever water is available in Sa'udi Arabia, fruit trees and the common vegetables can be grown. In the lowlands, bananas, mangoes, papaya and citrus fruits are cultivated; at higher altitudes, apples, pears, apricots, plums, peaches, guava, quinces, figs, grapes and pomegranates flourish in various sectors. However, outside of the grapes and pomegranates, none of these fruits are planted commercially.

During my visit to Tayif, a small, plateau-like area east of Mecca, with an altitude of about 5,100 feet, I found grapes and pomegranates which were the most luscious to be found in any country, thanks to the protracted summer season in a temperate climate. Yet, the condition of the orchards bespoke the effect of three consecutive dry seasons. Above Tayif, right through the valleys, small orchards are to be encountered with sufficient yield for this section of the Hijaz.

In the uplands of Asir, the coffee produced is of the blending variety, and compares favorably with the best in Yemen and Abyssinia; and, with proper guidance, coffee fincas could be profitably planted in that section. The Hiwar plant, which produces indigo, is also grown for local use.

Moreover, experiments of Egyptian experts have demonstrated that the sesame seed, peanuts, sugar cane, sugar beets, and the Egyptian onion do very well. Cotton has been successfully grown, but its desirability is doubtful. From my knowledge of tropical agriculture, I believe that cacao (the chocolate bean) could be profitably cultivated in the lowlands.

Asir, as we know, is mostly mountainous, but its small farms are more numerous than in the Hijaz, and the possibilities are greater. In the southern section, the valleys are broader, and the monsoon season brings more rain. Especially in the valleys of Najran and Dawasir is water more accessible, and the prospects of an agricultural revival in these ancient settings are excellent. Transportation is a problem in these districts today, but, with the building of better roads, the future is reassuring.

My own belief is that, in all of the aforementioned districts, tree culture should be the aim of the small farmer, for neither the size of his lands nor the other physical conditions will permit him to profit from raising grain for sale, although he can and should raise it to feed himself and his livestock.

I was especially impressed with this conviction when I revisited Lebanon after fifteen years, and was pleasantly surprised by the horticultural revival that had taken place. The best varieties of Italian and American fruit trees had been introduced and were flourishing, adding to the joy and profit of that beautiful country.

Conditions in Asir and the Hijaz are just as favorable to fruit raising as anywhere else; and, if canneries should be established at convenient points, the fruits of these provinces will hold their own in any market. As it is today, the shops

[214]

from Jiddah to Mecca and throughout the country are stocked with American canned fruit.

By the same token, there are very promising opportunities for livestock raising. Wherever sorghum grows sixteen and seventeen feet high, as noted in Asir, American maize or corn could be profitably cultivated to furnish food for men and livestock in that area. In addition, alfalfa grows in all parts of Sa'udi Arabia. When the livestock is improved by the introduction of better-bred cattle and sheep, the farmer may profit by converting the corn or sorghum and alfalfa into ensilage for food, as this will give much better returns than trying to raise these grains to sell.

In times past, wheat and its principal product, burghul, was the main commodity, after dates. Then, in the years before World War II, rice was imported in such large quantities and at such low prices that it put wheat in the background. The shipping difficulties during the war, however, cut down sharply the amount of rice that could be obtained, and the planting of wheat was resumed.

Burghul is made of hard wheat, which is boiled, then sun-dried, and put through the grist mill to come out as a coarse cereal, superior in all nutritive values to rice, and just as readily cooked. Today, in the United States, this crushed wheat is preferred and served in the Armenian, Syrian, Greek, and Turkish restaurants. Like rice, it is cooked with meat, and can also be used in certain desserts.

But Sa'udi Arabia will not, in my belief, be able to produce sufficient wheat or rice to feed its population. The deficiency in these staple products must be made up by imports. As a corollary, it would seem wise to establish strategically located warehouses to store wheat during harvests of plenty, when cheap prices prevail abroad. In this way, the Government could protect itself against greedy merchants, and could minimize the hardships which result when transportation is interrupted and the staff of life becomes scarce, as has happened more than once to the people of the Hijaz.

*   *   *

We have spoken now of many crops, but there remains the most important one of all, and I refer to a saying attributed to the Prophet Muhammad: "Honor thy cousin, the Palm."

Verily, the date palm is kin to the Arab. With the camel, it sustained him from the dawn of history. To this day, dry dates and milk form the principal diet of the nomad.

Sa'udi Arabia rates fourth in the world in date production, with an estimated ten million palms. From the shorelands of al-Hasa and the Oasis of Jabrin, throughout every altitude up to 4,500 feet, as at Bisha, the date palm reigns supreme. An Arab farmer is essentially a date planter, who may have a rice paddy in the uncultivated corner of his grove, with alfalfa covering his soil and a few vegetables scattered here and there.

While Sa'udi Arabia grows more than 150 varieties of the date, the khilas date of al-Hasa is unquestionably the finest to be found anywhere. Its pit is very small, and its substance is almost transparent. Our own excellent American variety, propagated in the Imperial Valley, and called deglet-noor, tastes rather salty beside the khilas.

The Buraidah date of the Qasim is recognized on any market, for this sun-dried variety looks bleached, woody and hard, but, in the mouth, it melts like a lump of sugar. At Medina, the dates are the longest known, exceeding in length the Zaglool date of Egypt, but they are eaten fresh and therefore are not sun-dried for the market.

Because there is not, at present, a surplus, the export of dates from Sa'udi Arabia is frowned upon by the Government, for, with milk, they are not only the main diet, particularly among the Bedu, but, in certain sections, a portion is given to the livestock.

In al-Hasa, where two million palm trees flourish, and where the best khilas date is grown, there is an abundance of flowing water; and Hofuf, Dammam, Qatif, and their environs are dense with small groves.

It is between Dammam and Qatif that the model farm and experimental station of His Excellency, the Finance Minister, is located. Here, Hussein Badawy Bey, Egyptian agronomist and expert horticulturist, conducts his scientific research and experimentation.

This gentleman, whose ability places him in the front ranks of tropical agriculturists, is the author of a book, *Modern Agriculture in Sa'udi Arabia,* in which he leaves very little for the student to desire. Men interested in argriculture, and ambitious to follow modern tree culture, come to him and are patiently and courteously instructed by visual demonstration. He has sought in other countries for disease-resisting trees and plants; and, with the Finance Minister's encouragement, he distributes these to the farmers at actual cost.

The tribesmen of banu Murrah have planted their palm groves in the Oasis of Jabrin, which consists of about 7,500 acres of soggy, alkaline soil, about 150 miles southwest of Hofuf. Because of its malarial mosquitoes, the tribesmen visit these groves only twice yearly: in the spring, to pollinate the palms; and in the fall, to harvest the crop. A reclamation project here and at Khaybar would result in untold benefit.

The Sa'udi settler, who dislikes to work for hire, is very

diligent when he tends a little grove of his own. Accordingly, the Government is ever ready to cede land from the public domain to the settler, provided that he will plant it; and will help him with the necessary animals, seed, and palm shoots, and an occasional loan when needed.

After ten years, the settler is expected to pay the Government one-fourth of the produce thereafter. This has been a wise partnership, and today whoever wishes to farm can designate and obtain land for that purpose.

In this connection, it may be of interest to note that, in Sa'udi Arabia, where the public domain belongs to the King and the people, no speculator, who is not going to work the land, is allowed to acquire it. Hence, no unearned increment can be garnered. Take, for instance, a boom city like Jiddah is today, or any other city in the country: Any Sa'udi may ask for and acquire an ample building lot for a nominal fee, provided he starts building and improvement within six months. If for any reason he fails to do so, within two years at the most, it will be taken away from him, and revert to the public domain.

Through the centuries, insecurity had developed in the Arab farmer an ingrained sense of impermanence; therefore, his methods lacked orderly development. Now, with the Government assuring him safety from depredation and raid, he is being led slowly into pursuing improved methods, with the guidance of the authorities.

This road to improvement is, very naturally, a slow and difficult one to travel. Anyone familiar with farmers knows their resistance to agricultural innovations, and can understand the difficulty—if not the futility—of trying to persuade the owner of a small orchard to thin out his bearing trees in crowded areas—to cut down "his cousin the palm," who bestows upon him a yearly income—in order to better the lot of the rest of the orchard. By way of parallel, we know how long it took the U. S. Department of Agriculture, the agricultural colleges, and the county agricultural agents to persuade the American farmer to plant alfalfa; yet now it is our greatest forage crop.

This writer considers that the real hope of making Sa'udi Arabia the leading producer of dates, and to increase its present output fourfold, lies in introducing modern methods of date culture in the four hundred settlements of Hijr, as well as in all additional communities where artesian wells or overflowing subterranean springs are to be found.

The life of trees falls short of expectancy in crowded and over-irrigated orchards, where three or four shoots grow out of the mother tree, leaning in different directions. This can be obviated by choosing sites on slight inclines, so as to obtain drainage; by selecting only the best varieties of shoots; and by spacing palms not exceeding thirty to an acre so as to avoid shading, because the life of the palm and the period of its fruition may reach a hundred years, and it should be provided with sufficient soil nourishment. These things, with other care which has no place in this book, could make Sa'udi Arabia the "Palm Garden of the World."

In offering these modest suggestions from time to time, on the basis of personal observations in Sa'udi Arabia, backed by experience as a farmer and planter, the writer is inspired by the great and sincere efforts which are being made everywhere in the matter of agriculture at the insistence of the King.

In a sense, the King's efforts mark a swing of the pendulum back fourteen centuries, for the Arabs were using science in those days to improve their agriculture, and now they are doing so again. Many people are not aware that it was the Arabs who built the greatest dam of antiquity, at

[219]

Ma'rib; and that, in Asir and the Hijaz, we still may see the sites of many of the ancient dams which helped to conserve the water, and, to a certain degree, to keep the wells supplied by seepage.

Mr. K. S. Twitchell, the American engineer, who, we remember, assisted Mr. Lloyd N. Hamilton in the negotiations that led to the Aramco concession, surveyed the water possibilities and investigated the dams at Tayif in 1945. He wrote in part:

"To sum up my findings briefly: There are eight dam sites in the region, several of them already containing dams of ancient origin. Sudd Sayaud (Sudd being the Arabic word for dam), about six miles east of Tayif, possesses Kufic inscriptions on its rocks which read:

" 'This dam, belonging to Abdullah ibn Muawiyn, Amir al-Mominin, built by Abdullah Ibrahim by Allah's instruction, 58 Anno Hogeira (A.D. 680).'

"The structure of the dam, in which no mortar or mud was used, is today in excellent condition, a 1,266-year tribute to the engineering skill of Abdullah Ibrahim."

But, as we know, the decline came for Arabia, and kept it submerged for many a century.

When Abdul Aziz came to power and accomplished unification of the country, one of the first tasks to which he gave his attention was the development of agriculture, for Sa'udi Arabia has always had to import the bulk of its foodstuffs.

He called for experts from Iraq, who labored for two years, and initiated a number of improvements in planting, irrigation, and cultivation. At the expiration of their commission, they were succeeded by a group of Egyptian agriculturists and irrigation engineers, who, during four years, advanced the work materially. Their scientific research and labor will redound to the benefit of the country for many years to come.

Meanwhile, Sheikh Abdullah Sulayman, the Minister of Finance, had seen the Kharj area and recognized the possibilities for developing it into a large farm project because of the large ains (water pits) which are located there, and because of the good farming soil which is created by the silt in the wadi. He spent an entire summer in al-Kharj, studying its possibilities, and toiled at the program almost as a personal project.

He asked Aramco for assistance in appraising the water possibilities: and, as a result of their studies during World War II, new diesel-driven pumps were installed, and an eleven-mile canal was dug, thus giving the project considerable stimulus.

During the war, al-Kharj was operated for a time by the U. S. Foreign Economic Administration. Agricultural experts, engineers, farmers, and mechanics were sent to Sa'udi Arabia to undertake additional surveys. Their reports and recommendations were gratefully received.

After the war, Aramco took over the operation for the Sa'udi Arab Government's account, and brought in trained personnel from the United States, mostly from New Mexico, Arizona, Texas, and elsewhere in the American Southwest, where similar conditions of soil and climate exist.

Now, at al-Kharj, modern agricultural methods have produced results which are the pride of the Kingdom. The project is actually three farms, spreading over an area of about thirty square miles. Each farm, in turn, consists of smaller, contiguous operating units.

Conceived originally by Sheikh Abdullah Sulayman as simply an agricultural development, al-Kharj has become a demonstration project, as well as a commercial farm. The people are enabled to see the improved results which can be obtained by proper methods and irrigation.

Here are grown watermelons, cucumbers, cantaloupes, honeydews, many varieties of pumpkins and squash, tomatoes, enormous and delicious onions (many of them eight inches or more in diameter), sweet green peppers, carrots, and okra.

There are excellent yields of alfalfa, which is harvested every thirty-five days in summer and every twenty days in winter, or an average of twelve cuttings a year, sometimes even as many as fifteen, compared with a maximum of eight in California. The Arabian alfalfa is somewhat coarser and stemmier than the American variety, but, since it is fed green to the livestock, this is not a handicap. Thus far, no American variety of alfalfa has been found which will yield as much tonnage per acre, not being as tolerant to sand and the saline content of the soil as that of Arabia.

Approximately ten thousand date trees have been planted under the Finance Minister's direction, and about half of them are bearing already.

It is believed that practically anything can be grown at al-Kharj which can be grown in the southwestern and southern United States, *if* it can tolerate the high saline content.

The project tries to "double crop" as much as possible: that is, growing wheat, alfalfa, et cetera, in the date groves, for example. This permits maximum utilization of the available land.

As of mid-1950, about 700 Arabs were working at al-Kharj, and they had demonstrated their ability to learn modern methods well. The Americans, in turn, are learning much about desert farming problems from the Arabs, so that, between the fellow-workers, excellent results may be expected.

[222]

An idea of the magnitude of the al-Kharj operation may be seen from the 1949 report on the value of crops produced:

Alfalfa and other grasses	$324,227
Watermelons and other melons	169,516
Wheat, barley, and oats	110,332
Vegetables	48,358
Squash	20,484
Dates and pomegranates	12,063
Total value of produce	$684,980

It should be emphasized that al-Kharj is entirely a Sa'udi Arab Government project; conceived by the Government and financed by it. Aramco's role has been simply to assist in the supplying of skilled personnel during the developmental period, and it has been reimbursed for all of these services.

The King, who built a residence at al-Kharj, spends some time there every year to look over this much-favored project of his, and to enjoy his thoroughbred stables.

But, al-Kharj was only a start. Under the direction of His Excellency, Abdullah Sulayman, another project, embracing seven hundred acres, was undertaken next at Khafs Daghara, thirty miles southwest of al-Kharj, where, among other crops, winter wheat, blue-stem, and seabreeze hard wheat are being experimentally cultivated.

The agricultural center at Hofuf was placed on an operational basis in the spring of 1949, and others were to be started at Qatif or Dammam, and Wadi Fatimah.

During 1949, the Sa'udi Arab Government Directorate of Agriculture was established, marking a definite step forward in the co-ordination and development of agriculture, with greater assistance from the United Nations Food and Agriculture Organization.

With this progressive development, the Directorate of Agriculture began a gradual transfer, to its own staff, of full control of the planning, administration, and operation of the demonstration projects. The Company will continue to assist in providing shop maintenance and other services which may be needed.

All of the expenses incurred by the Company are reimbursed by the Government out of royalties.

It was a pleasure and a revelation to visit al-Kharj, and to examine this cherished project of the King and the Finance Minister. When I was there, four turbine pumps, each with a minimum capacity of 4,450 gallons per minute and a maximum combined total of 20,000 gallons per minute, were being operated by Caterpillar motors.

The water at al-Kharj is derived from three spring pits, each with a diameter of approximately three hundred feet, and with respective depths of 531 feet, 400 feet, and 45 feet. The pit at Khafs Daghara is 150 feet in diameter and of undetermined depth.

At Aflaj, 156 miles south of al-Kharj, the largest pit of unknown depth resembles a lake, for it extends two thousand feet in length and has a width of eight hundred feet. This, with the other pits in the area, augurs well for its future, for the soil is even better than that of al-Kharj.

Aside from these abundantly flowing springs of al-Hasa, a number of which flow at a rate of twenty thousand gallons per minute, I have noted a number of small pits welling their good waters in the Island of Bahrein, twenty-two miles off the coast.

Enthusiastic in their desire to facilitate the King's wish to modernize his country's agriculture, Aramco engineers and geologists have continually searched the desert for water sources. Having carefully studied the greater part of the vast domain, they have concluded that the source of these water pits lies in the watershed of the Tuwaiq Mountain range, lying 150 to 200 miles west and southwest of the Gulf, and running in a north-south direction for 500 miles.

It is said that, in the early Islamic period, the al-Kharj region was able to provision the Holy Cities. I do not believe it can do so in the face of the large and growing population of today. The experts hope to increase the cultivable area of al-Kharj to eight thousand acres. The writer believes, from his personal observations along the base of the mountain, where vegetation indicates good silt soil, that the available farming land could be increased to twenty thousand acres.

Yet, it remains my considered opinion that there is much doubt whether sufficient wheat can be raised for the future needs of the country. It seems to me that the small planter of al-Hasa and Qatif can do best by raising sufficient rice in his paddies for himself and his family, while the farmer of Jabal Shammar and al-Qasim, as well as he of the terraced slopes of Asir and Hijaz, raises the corn, wheat, and rice necessary for local sustenance.

It is my judgment that the land under cultivation can be most profitably planted with the best varieties of date palm, and the surplus of dates will be sufficient to permit the importation of wheat and rice from other countries. In other words, I am thoroughly convinced that the agricultural future of Sa'udi Arabia depends much more upon its tree culture than upon anything else.

Besides the palm, study can profitably be given to the Australian pine, the eucalyptus, and the cactus which fruits the prickly pear, or, even better, the Burbank thornless variety if it is obtainable, as hedges for the protection of the irrigation ditches from the drifting sands. Such projects are

[227]

very costly, but is it not the part of wisdom to put back into the ground the wealth that has come from it, thus raising its productivity, and the standard of living and happiness?

All improvements will take time, and cannot be accomplished in haste. It may not be amiss to note that, if the Arabs are grateful for the opportunity to avail themselves of modern American agricultural methods, so may we in the United States remember with gratitude that it was the Arab who gave us, among so many other things, alfalfa, ensilage, and the windmill, which have been great factors in the development of our own agriculture.

The lot of the people has been hard in this desiccated land, but Allah, in his compassion, stored underground a compensating bounty of oil and water; and now we have the stimulating sight of a King with the wisdom and determination to tap them both and make the desert bloom.

CHAPTER TWENTY-ONE

Animal Husbandry

The camel might have continued to exist without the Arab, but the Arab could not have survived without the camel.

This sad-eyed, patient beast has been the Arab's faithful companion in prosperity and adversity; has swiftly carried him to safety when danger threatened; has borne his family and their burdens on the treks across the desert; has drawn his water from the deep wells, nourished him with milk, clothed him with wool, furnished him with meat, and sealed the sacrifice by donating his hide for sandals, water buckets, and saddle lining.

Such is the fate of a friendly animal, be it cow or camel.

One hardly needs to state that the camel is Arabia's No. 1 animal. Since time immemorial, indeed, a Bedu's wealth has been measured by the number of his camels.

The camel in Arabia is of the dromedary, single-hump type, and is bred for two purposes: racing and general utility. The greatest care is employed in the selection and breeding of the zalul, or racing camel, which not only moves with great speed, but is graceful as a greyhound. The best racing camels raised in Arabia are sorrel zaluls, of 'Omam.

As to the slow, heavy-boned (truck) camel, he may not have the glamour of the zalul, but he is irreplaceable as a means of commercial transport, and in carrying the Bedu in his endless pursuit of rains and fresh grazing areas. Even though the automobile and the airplane have become commonplace in Sa'udi Arabia, and railroad trains are now moving across the desert, the plodding camel continues to be the cheapest means of moving freight, and will almost surely retain his function in all cases where the time factor is not an element.

Certainly one can hardly foresee the time when he will vanish from the desiccated plateaus which are the open range of Arabia Deserta. There, camel and sheep raising will continue to be the care of the Ruhhal, with newly-drilled artesian watering places to make it less hazardous.

The once-heavy export of camels from Sa'udi Arabia to the Egyptian Sudan, Iraq, and Syria has fallen off considerably since the introduction of the motor vehicle into those countries, but they are still indispensable in many localities and on many routes.

Next in importance to the camel is the sheep, and millions of them are raised in the country, for mutton forms the principal meat diet. In fact, one can hardly imagine an Arab feast without the whole roasted sheep and the boiled rice or burghul.

Well-oriented to the dryness of the country, the Sa'udi Arab variety of sheep is well-fitted, too, to sustain human life. Besides supplying mutton, the ewes also provide milk, which is extensively used; and the cheese which is derived from it is of excellent flavor.

In addition, the Arab sheep have fat tails which, in themselves are quite an item of trade. The fat is heated to form a butter or lard-like substance known as "samn," which is highly-favored for cooking. The flocks of the nomads supply cities and towns in Lebanon, Syria, Iraq, and Trans-Jordan, in addition to what the growers use themselves and sell domestically.

The wool of the Arabian sheep is coarse: of the type

known in the United States as "carpet wool." Inasmuch as this kind of wool is imported by the United States from India and China, Mr. Twitchell suggests in his book, *Sa'udi Arabia,* that Sa'udi Arabia might well develop an export trade in this market. He notes, also, his belief that, if black-headed Somali sheep were introduced, they might well result in considerable export of the finer type of skin desired by American glove and handbag manufacturers.

I will go further and say that I believe that the people of the higher altitudes in Asir, Hijaz, and upper Najd would do well to introduce the Merino sheep, a favorite in Scotland, England, Canada, Australia, and the United States, for its finer wool would increase the industry of al-Hasa. In this province, a certain amount of wool is used, mixed with camel's hair, in the weaving of the mashlah', or 'aba, the outer Arab garment.

What many have forgotten is that it was the Arabs of al-Maghrib who introduced the Merino sheep into Europe during the reign of banu Merine.

Number three in importance among Arabian livestock is the black goat, raised for both its milk and its meat by the Bedu. It has one important advantage over the sheep: it can live on a diet which would cause a sheep to wither away. Its hair is used to make rope and coarse rugs, and also supplies the material for the famous "black tents of Arabia." In my opinion, the angora goat, which thrives in our Texas, could be profitably raised in the uplands of Asir and Hijaz.

Al-Hasa is famed for the excellence of its asses and mules. They are good-looking animals with worthy capabilities. The potentiality for further development of this necessary beast is excellent, provided that steps are taken to eliminate the breeding of small-sized donkeys, for the mule inherits from both parents.

[233]

Even as recently as the fall and winter of 1948, when I last visited Sa'udi Arabia, poultry-raising was done in a haphazard way. The chickens reminded one of the bantam variety seen in the United States, and the eggs were similarly small. At no place was I fortunate enough to observe modern methods except at the model farm of the Finance Minister, between Dammam and Qatif.

Now, it is a pleasure to relate, a new poultry project has been launched at al-Kharj at the request of Crown Prince Sa'ud. All buildings were completed and ready for operation in July, 1950. The start is being made with breeds of chickens developed by the Egyptian Department of Agriculture as a co-operative enterprise of the Egyptian and Sa'udi Arab governments.

The Cairo breed of chickens compares favorably with those of the United States in size and egg production, according to studies made by the Egyptian poultry experts. Eggs and baby chicks from other parts of the Middle East will also be used in experiments; and, later, efforts will be made to raise American varieties.

An attempt will be made to produce five hundred eggs daily and two hundred fryers a week.

I have deferred mention of the horse, from a vague hesitancy, possibly due to an ache of sadness over his impending fate. He is, to me, one of the most graceful and intelligent persons—not animals—in the world.

At eventide, he leaves his grazing and seeks the tent, for the milking by then is done, and a large wooden bowl of warm milk awaits him, with a few dried dates for dessert.

He is one of the family, tethered at the door of the tent by a halter—*not* a bridle—and *never* a bit in his sensitive mouth. The children play with and around him, and, should

[234]

the mistress of the tent pass him without a word, he appears hurt.

Professor Osborn's description of the perfection of the anatomical mechanism of the Arab horse is as follows:

1. Head and tail carried high when animated.
2. Skull short, but broad between the eye sockets.
3. Eye sockets high and prominent, giving the eyes a wide range of vision.
4. Facial profile, or forehead, concave.
5. Muzzle slender, but jaw deep and wide above the throat.
6. Round thorax, well "ribbed-up," and short back, with only five ribless, or lumbar, vertebrae.
7. Horizontally-placed pelvis (a speed characteristic) and very high tail region; few tail vertebrae.
8. Long and slender cannon bones, and long sloping pasterns.

Scientists say that the horse has been on earth for forty million years, during which he was well-distributed, and went through changes and variations according to climate and environment.

In prehistoric times, droves of diminutive horses and camels roamed the North American continent, and eventually disappeared excepting in our museums, where the fossilized skeletons show all of the essential characteristics of the horse and the camel in miniature.

In more recent ages, man bred him to serve his necessity, for the horse, with four feet, was able to travel faster than man, with two; and thus could carry him speedily in attack and flight, bear his burdens, and help him to domesticate other animals.

Thus, the horse is the only animal bred solely for energy.

When man domesticated the Arabian horse, he bred him for endurance and companionship. The nature of his

[235]

desert life, the scarcity of food, and the long distances between water holes all went to build up and shape his capabilities. Close dependence and association bred comradeship.

The Arabian horse is possessed of a balanced energy system, and a larger thyroid gland in proportion to his size than the modern thoroughbred, while the latter has a larger adrenal gland, and is therefore better equipped for a quick outburst of energy.

The development of the modern thoroughbred racer was arrived at by crossing the desert-bred Arabian stallion and English mares, for the mares of the north were larger in size, and had, accordingly, developed large brains, hearts, thyroid glands, and a greater volume of blood than the desert stallion. This proved to be a happy combination, resulting in a rangier breed, with a capacity for bursts of speed for short distances. This evolution came about during the period ranging between 1689 and 1734.

It was in 631 A.D. that the English first began to saddle their horses, but not until about 1689 that Captain Byerly brought to England the so-called "Byerly Turk," from whom the horse, "Herod," descended. The "Darley Arabian," bred in the desert of Palmyra, was imported into England in 1705, siring the Childers string. In 1794, Lord Godolphin brought the "Godolphin Barb" to infuse the blood to which the quality of the race horse is chiefly due, breeding the Matchem line.

The advance since then has been through selective line breeding from the offspring. This excellent blending, and resultant mutation, is now on its own.

We do not know when the Arab and his horse began their partnership. The ancient Egyptians do not portray the horse in their earliest paintings or sculpture, although the ass and other domestic animals are plentifully portrayed.

The first appearance of the domesticated horse in the Plains of Babylon was at the invasion of the Cassides of Iran, in the reign of Samsuiluna, son of Hamurabi, about 1,900 B.C. But, whether Arabia Deserta adopted the horse at that time or not, the Iranian horse was of the coarser and older variety.

This contention is supported by the findings, in 1928, in the valley inhabited by the Lur tribes, of many cemeteries, rich in bronze articles, especially those pertaining to the horse. In this verdant valley, one hundred miles by twenty, horse-raising people buried their steeds with their dead. Professor Hertzfield places this period before 500 B.C.

The writer, who had in his possession many Luristan bronzes which are now in our American museums, visited Teheran to inspect the collection in the National Museum, and can state that the heavy bronze bits, weighted by flat side ornaments, could never have been tolerated by the sensitive mouth of the Arabian desert horse. Some of these bits were joined in the middle so as to act like the American JC bit, which was used in breaking the wild bronchos of the West, and is strong enough to break the jaw of a horse. In contrast, we find that the sculptured horse of the Assyrians in 750 B.C. was of the finer Arab type.

Today, the world's armies have dropped the cavalry. Tanks, armored cars, guns that are accurate at thirty miles, airplanes, and guided missiles have put an end to the military usefulness of the horse. The Morgan horse, traditional pet of the United States Army, is in the discard. Trotters still enjoy a spotty popularity in America, Europe, and Australia, where the offspring of Hambletonian (1849-1876) by a Kentucky Arabian, Abdullah, have reigned supreme.

[237]

In the United States, you may cross many counties in farming states before discovering a horse, sadly reminiscing in a corner of some pasture. In our great cities, gone are the packing house trucks and the brewery wagons, drawn by four Percherons or Belgians, matched in color, size, and weight (more than two thousand pounds each). On our boulevards and avenues, one may look in vain for the four-in-hand and tandems, once driven by a proud master, but now gone where the pedigree Arab is going.

The desert horse is unfitted for polo: Its inherited traits in tournament or war, including the "karr" and "farr" (attack and escape), make it raise its front feet from the ground and turn on its hind feet at the least pressure of the body or halter. Crossing it with the Western broncho or the Australian pony does not harden the sensitiveness of its mouth to the toughness required of a polo pony.

Where, then, is this gallant and beautiful creature to find his niche in our world of today? True, in Najd, the home of the Arabian horse, King Abdul Aziz ibn Sa'ud has a great stable (at al-Kharj, as I have mentioned), and there his pedigreed horses live in the manner to which they are so truly entitled. Yet, there remains a sad sense of foreboding: my apprehension, expressed at the beginning of this discourse, as to the passing of the Arabian horse from the scene, still haunts me.

CHAPTER TWENTY-TWO

The Cradle of Gold

Back at the start of the '30s, Sheikh Abdullah Sulayman, the moving spirit in so many of Sa'udi Arabia's progressive projects, had been poring over some old Meccan archives. On the strength of what he had learned, he called Mr. Twitchell and asked him to take a journey.

And that is how it happened that the Mahad Dahab, or "Cradle of Gold," not many miles from Medina, was rediscovered and is now being worked by the Sa'udi Arabian Mining Syndicate, Ltd., to the benefit of both the entrepreneurs and the country.

Mr. Twitchell began his expedition at Jiddah on February 8, 1932. After crossing river beds, hills, lava flows, brush, and desert, he reached the ancient workings eight days later, having covered 426 miles. In contrast, a road now connects the two points, and the distance, reduced to 246 miles, is now generally traversed in about ten hours, including stops for lunch and water, even though a 3,700-foot summit is crossed.

The exploratory party was impressed to find approximately 500,000 tons of tailings, which had been dumped after the old milling and extraction. Subsequently, some 380,000 tons of these have been cyanided, averaging a yield of about 8 pennyweights of gold per ton.

The approximate dating of these tailings, according to the pottery findings, as well as the Kufic inscriptions, is 750 to 1,150 A.D. These are called the "modern" tailings, for, underlying this tonnage is a layer estimated at more than 100,000 tons which are known as the "ancient" tailings, possibly going back a thousand years earlier, for gold mining in Arabia was known to the Babylonians (2,000 B.C.). This ancient layer of tailings is yet to be worked.

The syndicate was formed in May, 1934, and a concession was granted December 24, 1934, under the terms of which 15 per cent of the stock was assigned to the Sa'udi Arab Government, plus 5 per cent of the gross production as royalty; and another 10 per cent of the stock was sold to Sa'udi Arab citizens.

The present company, before undertaking this expensive development, did about ten thousand feet of diamond-drilling to prove the existence of a probable ore extension underground. In 1948, four dividends were paid, or 40 per cent of the par value, so, even taking into consideration the high cost of the primary construction and installations, the showing augurs well for the stockholders.

The syndicate has constructed the aforementioned 246-mile road from Jiddah to the mine at a minimum grade of 7½ per cent, with a minimum radius of curvature of fifty feet. At present, fifteen-ton trucks constantly operate over it. Though the sand road is paved, it is macadamized over the lava flows; the rest is gravel surfaced and under constant maintenance by about seventy-five men under one superintendent, an Englishman. The mine is staffed by about twenty-four overseers, with five hundred workers on the mine and 125 at the Jiddah Terminal.

Ore is stoped underground, using machinery drills and blasting. The stoping is done by both shrinking and cutfill methods. Ore is crushed by jaw-crusher, conical crusher, and ball mills; then oil flotation is used to make concentrates and the tailings are then cyanided by agitation, filtered, and

[240]

precipitated by the Merril-Crowe zinc dust method. Both concentrates and precipitates are shipped to Perth Amboy, N. J., to the American Smelting and Refining Co.

The Syndicate's terminal improvements at Jiddah consist of storehouses, dynamite magazine, machine shop, staff house of sixteen rooms, with kitchen, food stores and servants' quarters, office, first aid, 2,100-ton and 500-ton diesel oil tanks, eight-inch pipeline, three 3,500-foot causeways to water's edge, then a 3,000-foot pier terminating in a 175-foot reinforced concrete pier on which are installed one fifteen-ton crane operated by a thirty-eight-horsepower diesel engine, and two five-ton land operated cranes.

A six-inch pipeline belonging to the Sa'udi Government also parallels the eight-inch line and is used to convey gasoline from tankers to the Government's six thousand-ton floating-roofed gasoline tank. There are indications of mineral deposits in different sections of the Hijaz and Asir.

Through the courtesy of Dr. George Miles, curator of the American Numismatic Society, of New York, we are reproducing a photograph of a gold dinar which bears an inscription stating that it is from Ma'din Emir al-Huminim B'il Hijaz, 105 A.H. Quoting part of the notes relative to the coin, Dr. Miles states:

"The mine of the Commander of the Believers in the Hijaz is undoubtedly to be identified with Ma'din (later Harrah) Bani Sulaim,* southeast of Medina and northwest of Mecca, on the route between Baghdad and Mecca, at

* The mine of the tribe of Sulaim.

[241]

approximately 41° 20′ east 23° 308′ north, according to calculations based on the literary sources and the accounts of travelers. The Arab historians record that Umayyad Calif 'Umar b. 'Abd al-'Aziz (99-101 A.H.) bought a piece of land, on which there was at least one mine, from the son of a certain Bilai b. al-Harith, to whom the property had been given in fief by the Prophet; and it has been amply demonstrated that this mine was the source of the gold as well as the mint of the coin in question. While this coin was struck five years after the death of the caliph whose personal property the mine was, it is not surprising to find the name of the mint still in use.

"There seems to me," continues Dr. Miles, "little doubt that the Ma'din Bani Sulaim is further to be identified with Mahad Dahab, the site of the gold mine now being worked by the Sa'udi Arabian Mining Syndicate, Ltd., under the management of the American Smelting and Refining Company."

I owe Mr. K. S. Twitchell the knowledge of many interesting facts in connection with this mine, located at 40° 52′ 45″ east 23° 28′ 52″ north. In 1941, Mr. Twitchell was kind enough to place at my disposition a photograph of an extremely interesting Kufic inscription found in the old tailings of the mine, and I hope soon to be able to publish this inscription, together with a further discussion of the probable identity of Mahad Dahab and the mine of the Commander of the Believers in the Hijaz.

The inscription, dated 304 A.H. (916-7 A.D.) records the building of a great highway for the pilgrimage to Mecca.

While Dr. Miles is awaiting a better photograph of the inscription, which he plans to publish and discuss in a future paper, he has been kind enough to furnish the writer with the following translation:

[242]

"In the name of Allah, the Compassionate, the Merciful: The Servant of Allah, Ja'far, the Imam al-Muqtadir Bi'llah, Commander of the Believers (may Allah prolong his life) ordered the Visier abu 'l Hasan 'Alib.'isa (may Allah cause his power to continue) to build a broad highway for the pilgrims of the House of Allah, in the hope of Allah's generous reward; and it was carried out under the administration of the qadi Muhammad b.Musa (may Allah strengthen him); and this work was entrusted to Abu-Ahmad b. Abd al-Aziz al . . . i and Mus'ab b. Ja'far al-Zubayri, in the year four hundred and three . . . (403 A.H.)."

CHAPTER TWENTY-THREE

The Safest Land on Earth

It was early in the days of Ibn Sa'ud's rule, and not all of his people had learned that crime was no longer something to be accepted or winked at. Some of them did not believe that the new ruler was really serious.

A poor barber from India was traveling on foot between Jiddah and Medina, on his pilgrimage. He was carrying a cheap, shiny valise, containing his personal belongings and the tools of his trade. Near the end of his journey, he lay down in the shade of a scrub tamarisk and fell asleep.

Soon thereafter, a Bedouin happened along, and was attracted by the shiny kit. He crept up to the poor barber, clouted him with his staff, and scampered away with his loot, leaving the victim unconscious and bleeding from a deep cut in his head. Hours later, he revived; and ultimately a passing caravan picked him up and took him on to Medina.

The report quickly reached Ibn Sa'ud, and his action was swift: he had all the Bedouin chieftains between Jiddah and Medina brought in and jailed. A month later, he called them before him and ordered each of them to send for his son to take his place in jail while they returned to their districts to find the thief. The order: None of the sons was to be released until the thief was seized. And what happened? Let there be no doubt: The thief was caught.

A sharp contrast this was with those other days, when lawlessness was commonplace in Arabia, and was the especial shame of the Holy Land of the Hijaz. The Turks and the sherifs made only feeble efforts to root out the evil, and sometimes tacitly acquiesced if their agents did not actually share the spoils.

Consequently, pilgrims who had already braved the piracy of the seas and the banditry of land travel in order to *reach* the Hijaz, found themselves exposed to robbery and assault after they arrived. The Bedouins got to the point where they looked forward to the period of the pilgrimage as a sort of annual hunting season: a kind of sport and special privilege. Had it not been for the pilgrims' great and all-pervading faith, they would assuredly have abandoned this great and sacred institution.

Those days have vanished. Abdul Aziz ibn Sa'ud has made *all* roads safe; and all communities, as well. All districts are apportioned under the authority of the chieftains, who are held strictly accountable to the Amir of the district. The writer had the privilege of participating in the pilgrimage of 1948, and saw eloquent evidence of the new order.

Several wealthy Indian potentates took part in the 1948 pilgrimage, and all of them carried small sacks of gold sovereigns to give as alms. In fact, every pilgrim, no matter how poor he may be, comes to the Hijaz carrying gifts of money, scraped together by himself and by his neighbors, to distribute in charity among the poor of the Holy Cities.

It is estimated that more than 300,000 persons attended the 1948 pilgrimage, yet *not a purse was snatched or an article stolen.* Money changers in the open market left their stands to pray, and returned in the confident knowledge that nothing had been taken.

Is there any other land where this could be duplicated? And, is it any wonder that the lawfulness that he has established has endeared Ibn Sa'ud to the four hundred million Muslims?

[245]

Earlier in this narrative, it was noted that the two principal law enforcers for Ibn Sa'ud were Abdullah ibn Jlewi and Abdul Aziz ibn Ibrahim. Indeed, Ibn Jlewi was the right hand of Ibn Sa'ud from the earliest days. It will be recalled that he and his two brothers were by the side of the king-to-be when he slipped through the darkness into Riyadh on that historic night of January 15, 1902; it was Abdullah who accompanied his leader into the chamber of 'Ajlan; and it was Abdullah again who braved the fire of the garrison to storm into the citadel and kill 'Ajlan.

It was Abdullah whose exploits made him the natural choice to govern the then-lawless province of al-Hasa, after its capture from the Turks; and he who was given the rugged task of taming the 'Ujman and the wild banu Murrah. Many are the tales of his severity, but none can deny that he brought lawfulness, peace, and security where none existed before.

Hafis Wahaba, Sa'udi ambassador to the Court of St. James, told how, in 1916, a peasant of al-Hasa complained to Ibn Jlewi that one of the Amir's servants had beaten him and his sons. The Amir ordered a roundup of all of the servants in order that the accuser might identify his attacker. He could not do so.

It then occurred to the Amir that one of his own sons might have committed the abuse, and he thereupon ordered his sons brought before him. Promptly, the peasant pointed to the guilty one. Then, when he realized that this was the son of the Amir, he withdrew his complaint and apologized, saying that he had not known the true identity of the one he had identified.

Abdullah reprimanded him, saying:

"If we are not an example of justice, how can we expect the people to respect the law? In the past, nations have perished because of injustice. As to you, the guilty one (addressing the son), you shall receive your punishment."

With that, he arose from his divan in court and himself dealt the young man a severe beating with his cane.

"It behooves us," he asserted, "first to correct ourselves before attempting to correct the people."

Occasionally, Ibn Jlewi's severity got him at cross purposes with the King; for Ibn Jlewi saw no excuse for intentional wrong-doing, and he meted out justice according to the Shar' (Koranic law). In contrast, while Abdul Aziz is stern and unyielding when necessary, he is also ready to forgive or to compromise, for he has that far vision which causes him to take the long view of all things, be they important or seemingly trivial.

One time, Ibn Jlewi sent out three young officers to bring in some 'Ujman for some infraction. But, when they arrived, and the 'Ujman learned of their purpose, they fired upon the officers, killing one and wounding another, who died on the way back to Hofuf. Ibn Jlewi immediately sent out a large contingent of soldiers, who brought in twelve of the young men. The trial court exonerated nine of them, and convicted three, who were, of course, sentenced to death.

It so happened that the King arrived at Hofuf that day, and the chiefs of the 'Ujman came to the evening Majlis to ask mercy for their sons. He agreed to intercede with Ibn Jlewi in the morning.

So, when the Majlis assembled in the morning, and the elders gathered, Abdul Aziz begged Ibn Jlewi to modify the punishment. Manifesting great surprise and regret, Ibn Jlewi replied that he wished that the King had made his desires known earlier, because the men had already been executed.

[247]

What had happened was that Ibn Jlewi had gotten wind of the chiefs' intercession, and had carried out the execution at dawn.

Another time, a farmer from the outskirts of Hofuf brought a Bedouin and his camel to Abdullah ibn Jlewi with the complaint that, while the Bedouin was camping in the vicinity of his grove, he permitted the camel to graze in his date orchard, where it reached the ruttub (ripe dates) and ate bunches of them.

The Bedouin, on his part, declared that he never let the camel out of his sight, and that the animal did not trespass upon the orchard.

With each man equally vehement in his assertions, it appeared to be quite a problem. Finally, the Amir inquired of the farmer:

"What is the amount of the damage?"

"Thirty riyals."

"What is the value of the mount?"

"Three hundred riyals," the Bedouin answered.

"Slay the camel," the Amir ordered.

The camel was killed and its stomach opened, but no dates were found.

"Give the Bedouin 300 riyals," the Amir ordered, "and let him have the meat to sell."

As to the farmer, he was sent to jail until he had paid the 300 riyals, plus a 700-riyal fine.

On Thursday, December 2, 1948, I took leave of the Amir Sa'ud, whose guest I had been, and returned to Dhahran, the administrative headquarters of Aramco. I learned that there was to be an execution during the afternoon.

I did not care to witness it, and I, therefore, went over to Dammam to visit and to bid farewell to Amir Abdul-

Muhsin ibn Jlewi, brother of the Governor; and arrived back at Dhahran after the scheduled event to find hundreds of persons still gathered at the scene.

The story of this affair was that of a Somali employee who had suddenly gone berserk and stabbed to death a boy of fifteen. Of course, the Muslim law, like our American law, condemned him to die; but, instead of hanging or electrocuting, the sentence was to be carried out by the swordsman.

Somali employees had collected funds for ransom, but they were refused by the mother of the murdered boy, and, accordingly, the brother and cousin went along to witness the execution.

Scheduled for punishment, also, were two Somalis, who had stolen a Company automobile, painted the markings and driven it northward hoping to cross the border and profit by their theft. Somewhere in the desert the machine stalled and they left it and traveled away on foot. By the time the car was discovered the traces had been obliterated by the wind and sand. Sa'ud ibn Jlewi sent for two trackers of the banu Murrah, famed among the Arabs for sign reading. Like hounds they searched the ground, circled and traveled until they caught up with them.

Of course, the penalty for theft was the amputation of a hand by the swordsman, and these two events were scheduled to take place at the site of the crime.

On Thursday afternoons in Sa'udi Arabia, work ceases in order that the Muslim workmen may go to their homes and prepare for their Friday congregational prayer, for Friday is the Muslim day of worship, and, in deference to the people of the country, Aramco conforms to their custom by resuming work on Saturday and Sunday.

The Amir ordered that all employees be present at the

public execution. Of course, this did not please the American officials but they had no say in the matter, for this was not a matter within Company jurisdiction, but one involving the law of the land.

In talking with some of these officials I ventured to say that this was an historical occasion, for it was the first stolen automobile in Sa'udi Arabia, and that it would be a devil of a long while before another was stolen. Ibn Jlewi stands between them and insecurity, as their equipment stretches over a hundred miles, and could not have been protected so well had they assumed their own responsibility with three thousand military police.

These banu Murrah trackers, incidentally, are simply phenomenal operators. On one occasion, a group of Egyptians, who were guests of the King, indicated a certain skepticism concerning the reputed feats of these men. The King decided to give them a demonstration.

He summoned five of his trackers, and then asked one of the Egyptian guests to remain with them, in a room inside the palace, while the rest of the party went out into the courtyard. There, a group of about two hundred townspeople was instructed to mill around in the sand until a hodgepodge of footprints had been created. Finally, one of the crowd was asked to stop, and a circle was drawn in the sand around his footprints.

Everyone was then asked to retire to the edge of the courtyard, and the trackers were summoned. The King pointed to the encircled footprint and told the trackers: "Find this man." The footprint was then obliterated.

The crowd was then instructed to begin milling around again, as the trackers peered at their footprints. Whenever a print resembled the one in the circle, the trackers would smooth out a patch of sand and ask the individual to make

Murra

a clear print. This work moved swiftly, and one after another "suspect" was rejected until—in less than two minutes—a tracker looked at one track, pointed to the man who had made it, and exclaimed:

"It is he."

It was.

And, so, justice in Sa'udi Arabia is the foundation of the state. Trials are never protracted, perjury has been found to have unpleasant consequences, and no welcome has been proffered to criminal lawyers, performing emotional acrobatics. Simply and directly, the judges arrive at the truth and deal with the issue.

Is the system effective? Well, no country on earth can boast of the safety of person and property that exists in Sa'udi Arabia today. Caravans travel the length and breadth of the land in peace and perfect security, praising Allah and praying for long life for Abdul Aziz ibn Sa'ud.

CHAPTER TWENTY-FOUR

The King's Men

It was just before one of the most crucial undertakings of World War II, and one that was certainly among the most decisive: the Battle of El Alamein.

Tensely waiting to move forward with General Montgomery in the great adventure were the Indian forces who had been so effective in clearing East Africa of the Italian troops, and whose comrades rendered such valiant service in the China-Burma-India theatre, and later against the German armies.

On the eve of El Alamein, King Ibn Sa'ud sent his son, the Amir Mansur, to review and encourage the Indian Muslim officers and men as they awaited the venture that was to mean death or glory. The appearance of the son of the ruler of the Sacred Cities of Islam, his conversations with the fighting men, and his encouragement, were a most effective stimulus for the Muslim forces.

The role played by the Arabs in the first World War was well chronicled, but, for one reason or another, their part in the second World War, although most effective, seems to have been sidetracked from the American public.

The casualties of the Syrian and Lebanese soldiers, fighting under French leadership at Bir-Hakim, reached six thousand. At the Battle of Tunis, the casualties among Algerian, Tunisian, and Moroccan Arabs were reported at sixteen thousand, of whom three thousand were left dead on the battlefield. These were Muslim Arabs, yet this fact seems to have been ignored.

After Sicily and Corsica, their valor and sacrifice in obliterating the Gustav Line, in the vanguard of our Fifth Army, has been given no recognition; and the fact that they were Arabs and Muslims has, to the best of my knowledge, never been mentioned.

The First French Army, composed of these fighting Muslim Arabs, reported casualties of 33,000 in the late war, to say nothing of their terrific losses in Belgium and France during the German onrush of 1940, but they were designated as French—fighting for the mother country, France.

During the formative period of the Kingdom of Sa'udi Arabia, the only available forces to be mobilized were partisan settlers and tribesmen who went out to fight for their religious faith and for spoils.

Abdul Aziz, the experienced fighter and strategist, realized the futility of the old order, and directed his energies to creating a modern army. He realized that the process, under the circumstances, would be slow, and so he hastened to lay the foundation by establishing schools for officers, providing instruction in light and heavy arms, artillery, and armor. He sent groups abroad to study mechanized warfare, established military hospitals and a medical corps, and called upon Americans and the British to assist in creating a modern force.

A master of mobility in his warring days, the King early acquired tanks and armored cars, but knew that airplanes were also essential. He is, therefore, making this arm of the service a prime objective, and, in this effort, he is unsparingly encouraging civil aviation as a step in that direction.

In 1945, he appointed the since-deceased Prince Mansur as Minister of Defense, and he devoted his energy with great

[255]

effectiveness to fulfilling his father's desire for a modern air fleet. On account of the vastness of the Sa'udi Domain of 2,600,000 square kilometers, its stretches of mountain and desert, and the difficulty of travel, the utilization of air transportation will accrue to its advantage.

Of course, the camel corps of fifteen thousand, strategically posted, will continue to be indispensable, as well as the border posts of thirty thousand and the shore patrol of two thousand. Under the management of Prince Mansur, infantry, tanks, and planes were increased as rapidly as officers could be trained to man them.

Every able-bodied man between the ages of fourteen and sixty-five is subject to call in time of war. One might add that, as far as Najd is concerned, all able-bodied men are not only always *subject* to call, but always *ready*. From early youth, the Najdis practice marksmanship and riding, and experience the hardships of the desert; they are equipped with sword, gun, and ammunition, furnished by the Government, while every man has his own horse or fast camel, carries a bag of dried dates and is thus ready to take to the field.

Under this paternal government, the King says: "We take care of them in peace and they take care of us in war."

The "Najdi Army" is divided into the following sections: (1) The Men of al-'Aridh, (2) The Men of the Towns, (3) The Men of the Ikhwan Colonies (Hijar), and (4) The Bedouins.

(1) *The men of al-'Aridh* (Ahl-Al-'Auja), which comprises the District of Riyadh and environs, are the elite of the army, for they have always been the valiant partisans of the Sa'uds and have fought for Abdul Aziz throughout his career.

During my visit to the Crown Prince I attended with

[256]

him a celebration where two hundred of these doughty warriors, with drawn swords, were chanting their war song, and he pointed to them, saying:

"All these Khwayah (Sworn-brothers) are the sons of men who died in our wars."

The guards of the King and Princes are selected from al-'Aridh; never leave the person of their royal charge unguarded; and are always under arms, ready for the call, even while asleep. The civil officials, in time of war, assume military duties in addition to their civil posts, and all warriors in the district are recorded, equipped and given regular grants.

The warriors of the district fall into three classes:

a. *The Royal Guard.* The guard of the King and the Princes of the Royal Blood, men who never lay aside their weapons, even while asleep.

b. *Government Officials.* All Government officials except the foreigners among them are liable to military service in case of need.

c. *The Men of the Jihad.* All Men of the Jihad bear weapons stamped with the King's brand. The Royal Guard are Men of the Jihad, differing only in that they are never separated from the person of the King or the Princes.

The other Men of the Jihad may not leave Riyadh except at the King's command. There is a special office (Diwan of the Jihad) for them in the Royal Cabinet, that looks after their affairs and weapons and remuneration. A register is kept for all types of weapons and equipment. Ownership and distribution of weapons is a monopoly of the Government.

(2) *The Men of the Towns.* All male inhabitants of the towns and villages of Najd fall into this category. In

[257]

battle they form the right and left wings, with the Men of al-'Aridh in the center. Their military service goes according to four different states of affairs:

a. *The State of Prolonged Lasting Peace.* When no threat of war is apparent, each village is under obligation to provide a certain number of men with their supplies and provisions for a period of four months out of the year. If there is no need for the men, the people of the village pay a sum equal to the cost of maintaining them into the treasury of the State, which uses it for the benefit of Moslems.

b. *The State of Light Campaigns.* In this case, each village furnishes its specified number of men with their supplies. The Treasury provides them with weapons and military equipment and, if they remain in the field more than four months, their food for the additional period.

c. *The State of Heavy Campaigns.* In this case, the Secondary Jihad is proclaimed and the towns and villages are required to double the number of men they put in the field.

d. *The State of Great Emergency.* If danger threatens the existence of the Kingdom, the general call to arms is sounded summoning everyone capable of bearing weapons.

(3) *The Men of the Ikhwan Colonies (Hijar).* The inhabitants of these colonies were originally Bedouins who were settled as a means of bringing an end to the raids and dissensions of Bedouin life. Unlike the people of the other towns, the colonists turn out en masse in answer to a military summons, every man of them bearing arms.

(4) *The Bedouins.* Despite the fame in warfare of many of the tribes, the custom is to use the Bedouins only as

[258]

scouts and skirmishers. One of the King's main tasks as a ruler has been to put a stop to the raids of the Bedouins in time of peace; in order to break them of the habit it has been necessary to limit their role in the military forces.

Every division of the army has its own battle flag, while all fight under the banner of the Commander in Chief, usually borne in the center.

Each division also has its own battle cry, by which it is recognized, while the common battle cry that binds all the soldiers of the Army together is "Knights of God's Unity, Brothers of those who obey the Lord." During the Second World War, both the United States and Great Britain sent military missions to aid in training the Sa'udi Army in the use of modern weapons. Tayif, the summer resort for Mecca and Jiddah in the hills of the Hijaz, was the site selected for the work of the missions. The American mission gave hundreds of officers months of intensive training in the use of small arms, such as Browning automatics, and communications equipment, such as walkie-talkies. A considerable amount of up-to-date equipment was supplied by the United States under the Lend-Lease Act. The British concentrated on giving instruction in the use of light ordnance such as mortars and in military transport.

CHAPTER TWENTY-FIVE

From These:
Strength to His Hand

The day of January 15, 1902, was a doubly auspicious one for Abdul Aziz ibn Sa'ud: First, of course, it was that day on which he recaptured possession of the Sa'udi capital, Riyadh, and laid the foundation of his kingdom. But, also, it was the birthday of his third son: the Crown Prince and successor to the throne, His Royal Highness Sa'ud.

The Crown Prince is ranking member of that group of strong, able men who have been support and comfort to the King in his enormous task of building a new and greater Arabia.

The eldest son of Abdul Aziz was Turki, but he died in 1919, during the influenza epidemic; the second born, Khalid, had died previously, at the age of seven.

Sa'ud's mother was the daughter of the chief of the powerful tribe of banu Khalid, who ruled al-Hasa. The infant prince-to-be was brought to Riyadh by his grandfather, Imam Abdul Ruhman, when the Imam made his triumphal entry into the city.

Schooled at an early age in the Arabic language and the Holy Koran, Sa'ud then was put through the training in hardship which his father enforced upon all of his sons: going barefoot in the burning sands, riding bareback, learning the use of arms, and experiencing, in general, all of the

[260]

discomforts which must be faced and endured by a warrior.

Well it was that he had this training, for he was to need it on more than one occasion. From 1915 forward, he participated in the wars of his father. He accompanied him in the invasion of the Hijaz; and, after the Battle of Turbah, led an expedition against the 'Utaibah and other tribes which were affiliated with Hussein. Notable among his victories was the Battle of Dafinah, where he distinguished himself by his initiative and bravery.

On his first expedition to Haiel, he surprised a section of the Rasheed Army, defeated it, and enriched his followers with the spoils. He returned to Riyadh, and later headed five thousand men in raiding Shammar far and wide, preventing reinforcements or provisions from reaching Haiel, which, as related earlier, was being besieged by his uncle, Muhammad ibn Abdul Ruhman. It was to Amir Sa'ud, it will be recalled, that Abdullah ibn Mut'ib surrendered, in 1920.

Sa'ud's strong hand was needed again in 1924, when he made his first pilgrimage to Mecca with his father.

During this pilgrimage, the intolerant Ikhwan objected to the coming of the Egyptian Mahmal, accompanied by a military escort with music and dancing. This was considered by the Ikhwan to be a pagan innovation, and feeling ran high. Hearing of this, Abdul Aziz dispatched Sa'ud, who drove back the belligerent Ikhwan, and protected the Egyptian pilgrims from possible serious trouble.

Many another call to arms was answered readily and effectively by the warrior-prince in the ensuing years, including participation in the Battle of Sabla (1929), which marked the beginning of the end of the Ikhwan rebellion; command of the Najdi troops in the campaign against

Yemen (1933); and command of the Sa'udi Army in the 1934 hostilities, resulting in annexation of Najran and the Country of Yam, in the south.

It was on May 11, 1933, when the Royal High Council decreed that Sa'ud should be designated as Crown Prince of the Kingdom. The decree was signed by all members of the Council, headed by Prince Faisal; and received the consent of the King, and the approbation of Sa'ud's other brothers and of the public.

He had already proved himself worthy of the honor. Within a year, he was to do so once more, during his 1934 pilgrimage to Mecca with his father. The dispute with Yemen had been terminated only a short time before, and the tense feelings had not fully subsided.

So it was that, while the King and the Crown Prince were making the circuit of the Ka'ba with the multitudes, one of the crowd, a Yemenite, made a sudden frontal attack on His Majesty.

The King stood still while one of his retinue cut the man down. A second attacker, trying to get close to the King, was blocked away and started to flee, but was caught and killed.

Then, in the course of this excitement, a third assassin suddenly appeared from behind, raised his dagger, and was poised for the lunge when the Crown Prince saw him, and threw himself between the assailant and his father just in time to receive the thrust of the blade in his left shoulder.

The Prince's bodyguard, a soldier named Kheirallah, shot and killed the Yemenite; the Prince was given emergency treatment; and the King, shocked by the sacrilege of bloodshed within the Haram, immediately ordered all gates to be closed. Then he took two actions. First, he dispatched fast riders to Mina, where he knew that twelve thousand

Yemenite pilgrims occupied their allotted section, with a message to the two leaders there, Amir Faisal and Abdullah Sulayman, saying: "Thanks to Allah, I am unharmed, and I hold both of you personally responsible for the slightest harm that may befall a single Yemenite pilgrim."

Only after this was done did he take the second action: "Order a thorough search for possible additional plotters."

Throughout these years of war and adventure, the Crown Prince had become his father's confidant, participating in all important affairs, and preparing himself with characteristic thoroughness for the great responsibility assigned to him. He had entrenched himself thoroughly in the hearts of the Najdis.

Travel has been an integral part of his training. His first trip out of Arabia was in 1925, when he went to Egypt and submitted to two operations on his eye. After his recuperation, he visited King Fuad and his ministers, and became acquainted with the notables of Cairo, both Egyptian and foreign.

In May, 1935, the Crown Prince left Sa'udi Arabia again, on a three-months tour of Europe, visiting Italy, Switzerland, France, Holland, Belgium, and England, where he was well received by the governments and people.

In January, 1947, he came to the United States at the invitation of the President, and spent six weeks touring the country by air, visiting Kansas City, Houston, Phoenix, Boulder Dam, Los Angeles, San Francisco, Chicago, Detroit, Princeton, New York, and Washington.

He showed unflagging interest in the U. S. Government's experimental farm outside of Washington, in the irrigation developments of the Southwest, and in the advanced agricultural and horticultural methods of the University of California. Tree culture and stock breeding received his close attention. He visited military and naval installations, saw steel made at Gary and automobiles manufactured in Detroit, inspected the great nuclear physics installations at Berkeley, and enjoyed immensely the Middle Eastern cultural treasures at Princeton University.

Despite the barriers of language, the Crown Prince's immense personal charm and innate courtesy won a great new body of friends for himself and for his country: high U. S. Government officials, leading members of the diplomatic corps, important corporation executives, and plain men and women from coast to coast.

An American member of the Crown Prince's entourage recalls how a police motorcycle escort, sirens screaming, had led the official motorcade through the streets of New York, first stop on the tour, after the party left Washington. His Royal Highness seemed considerably amazed by this procedure, but tactfully said nothing, probably assuming that it was a peculiarity of the biggest United States city.

But, when the same procedure was repeated at the second stop, Kansas City, the Crown Prince asked a State Department security officer, who was traveling with him, to see that the practice was avoided thereafter.

"We do not have to hurry," he explained through one of the interpreters, "and we do not have to cause disturbance and inconvenience for other people."

Like his father, he has a deep-seated love of people and a constant desire to help them in their troubles. One small example: During the 1948 pilgrimage, he learned that a motorcade of Persian pilgrims had encountered difficulties in crossing the Dahna. He immediately dispatched fifty automobiles, twenty ten-ton trucks, and six wrecking trucks with crews and mechanics to extricate the pilgrims and send them on their way in time for the official ceremonies.

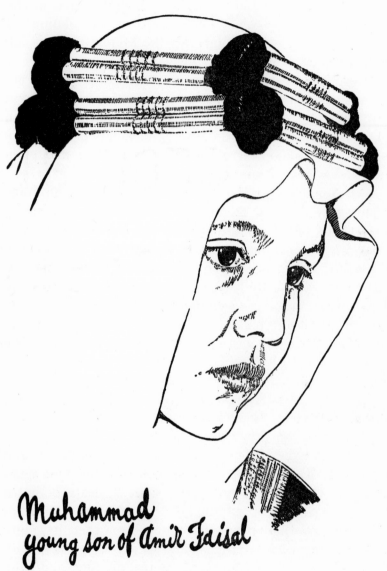

Muhammad
young son of Amir Faisal

After the 1948 pilgrimage, the writer visited the capital city of Riyadh while the King and most of his family, court, and retinue were still in the Hijaz, and so had an especially privileged opportunity to observe the Crown Prince at close range: watching him presiding with sagacity at the Majlis in the King's absence, dispatching the affairs of state with confidence and ease, and presiding as gracious and versatile host: first at his table, served in the best European manner, and then at an Arab-style banquet in the open country, where the guests enjoyed the most succulent and delicious food in Sa'udi Arabia, the tenderloin of a young camel. At his model gardens, al-Badi'ah, at Wadi Hanifah, his attention to, and pleasure in, every shrub, fruit tree, and flower reflected the artistic nature which a life of adventure has never subdued.

Warrior, world traveler, administrator, His Royal Highness has never lost the essential humility which is inherent in his Faith.

In his own words: "Man should advise himself before advising his brother Muslims, and likewise purify his intentions that his good deeds may be acceptable to God."

*   *   *

H.R.H. Amir Faisal

If the day of January 15, 1902, was a doubly auspicious one for Abdul Aziz ibn Sa'ud, no less was that of April 14, 1906.

This was the day when the king-to-be overwhelmed the ferocious Abdul Aziz ar-Rasheed at the Meadows of Mhanna, to deal that rival tribe a blow from which they never recovered, and to put an end to Turkish influence in Najd.

This was the day, as well, when another son of destiny was born to Ibn Sa'ud, and they named him Faisal, the same

[267]

as that great Amir and Imam who brought such lustre to the family name between 1830 and 1865.

Of all of the sons of Ibn Sa'ud, Faisal is unquestionably the most widely known in other lands; for, besides being Viceroy of the Hijaz and Chief of the Royal Council, he is also Minister of Foreign Affairs. As such, he participated in the organization of the United Nations at San Francisco, and has been his Nation's delegate to that body ever since. He has visited virtually every country in Europe, including Russia and Poland.

The handsome, sartorially flawless Faisal is the cosmopolite of his family: thoroughly versed in world affairs, quick-thinking, shrewd, self-assured; his healthy fondness for gayety is well balanced by a native dignity and sense of proportion.

One recalls his impressive demonstrations of military skill and daring: in the campaign to annex Asir, in 1922, when he was only seventeen; in the siege of Jiddah, in 1925; and in the invasion of Yemen, in 1933.

If his prowess as a warrior was a natural heritage from his father, then his facility with book-learning came with equal appropriateness from his mother; she was a daughter of that venerated family of Sheikh Muhammad ibn Abdul Wahhab, founder of the Reformation; and Faisal was brought up in the traditions of that house of learning.

Making remarkable progress in his early youth, he was well able to fit into the Arab pattern of assuming responsibility in those years when we in the West are still occupied with games and carefreedom.

Thus, he was still a youth in his teens when the King, realizing his precocity, commissioned him to go to London and learn, at first hand, Downing Street's stand on basic Arabian matters.

[268]

There, he was received by Lord Curzon, then Minister of Foreign Affairs, who could not persuade himself to give serious regard to this lad in Oriental costume; but who, instead, spoke patronizingly, and offered Faisal the abruptly-rejected hospitality of bonbons and passed jestingly over the questions which his visitor had come to discuss.

The keen and sensitive youth left in anger, but not without gaining the conviction that the Foreign Office was Al-Hussein's partisan in all Arab controversies. Ibn Sa'ud, wise and practical, comforted Faisal, and bided his time.

The episode of the Foreign Office is illustrative of a characteristic attitude of youth in the Middle East: their seriousness, when not at play, and their attention to proprieties. The writer had the opportunity to witness a delightful example of the latter during a visit to Amir Faisal.

The Amir was absent at the moment, and I was received by his little son, Muhammad, aged nine. He welcomed me with the ease and dignity of an ambassador, led me to the salon, and refused to be seated until I had settled myself comfortably. He then ordered coffee to be served, and presided throughout the visit with the graciousness of his father.

This dignity was well evidenced when the Amir Faisal, on his first visit to the United States, a few months after war's end, was acclaimed by Americans of Arab descent at a banquet in New York. Deeply grateful for this affectionate tribute from men of his own derivation, he spoke his sincere appreciation, but none the less reminded them: "You owe your undivided fealty to the great and hospitable country which opened its arms to receive you. I am gratified to learn of your excellent response to the call of your country in its hour of need."

A man whose feet are always firmly implanted on solid ground, Faisal evoked memories of his father when he told a meeting of the Royal High Council: "I am fully aware of my shortcomings, and value most he who points out to me my errors. I would welcome being admonished of fault or omission by any person outspokenly, not by hint. I vow by Allah that I bless the moment in which one comes to say: 'You are mistaken or deficient.' In my innermost consciousness, I am aware of my deficiencies, and yet I have never heard this from you. I ask you: Is this trustworthy on your part?"

Ready at all times to acknowledge and applaud the virtues of the many lands which he has visited, he is equally ready to defend the virtues of his own. For example: "We have seen in different countries people who mount the rostrum, criticizing the head of the government and its leaders. This is not current in our land, and it is said that we have no freedom of expression. This can be answered as follows: "What country can claim the liberty that we possess? Any man may stop the King on the road and voice his complaint freely. Is there any greater freedom than this? Does one mean by freedom the establishment of a tournament of personal quarrels and an exchange of vilification? That is not freedom. Freedom consists in giving free vent to sincere views."

H.R.H. Amir Sultan

The Amirate of Riyadh governs the Province of Najd from north to south, and includes the districts of Haiel, Qasim, Sadir, Mahmel, Wadi-ad-Dawasir, al-Yamama, and Tabbak, with their cities, towns, and deserts, their townsfolk and Bedu. It constitutes the heaviest administrative responsibility within Sa'udi Arabia.

Yet, the man who is Governor is only twenty-eight years of age: the Amir Sultan ibn Abdul Aziz. The writer has never

[270]

been so impressed with the personality and ability of a young executive.

Prince Sultan devotes five hours daily to reviewing all reports, petitions and communications received during the preceding twenty-four hours. These, he assigns to the appropriate official for action. In addition, he daily holds his own Majlis, where he receives the tribal chieftains and Bedouin delegates who come to visit the King, and to discuss their tribal and regional problems. This is a most delicate task, but the young Prince has so acquitted himself as to win the complete confidence of the King and the Crown Prince.

He has that rare quality of being able to concentrate completely upon the matter at hand, as the writer has observed at first hand: studying a document seriously and intently; listening to an excited petitioner calmly and patiently; or relaxing in high spirit at a horse race or sword play. He is a true Najdi.

Amir Abdullah al-Faisal

H. H. Amir Abdullah al-Faisal, son of H.R.H. Amir Faisal, is charm personified, handsome, alert, and gracious. In spite of his youth, he has proven himself a competent administrator, for, in the absence of the Viceroy of Hijaz, he assumes the task of governing the most populous section of Sa'udi Arabia.

During the annual Pilgrimage, the influx of 300,000 for the Hajj creates a heavy responsibility. Potentates and paupers from all countries must be looked after and properly directed. During the Pilgrimage of 1948, Abdullah spent four days and nights in continuous activity, re-routing jammed traffic and looking after the needs of the vast multilingual crowds: their water supply, clinics, hospital posts,

[271]

sanitary welfare, relocating the strayed and lost, et cetera, et cetera. At the end, his vigilance and devotion to duty landed him ill in bed, and the King ordered him and his family to be flown to Egypt for a rest.

Abdullah, like his father, is a poet of talent. The writer had the good fortune to have him recite some of his verses to him and was delighted with the delicacy of his imagery and eloquence of expression. At present, he is engaged in collecting an anthology of Najdi poems in Najdi dialect, which should be invaluable to the research student of Arabic poetry.

During a visit with Abdullah, I noticed his seven-year-old son, and remarked that he seemed too young to have a boy of that age:

"Well, ya ustath (O professor)," he replied. "I was sixteen when I fell in love with a cousin of mine of fifteen. My father said 'no,' that it was the time for study, not for marriage, should I hope to attain a measure of respectability in life.

"I took it hard, and ran away from school and went to my grandfather, the King, who inquired why I was not at my studies. I answered that I was in love with my cousin and wanted to marry her.

" 'Who is the girl?' he asked.

"I named her.

" 'Good,' said the King, 'that is fine. I will see to it and will make all arrangements.'

"Of course, neither my father nor anyone else could gainsay him, and I was married and have had five children."

His Excellency, Sheikh Abdullah Sulayman al-Hamdan
He will tell you: "I am the Minister of Finance, and concern myself with nothing else."

[272]

But, the fact is that there is no busier man in all Sa'udi Arabia than this able, tireless Finance Minister, Sheikh Abdullah Sulayman, nor is there a keener or a more dynamic personality.

A Najdi of 'Unaizah, whose people originally came from Dur'iyah, the old Sa'udi capital, he has been at Ibn Sa'ud's side for over thirty-five years, first as secretary, then as Chief of the Diwan, and finally in his present Cabinet rank.

Despite his modest disclaimer of all responsibility except the Ministry of Finance, he is continually assigned to a variety of major undertakings. His was a major role, from the beginning, in the efforts to determine Sa'udi Arabia's oil possibilities.

He has a great deal to do with provisioning the country, with planning and making contracts for the many modernization and improvement programs, and arrangements for the comfort of the pilgrims. In fact, most public works must eventually have his scrutiny and approval before they materialize. And these duties, of course, are all in addition to those incident to the direction of the country's machinery for the collection and disbursement of revenue.

Quiet and courteous by nature, Abdullah Sulayman has, nevertheless, demonstrated, on more than one occasion, that he can flare up when necessary with spirit and force which tolerates no trifling.

Having accompanied Ibn Sa'ud with unstinting devotion through the worries and hardships of the lean, uncertain years, he now enjoys the King's complete confidence.

The Minister, himself, says only: "We have worked together for many years for the good of the country and the benefit of its people, and through it all my ambition has been to serve my King faithfully and to please him."

He has achieved both ambitions.

[273]

His Excellency Sheikh Yusuf Yasin, Vice-Minister of Foreign Affairs

Sheikh Yusuf Yasin, Vice-Minister of Foreign Affairs, is one of the most devoted and hard-working officials of the King. He was born in the Ladikiya, Syria, studied in Egypt at the school of Sheikh Ali Ridha, and a short time at the University of al-Azhar. Later he studied law in Damascus and joined the Revolt in the Desert by going with Sherif Zaid, the son of Al-Hussein, to the Aqaba, ending the campaign with the Arab Legion in the reconquest of Syria. From there he visited Mecca, where he resided six months; then Amman before the entry of Amir Abdullah, with whom he could not agree, and so returned to Jerusalem, where he spent four years, during which he organized the Arabian Political Club. He returned to Damascus, then to Baghdad and to Najd, joining Sultan Abdul Aziz in 1923. A young man then, he was imbued with the revolutionary spirit of independence and was eager to help to bring liberty to his people, for which he suffered imprisonment by Turk, Frenchman, and Englishman. In his travels from place to place he was always thwarted by the colonizer and sought at long last the only independent spot in the Arab World. It is needless to recount the different positions, missions, and titles that he has had during his twenty-six years of service to Ibn Sa'ud, but through it all no one can claim a greater devotion to the King or enjoys a closer relation with him than Yusuf Yasin.

CHAPTER TWENTY-SIX

A Visit
to a Leading Merchant

The writer's first impressions of Jiddah were gleaned during the Pilgrimage season, when fifteen to twenty steamers were busily unloading the Hajjaj, swarming in by the thousands from India, Indonesia, Java, Port Sudan, Egypt, Turkey, North Africa, and other points. At such a time, Jiddah, with its inadequate accommodations and narrow thoroughfares, is packed with surging pilgrims.

I was fortunate to be the guest of Sheikh Muhammad Alireza, whose villa was opened to his friends from all countries. The Alirezas, of the House of Zainal (abbreviated from Zain-al-Abideene), is one of the oldest and most prominent houses in the Hijaz.

At the season of the Hajj, the homes of the various members of this house in Jiddah, Mecca, and Mina, and their tents in Arafat, are famed for their open hospitality. Eminent Egyptian intellectuals, prominent nobles from Pakistan, merchant princes from India, literati from Persia, and statesmen from Syria are to be found among the guests.

We, the Hajjaj, were expected to endure hardship when we humbly and penitently made the Pilgrimage, but alas, as the guests of Muhammad Alireza, partaking of black caviar flown from the Caspian Sea, with other delicacies, we experienced no hardship; and our progress throughout the Pilgrimage was an occasion to be remembered.

[275]

Such was the hospitality of Al-Zainal with Uncle Yusuf presiding over the welfare of his guests and showering them with attention. Uncle Yusuf is recognized as a man of learning and culture, mellowed by experience and travel. He is one of the most gracious and versatile gentlemen whom I have ever encountered.

The Hijaz is indebted to the Alireza family, for it was Muhammad Al-Zainal, the pearl merchant, who established the Falah (Progress) elementary and secondary schools in Jiddah, Mecca, Bahrein, and Bombay.

In spite of Turkish suspicion of such philanthropy and the non-co-operative spirit of the sherifs and their agents, the enrollment exceeded three thousand pupils. Today most of the Sa'udi Government officials and teachers can be counted among the former students of the Falah Madrassas. Indeed, the Sa'udi Government would have been at a loss, in 1925, to staff its administrative offices had it not been for these students.

The philanthropy of the Zainal family in encouraging education extended to Makala, in Hadrumut, and to Java, and all of this at a time when absolute ignorance and neglect pervaded the Hijaz. At the present time, the Sa'udi Government, handicapped in personnel, is bending its efforts to fast remedy this neglect.

But, to return to our host. . . .

After mounting the broad stairway to the first floor of the Bait Zainal's main offices, one passes first the salon where Uncle Yusuf presides: friends, guests and visitors come in, exchange salutations, chat, or take their ease on the cushioned divans that line the room.

"Ya walad!" ("O boy!"). The call is echoed by the hall porters and immediately the coffee boy enters with the brass service pot and tiny cups in which the coffee is served. As in all Arabia, it is brewed with cardamon seed as much as coffee and is poured in small measure to the guests. The latter, using the right hand, sip and return the cup for an additional helping, and the attendant will continue to serve him in installments until the guest shakes the tiny cup in token of satisfaction and then the attendant moves on to the next guest. A moment later, sweetened tea is served in small glasses.

The few hours during which Uncle Yusuf receives are more of a social court than the Western idea of business. He is consulted only on important matters. The business is conducted in the spacious offices back of the salon. Muhammad Abdullah Alireza, Ahmad and Muhammad Yusuf, and their secretaries, direct the affairs of the various projects and undertakings.

Much in the same ceremonial manner is the office business conducted. Notables and business men from many countries come in and, during the coffee and tea service, state their business. Secretaries are called to take instructions, and are placed in charge of the person or case while, on the right side of the house, the many offices are crowded with managers, accountants, clerks, and messengers. This cosmopolitan house carries on its business in the languages of Hindustan, Indonesia, Persia, and all European tongues.

The upper floors are equipped with sleeping quarters, kitchen, and dining service, and are ever ready for the comfort of the usual business traveler, while the more prominent ones are taken into the homes of the various members.

The writer was extended the courtesy of a desk, and watched the ebb and flow of the business hours which ended at 12:00 noon, to be resumed at 3:30 p.m., after the midday meal, the siesta, and shower. The waste of time is appalling to Westerners but—ah!—the people who practice this live as long, do as well, and possibly "live by the way."

All during business hours, old men, cripples, and, occasionally, women come seeking alms. The hall porters have their orders not to keep anyone away and so they freely saunter in ones, twos, and threes to the doors of the busy offices seeking Mal-Allah (the Bounty of Allah). The secretary without a word, reaches into the silver drawer and quietly gives one, two, or three silver riyals, according to his judgment and the beggar's needs, and this continues all through the business hours.

No one is turned away, for these people who have no organized charities believe in the personal touch which benefits the giver as well as the receiver. I was told by the porters that, during Ramadhan, the month of fasting, a line of fifteen to twenty is constantly forming while business goes on as usual.

The sills of the windows in this office are four feet wide and are covered with rugs. During working hours, some of the employees, after performing their ablutions, come to these and like-situated fit places, shed their slippers, and begin their devotional prayer. No one heeds them, nor do they pay any attention to others, and, when they have finished their genuflections, they go about their business without eliciting any attention or comment.

This procedure can be noticed anywhere and everywhere. The host in a home may excuse himself for a few moments or the guest may do the same for, scandalous as this may seem to a Western business man, they really believe and are not ashamed of asking forgiveness or grace; and whether it is fitting or not to carry one's prayer to business or to mix business with godliness is up to one's individual self.

Another observation: no employer or patron is spoken

to, or about, as "boss." The servant or Ethiopian slave calls the head of the house or the Amir "Ammi" ("My uncle") and, when I asked the manager of a workshop the number of men he employed, he always spoke of them as so many "anfus" (souls), never hands. In the West we fight for something that we may find ingrained in the East.

In such an old-fashioned and yet up-to-date business institution as this, there is a small room in the hall where attendants are constantly brewing the fragrant coffee and where the samovar is steaming, they are on the alert for the call of "Ya walad" while business goes on as usual.

CHAPTER TWENTY-SEVEN

The Island of Bahrein

The Island of Bahrein, lying off the coast of al-Hasa, has an area of about twenty-eight miles by ten, and is the chief of a group of fifteen small islands constituting the independent Sheikhdom ruled by His Highness, Sheikh Selman ibn Hamad al-Khalifa, K. C. I. E. Here, as in Kuwait, the Sheikhdom claimed the protection of England, which is represented by a political agent. The family of Al-Khalifa and that of Al-Sabah, of Kuwait, are tribally related to the Sa'uds.

At the northern tip of Bahrein Island, its principal town, Manama, is located. This tip of the island is fertile and well dotted with palm groves and gardens and has an excellent harbor.

Bahrein, famous for its pearl fisheries, gives the visitors a delightful vista, with its public buildings, its modern institutions, its well-laid-out paved streets, and its regulated traffic.

The two main islands are joined by a modern causeway, and its markets and shops are stocked with Indian and Eastern merchandise as well as European and American goods, making it the shopping center for the American employees of the mainland.

During my visit to Bahrein, which occurred in the absence of the ruler on a hunting trip to the mainland, I was met and received at the pier by Sheikh Muhammad, the elder of the family, whose hospitality and that of his cultured sons overwhelmed me with its graciousness. Aside from inspecting the governmental projects, the modern American settlement, the agricultural undertakings, and the wonderful clear springs welling out of the depth of the earth, I was gratified to view the Necropoli of the Ancients where, for miles, over fifty thousand tumuli are to be seen, and they make it unique, and the most impressive cemetery in existence. My delightful visit to Bahrein ended after a hunt with falcons.

The Ancient History of Bahrein, called "Dilmun," goes back to three thousand years before the Christian era. Cuneiform inscriptions from Mesopotamia, business documents, letters of merchants, and boastful annals unfold the history of this "Arab State at the Dawn," as Dr. Peter Bruce Cornwall, the brilliant young archaeologist, names it in his article contributed to the Arab World, as well as in his other writings in various publications in which he unraveled its past.

Today the Bahrein Petroleum Company is working in conjunction with local governmental agencies and members of the ruling family for the welfare of the native population. This ranges from direct contributions of cash to the performance of various engineering and technical tasks relating to civic projects, such as the construction of roads and bridges, drilling water-wells, malaria control, and a general interest in hygiene and sanitation which has generally raised the standard of living throughout the island.

The Company has modern, well-equipped hospitals as well as outlying dispensaries for its employees, staffed with skilled surgeons, physicians, and nurses, free medical care being provided for all employees. In addition to this, the

Bahrein Government has a hospital for men and another exclusively for women, and the Dutch Reform Church of America has maintained a Mission Hospital.

All of these institutions give free medical care and hospitalization for the poor to the limit of their facilities. The Mission Hospital has been in operation for many years and has been instrumental in creating good will. The Oil Company subsidizes the Mission Hospital to a varying extent and works in close co-operation with the governmental medical personnel in all matters of public health, sanitation, and mosquito control, for which the Company maintains a qualified entomologist and sanitation expert. The mosquito abatement program is maintained by the Company, covering not only the Company area but the adjacent native villages and gardens.

The Government of Bahrein operates primary and secondary schools, including a technical school. The Oil Company has established several scholarships for worthy students in these schools, and aids the development of these institutions. In addition, the Company regularly imports and distributes literature concerning modern methods to the more enterprising farmers, while the Government runs an experimental farm and is quite interested in improving agriculture and animal husbandry.

The Bahrein refinery, which was designed for a capacity of 10,000 barrels per day in 1937, was extended in subsequent years, and today it is processing crude oil at the rate of 178,000 barrels per day.

In 1944, a twelve-inch, thirty-four-mile pipeline was laid from the Dammam field, in Sa'udi Arabia, to the Bahrein refinery. This pipeline is under water for seventeen miles. During 1947, the land portions of the line were looped with an additional twelve-inch pipeline. This line, with a capacity

H.H. Sheikh Selman ibn Hamad Al-Khalifa, K.C.I.E.

of approximately 115,000 barrels per day, carries Sa'udi Arabia crude oil under the waters of the Persian Gulf, to be processed in the refinery on Bahrein Island.

A new four-berth wharf, plus the older two-berth Island wharf, is supplied by thirteen oil lines varying in size from six to eighteen inches, and runs three miles to a deep-water pier. Six tankers can be accommodated at one time at these wharfs. The new one is located in six to seven fathoms of water and is capable of handling the largest tankers; the present loading rate is approximately five thousand barrels of petroleum per hour.

CHAPTER TWENTY-EIGHT

Unchanged by Change:
The Pilgrimage

It was nearly fourteen centuries ago. From every corner of the Arab world they were making their hot, weary way toward a single goal. A few miles away they stopped and made their devout preparations. And then, their hearts stirred with exaltation in their Faith, their arms stretched forward and upward in piety, they presented themselves to their Maker:

"Labbaika Allah-Umma Labbaika!" ("Here we are, O Allah! Here we are in Thy great august presence.")

Then:

"Inn-Al-Hamda wal-ni'mata, wal-mulka la-ka, la-sharika la-ka!" ("Surely all praise is Thine, and all favors are Thine, and the Kingdom is Thine. There is no associate with Thee.")

For this was The Hajj: the Pilgrimage, one of the five great Pillars of Faith of the true Muslim. As the rites were performed fourteen centuries ago, so are they performed today, and so they will be as long as Muslims live and breathe on this earth.

Now, as then, men from every direction have turned their faces toward the Ka'ba, the House of God in Mecca, with the hope and anticipation of performing the Hajj: wealthy merchants from China, princes and paupers from India, Morros from the Philippines, Javanese and Malayans,

[286]

learned men from Samarkand and Bokhara, Cossacks and Tartars from the steppes of Russia, Turkomen and Persians, men from the mountains and plains of Poland and Hungary, the Balkans and Sicily, erudite 'Ulamas from Cordoba and Granada, Berbers from the Riff or Sus, the blue-veiled Tuarics from the African desert, Arabs from Fez, Tunis and Kairawan, Negroes from Lake Chad and Equatorial Africa, Swahilis and Senegalese, traders from Zanzibar—rich and poor, civilized and primitive, black, white, brown, and yellow, all possessed of the one purpose of meeting and performing their devotions at this one holy place.

Actually, the Hajj had its beginnings as a pagan institution of the Arabs, and it was an event of first importance to the scattered tribes. It provided a truce in their wars and blood feuds, a market for exchange of their goods, a fair for their pleasure, a forum for their poetry, and a source of news from the outside world.

Islam retained and remodeled the institution, making it a means of religious exaltation and a democratic leveling process which drew men of every race, color, and station from every known corner to meet as equals before the eyes of Allah, and to go back to their communities as apostles of a practiced brotherhood of men.

The Hajj is performed, in accordance with the Koran, during the "well known months," or the months that were well known at the time when the Koran was revealed. These are the months of Shawwal, Dhul Qa'dah, and the first ten days of Dhi-l-Hijjah. This is the period of the *great* Pilgrimage, although Islam also recognizes the merit of the "umrah," or lesser Pilgrimage, which may be made at any other time of the year, and in which most of the ceremonies of the Hajj may be performed.

The Pilgrimage proper is limited to six specific days in each year. A pilgrim may enter into the state of ihram (purity) at any time during the "well known months," but the actual congregational devotions for the Hajj are from the eighth to the thirteenth, inclusive, Dhi-l-Hijjah.

When the pilgrim is ready to leave his home, he speaks the prayer for the journey, saying: "O God, You are my Companion on my journey, and You are the One who remains with my people. O God, roll up the earth for us . . ." At the door of the house, another prayer is said, beginning: "In the name of Allah, I place my trust in Allah . . ." Upon boarding or mounting whatever conveyance he is using, the pilgrim repeats "Allah akbar" ("God is greatest") three times.

At the port of embarkation, which will probably be Suez for those from North Africa or Egypt, the pilgrim and his companions will join many similar parties aboard a pilgrim ship bound for Jiddah. The well-to-do pilgrim may prefer to go by air, but most of those who fly will wait until later in the season.

Before the recent years of easy transportation and communication, the journey was long and hazardous. Men bade farewell to their loved ones, never certain of their safe return. Yet, they started their perilous mission undaunted, to travel for many months, and in some cases for years, motivated solely by the spiritual hope of treading the ground that the Prophet trod, and of emulating him by circumambulating the Ancient House and to worship God, who is everywhere, at the spot where Ibrahim, Ishmael, and Muhammad worshipped.

Today, science and commerce have solved the transportation and communication problems, and Abdul Aziz ibn Sa'ud has provided the safety which, through the intervening centuries, had been non-existent. More than 100,000 came by sea to the 1950 Hajj.

In earlier years, the majority of the pilgrims traveled from Jiddah to Mecca in litters on camelback, and some of the poorer ones still travel this way, or even on foot. But, there is now a hard-surfaced road over this important seventy-four-kilometer route, built a few years ago by Egyptian engineers. Buses and automobiles have largely replaced the long, picturesque camel trains of former times.

For those who walk or ride animals, the King has provided fresh water fountains along the first thirty miles, that they may refresh themselves and make their ablutions before prayer.

"Long may he live!" is often repeated by the Hajjaj in appreciation.

In these respects, alone, has the Hajj changed since the days of the Prophet. Now, as then, the pilgrim comes ultimately to that designated point along each principal route where he enters into the state of purity known as "ihram," which consists in the adoption of a mode of dress and living designed to attune one's being to spiritual receptiveness.

Generally, Islam discourages asceticism, yet it lays great emphasis upon spiritual development through its institutions of prayer, zakat (annual charity tax of 2½ per cent on capital), fasting and the Hajj. All of these require material and personal sacrifices and denials, yet all such sacrifices (except those involved in the Hajj) are interwoven with and made a part of every-day life, without disrupting its order. Instead, they continually mellow and leaven it.

During the Hajj, however, the banning of certain ordinary, lawful acts during the state of ihram is intended to underline the serious intent of the pilgrim.

The pilgrim's first act in entering upon ihram is to bathe,

[289]

face the Ka'ba, and say his Talbiya (supplication), followed by two rak'as of prayer. He then clips his nails, cuts or shaves his hair, and discards his regular garments, be they silken robes and finery, or tattered rags of a beggar. He dons, instead, two seamless white wrappers, one from the waist down ("izzar"), and the other draped over the shoulders ("rida' "). Headgear must be discarded, and sandals ("khuff") substituted for shoes or slippers.

Women may wear ordinary clothes, black or white, but they must be simple, with face and hands uncovered. Change of clothing is permissible.

Thus, nothing remains that may tend to distinguish rich from poor, great from humble, or one race or nationality from another. All stand equal during the rendering of homage to their Creator.

The Muslim in ihram is forbidden to indulge in any pleasures of the flesh, to use perfumes, to wear garments with seams, to clip his nails or cut his hair, to hunt wild beasts, or to cut, or uproot any trees or plants growing in Sacred Territory.

It is when he has donned his seamless garments and completed his other preparations for ihram that he intones the Prayer of Intent: "O God, I have dedicated myself to Thee, and I intend to make the Pilgrimage, so do make the way easy for me and accept my Pilgrimage." He is then ready, with his fellow pilgrims, all standing together as equals, all actuated by singleness of intent and imbued with mass exaltation, to enter the Holy City of Mecca and to perform his devotions.

"Labbaika Allah-Umma Labbaika!"

This is his cry as he sets forth for the city, and this is his cry frequently during the Pilgrimage.

The pilgrims are assigned in groups to their "mutaw-

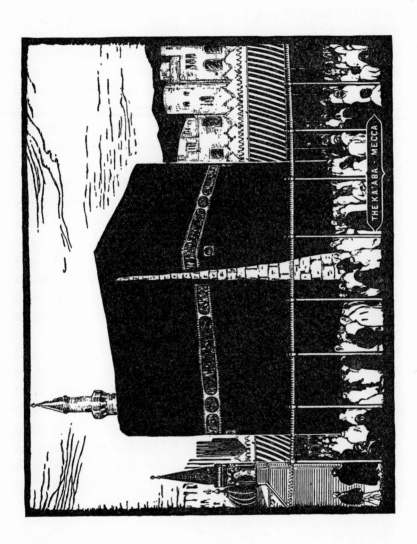

THE KA'ABA   MECCA

wifs," who are professional conductors or guides, responsible for their spiritual and material welfare. The mutawwifs and their assistants arrange lodgings, advise and guide the pilgrims in their religious rites, and otherwise minister to their needs during their stay in the Holy Land. They represent an old and important guild in Mecca, and are usually versed in the language spoken by the pilgrim.

Guided by their mutawwifs, the pilgrims preferably enter Mecca on foot, and preferably, though not necessarily, in the daytime. As soon as possible thereafter, they commence the Pilgrimage ceremonies.

They go directly to the quadrilateral enclosure, Al-Masjid al-Haram, or Sacred Mosque,* which embraces within its confines the Ka'ba, the Miqam Ibrahim (Station of Ibrahim) and the Well of Zem-Zem buildings. Here, in pre-Islamic days, was the administrative seat of the Quraish tribe, the site, among other things, of the Dar-al-Nadwa, or Council Hall. In Islam, it became the pivot of religious learnings, and of far-reaching activities for all Muslims.

Most sacred of the edifices is the Ka'ba, "Al-Bait al-'atiq," or the Ancient House, reared by Ibrahim and Ismael for the worship of The One God. The Arabs, as well as the Hebrews, trace their ancestry back to the Patriarch Ibrahim (Abraham), and the courtyard of the Sacred Mosque is believed to contain the stone (the Miqam Ibrahim) upon which he and Ismael stood when the Ka'ba was built. Nearby is the Well of Zem-Zem, the waters of which saved the life of Ismael as a child.

Hagar, the handmaiden of Ibrahim's wife, Sarah, who had borne him Ismael, had been driven into the wilderness with her child. Before the angel, Gabriel, appeared to guide

---

* Al-Masjid al-Haram, or the Sacred Mosque, is constructed in a quadrilateral whose dimensions are as follows: northwest side, 545 ft.; southeast side, 553 ft.; northeast side, 360 ft.; and southwest side, 364 ft.

her, Hagar had run seven times between two hills, As Safa and Al Marwah, in her search for water. The well which Gabriel showed her was the Well of Zem-Zem, from which pilgrims now drink as one of the privileges of the Hajj.

The well, in time, became filled in, but according to tradition it was rediscovered and reopened by the grandfather of the Prophet Muhammad, who, in turn, was told in a vision that it would furnish water to all pilgrims.

The Ka'ba, located in the center of the masjid (place of worship) is a rectangular building, whose front and back walls are each forty feet long, and the side walls each thirty-five feet, the height being fifty feet. The four walls face northeast, northwest, southeast, and southwest. It is shrouded in a covering ("kiswa") of black silk, beautifully embroidered with inscriptions in ornamental Arabic characters.

Each of the corners of the Ka'ba has its name: the north, "al-rukn al'Iraqi" after Iraq; the south, "al-rukn al-Yemen" after Yemen; the west, al-rukn al-Shami" after Sham or Syria; and the east, "al-rukn al-Aswad" after the Hajar al-Aswad, or the Black Stone.

The Black Stone, actually a reddish black, is a meteorite about eight inches in diameter, believed to have been sent down from Heaven by God in ancient times as a sign to man. Over the years, it has become broken into pieces, which are now held together by a silver band. It is now set into the wall in the east corner, at a height of about five feet.

It has long been the custom of the pilgrims to try to kiss or touch the stone as they circumambulated the Ka'ba, although often the crowds have been so great that many pilgrims had to be content to touch the stone with a stick and kiss the stick, or even to salute the stone with the hands and kiss the hands. This practice is now forbidden by the puritanical Wahhabis.

The door of the Ka'ba is in the northeast wall, about seven feet from the ground, nearer to the Black Stone than to the middle of the wall. A staircase is used to reach the entrance.

The pilgrim's first duty after entering the sacred enclosure is the circumambulation (Tawaf al-Qudum) of the Ka'ba, as it is the last upon leaving (Tawaf al-Wida'). The Tawaf begins at the Black Stone, and is performed in seven rounds, the first three at a running walk (harwala), and the others at an ordinary walking pace, with the Ka'ba to the left throughout the circuits.

The old, crippled, or infirm pilgrims make their Tawaf on short litters, carried on the shoulders of four men, who travel along the outer edge of the surging throng.

During the Tawaf, each person offers his supplication and prayer, reading the Koran or repeating whatever Sura (chapter) or verses he has learned. The mutawwif who accompanies each group or individual may, if the pilgrim is untutored in Arabic, offer the supplication or read in a slow clear voice, and the pupil repeats after him.

It is an unforgettable experience to be present with these thousands of men and women, from every part of the world and from every station in life, with all distinction erased as by death, as they stand in humility, with hands extended, tears streaming from their eyes, fervently pleading for mercy, guidance, and grace. Earnest prayers pour forth like a surging flood: a stupendous force that no barrier can stay.

After performing the Tawaf, the pilgrims visit the Station of Ibrahim, in the courtyard of the Sacred Mosque, and say a prayer, after which they may visit other sacred spots, including the Well of Zem-Zem.

They are *then* conducted to the performance of the next rite: the "Sa'y," or running. This takes place between the two small hills, As Safa and Al Maruah, situated outside the Haram, 380 yards apart. Fifty-three paces of the distance are marked for harwala, and the rest is traversed at normal walk, during which the pilgrim and his mutawwif recite their supplications. The running is, of course, in emulation of the distressed effort of Hagar to find water for her infant, Ismael.

Thus far, the pilgrim has covered the duties of the "umrah," or lesser pilgrimage, which may either be combined with the Hajj proper, or, as we have noted, may be performed at any time of the year.

Should the pilgrim enter into ihram during Shawal or Dhul-Qa'dah, or any other time prior to the Congregational Hajj proper, which is limited to the period from the eighth to the thirteenth of Dhi-l-Hijja, and should he wish to continue in the state of purity until he participates in the finals, he is at liberty to do so. This is called Qiran (joining together), and the interval is usually spent in meditation, prayer, and study.

Otherwise, should he wish to resume his usual state of living after the umrah, he may do so and then re-enter ihram on the eighth of Dhi-l-Hijja, and commence anew by circumambulating the Ka'ba, doing the Sa'y, and proceeding with the multitude. This is called the Tamattu'.

He is now ready to move on the eighth into the Plain of Mina and toward the final goal, Mt. 'Arafat, eighteen miles from Mecca.

The majority go on foot, for Muhammad said that every step of a man who walks is a hundred times better than the step of a mount bearing a rider. On the way, they pass over the Hill of Aqaba, where the people of Medina exchanged their pledges with the prophet. They must reach the Plain of Mina, halfway to 'Arafat by noon, so that the Zuhr prayer may be said there; and there they spend the night on the eve of the Standing on 'Arafat.

After spending the night at Mina, the pilgrims proceed on the ninth of Dhi-l-Hijjah to the Plain of 'Arafat. Mt. 'Arafat, rising about two hundred feet above the plain, is called "Jabal al-Rahma" (the Mount of Mercy). Here, from a pulpit, a sermon is delivered to the multitudes.

He who reaches 'Arafat on the ninth and stands to pray there, has performed the Hajj!

The pilgrims remain on this Plain throughout the afternoon and until sunset, facing toward Mecca and repeating prayers. Many weep as they pray, for the Prophet told his followers: "The best of prayers is the prayer of the Day of 'Arafat." The most desirable place to be is near the Mount of Mercy. The Prophet remained on the back of his she-camel during the sermon of his farewell pilgrimage.

After sunset, the pilgrims go to nearby Muzdalifa, headed by the King or his deputy, and there they perform their combined Maghrib (after sunset) and 'Isha (night) prayers. There the night is passed.

The following morning, the tenth of Dhi-l-Hijjah, is the day of the Feast of the Sacrifice ('Id al Adhha), and for this the pilgrims return to Mina, where the prayer for this occasion is recited.

At Mina, there are three stone pillars standing near the highway, each representing a devil. The stoning of these is one of the rites of the Hajj, and, so, in the preceding days, the pilgrims have gathered and brought with them a number of small pebbles. On this Day of Sacrifice, each pilgrim throws seven pebbles at the Great Devil, the one nearest Mecca.

Following the stoning, each pilgrim sacrifices a goat,

sheep, or camel in commemoration of God's sparing Ibrahim the sacrifice of his son by telling him to slay an animal instead of his first-born. The meat of the sacrifice must be divided with the needy of Mecca, for this is the day when Muslims the world over sacrifice in order to feed the poor.

After the sacrifice, the Pilgrims return to Mecca to perform the Tawaf al-Ifadhah ("for good measure" circuit) of the Ka'ba, and thereupon to emerge from the state of ihram. They now may shave again, cut their hair, clip their nails and don ordinary dress for the three remaining days—eleventh, twelfth, and thirteenth—which are called Days of Drying of the Meat, to provide jerked meat for the desert journey ahead.

During these final days, two more acts are expected of the pilgrim, in following the example of the Prophet. First, he must return to Mina and stone the devils: this time, all three of them. This ancient rite, accompanied by takbir (Allah-u-Akbar)—"God is Mightiest"—is symbolic of the fight against evil.

Finally, on the thirteenth day of Dhi-l-Hijjah, the pilgrim returns again to Mecca for his farewell circumambulation of the Ka'ba, "the noblest spot on earth, which Allah has chosen."

Although it is not obligatory, many of the pilgrims also go to Medina, either before or after the Hajj, to visit the Tomb of the Prophet in the Great Mosque, which is one of the two holiest shrines of Islam. The city also contains many other shrines and places of interest associated with incidents in the Prophet's life. In a sense, it is a great historical museum of the early days of Islam.

May Allah Bless Zubaidah

For more than eleven hundred years, the pilgrims have

called down the blessings and grace of Allah upon the Empress who quenched their thirst with sweet, refreshing water in this parched land of intense heat.

The Empire of the Arabs reached its zenith in the glorious reign of Harun ar-Rasheed and Zubaidah, his queen. His domain, station, and wealth were greater than those of any monarch who had preceded him; yet, in 790 A.D., he made the Pilgrimage on foot, a distance of eleven hundred miles. In humility he trudged along the trail, suffering the hardships endured by the poorest Hajj to perform his devotions.

Harun is credited with six to nine pilgrimages, and Zubaidah, who accompanied him on the first one (790 A.D.), is credited with six.

Having traveled this difficult road, crossing, as it did, the two ribbons of the Dahna, where men and beasts were subjected to untold hardships and grievous risks, Zubaidah ordered engineers to build the road, ever since named after her, and to mark it with a wall that even a blind person might follow without losing his way.

The traces of the wall remain to this day, extending in places for many miles (this according to the pilgrims from Iraq and Iran). This road is now followed by auto vehicles, via the Qadisiyah-Najef Road, to Haiel, thence to Ma'den al-Naqira * where it branches off to Mecca and Medina.

Zubaidah left endowments for the maintenance and repair of the road as well as of the water canals and cisterns. The water of the Sacred Well of Zem-Zem is not the best tasting water, and was insufficient for the inhabitants of Mecca. During the Hajj, the water problem became serious.

* Undoubtedly Mahd ath-Thahab, which is now mined by the Sa'udi Mining Syndicate, Limited, and where Mr. K. S. Twitchell found, in the old tailings, a Kufic inscription dated 916-7 A.D. recording a broadening of the road in Ma'den al-Naqira.

In 805 A.D., both Zubaidah and Harun witnessed the great suffering of the pilgrims from the effect of drought and jointly they undertook to relieve it by increasing the depth of the Sacred Well of Zem-Zem. The story is well continued by Dr. Nabia Abbott in her *Two Queens of Baghdad:*

"Perhaps it was the above experience that led the queen to undertake, on behalf of the Meccans and the annual pilgrims, waterworks that were bolder in conception and more extensive in scope than anyone had previously considered.

"The ambitious project included the central waterworks around the Spring of Hunain, some twelve miles east of Mecca, a number of smaller springs, large water reservoirs, and a subterranean aqueduct that brought water to Mecca and to the precinct of the sacred territory.

"Famous among this complex of waterworks was the 'Spring of Zubaidah' on the Plain of 'Arafat—a priceless boon to the tens of thousands of annual pilgrims. Equally famous was the Mushshash Spring in Mecca itself, which ministered to the inhabitants the year round.

"The magnitude of the task can be understood only when one considers the extremely difficult terrain of mountain and hard rock that had to be cut through and under before success could be achieved. Neither was success achieved with the first trial. But Zubaidah, once committed to the meritorious task, would not be discouraged by either technical difficulties or excessive costs.*

"She urged the engineers to greater effort and declared she would go through with the project were every stroke of the pick-ax to cost her a gold dinar. The engineering feat

* The waters of the Nu'man Springs, originating from Mount Karu, situated between 'Arafat and Tayif, are brought to 'Arafat and Mina. The springs of Hunayn, called today 'Ain As-Zaefaran from Wadi Nakhla, are brought to Mecca. Al-Asraqi says: "The people of Mecca and the pilgrims live by her grace, after that of Allah the Exalted, the Mighty."

was accomplished at a cost of some one and three-quarter million dinars, including gifts and charities incidental to the occasion.

"Work on this project already begun in the reign of Harun, was in progress at the time of his death. Zubaidah, shortly after her arrival at Baghdad from Raqqah with Harum's great treasure, left for Mecca in Ramadhan of 193, (June-July, 809). She took with her Amin's gift to the Holy City: some twenty thousand dinars' worth of gold bullion which was used as nails and gilding for the door of the Sacred Ka'ba.

"While in Mecca she, herself, witnessed the erection of fortifications, tanks, and canals in connection with her project. However, it was not finished until the following year after she had returned to Iraq. On the arch over the gate of the reservoir in Mecca the following inscription was placed:

" 'In the name of Allah, the Merciful, the Compassionate. There is no God but Allah alone without any partners. The blessings of Allah be on Muhammad His servant and messenger. The grace of Allah (be with us all)Umm Ja'far (Zubaidah)* the daughter of Abu al-Fadl Ja'far the son of the Commander of the Believers Mansur—ordered the construction of these springs to provide water for the pilgrims to the House of Allah and to the people of His Sanctuary, praying for Allah's reward and seeking to draw nigh unto Him. By the hand of Yasir, her servant and client in the year one hundred and ninety-four (909-10).'

"The task accomplished, Zubaidah's chief agents and workmen presented themselves at her palace overlooking the Tigris to render an account of their expenditures. She

* Zubaidah, meaning "Little Butter Ball," was the name given to her by her grandfather, then the Caliph.

received their ledgers and promptly cast them into the river, announcing regally, if not indeed piously:

" 'We have left the account to the Day of Accounting. Let him who has a cash balance keep it, and he who is our creditor, him we will repay.'

"Then having bestowed upon them suits of honor, she dismissed them and they departed full of praise and thanks.

"Parallel with her interest in Mecca went her concern for the welfare of the pilgrims on the road that she herself no doubt traveled, namely that from Kufa to Mecca, a distance of some nine hundred miles.

"It is interesting to note that though she did at times undertake philanthropic work at some well-known station on the road, such as Haitham, her main concern seems to have been the poorer or more pious pilgrims who, either from necessity or from choice, made the long Pilgrimage on foot. For, as one follows the course of her 'stations' on the Mecca Road, it soon becomes apparent that these were located mostly at some half-way spot between older established stations and towns.

"At least nine cities are associated with her activities on the road between Kufa and the southern junction of Ma'dan al-Maqirah, where the road branches off to Medina and to Mecca. A tenth station, Mulldath, lay beyond this on the way to Medina. Three of the sites, all in the first third of the road from Kufa, were named in her honor, the best known of the three being the first.

"At all these places was to be found at least either a well or a cistern, though some, as at Haitham, had in addition a shelter for rest or prayer and a fortification of some sort, while one station boasted still further, a mosque.

"Her philanthropic interest continued throughout her life and took the form of endowments for the upkeep of her

[302]

establishments and public works and a readiness to supplement these. A touching story is told in this connection. Ma'mun's governor of Mecca, (Salih ibn al-Abbas) wrote that caliph in 210 A.H. (825-6 A.D.) of the need for some supplementary cisterns and canals in the city itself and was told to undertake their construction. The work was completed and the occasion was celebrated with public festivities.

"When Zubaidah heard of the new project, she was much pained. It was probably in connection with this very project that she was anxious to make the Pilgrimage once more and used Buran's influence with Ma'mun, on the happy occasion of their wedding later that same year, to secure that end. When she did make the Pilgrimage the very next year, the governor came to pay his respects. She took him to task thus:

" 'Why did you not write me so that I could have asked the Commander of the Believers to assign that project to me? I would have undertaken its cost as I undertook the expense of the other cistern so as to carry out in full my intentions toward the people of the Sanctuary of Allah.' "

Lady Fatimah, mother of Sultan Sulayman, "The Magnificent," brought the water of Ayn-Zubaidah from Mina to Mecca at a cost of thirty thousand gold dinars.

Such then, is the Pilgrimage. The Christian can see many things in the Muslim faith to admire, without acknowledging any disparagement of his own. Indeed, Abdul Aziz ibn Sa'ud has said: "A Muslim is not a Muslim until he believes in Issa (Jesus) and what was revealed through him in the Gospel, and Musa (Moses) and what was revealed to him in the Torah, and Muhammad and what was revealed to him of the Koran, and he who believes not in Issa and Musa believes not in Muhammad."

[303]

CHAPTER TWENTY-NINE

Mission Accomplished

As this volume was written, Abdul Aziz ibn Sa'ud had completed his fiftieth lunar year of leadership in Arabia Deserta.

He had begun, we recall, with that little band of forty devoted followers who slipped across the desert with him in that January of 1902, and fought with him to his first triumph: the recapture of Riyadh.

In the intervening years, with much warring and much disappointment, he had unified Najd, conquered al-Hasa and Asir, settled his boundary troubles with the Yemen, and made himself master of the Hijaz.

He had unified Arabia, and then he had set out to give it a rebirth: to bring to his people an end of lawlessness and fighting, and a beginning of a better life: enough shelter, enough food, enough clothing—schools, roads, mosques, abundant pure water, agricultural development, industry, expansion of trade, sanitation facilities, hospitals, and medical care.

All of these goals he has achieved; and, today, as he contemplates his domain, he must surely know that he has made himself one of the great men of our century.

Even with all of his increased responsibilities, the King has never lost his love of the lighter side.

The writer recalls an occasion when, at dinner, the King good-naturedly taunted Sir Abdullah Philby about the superiority of American automobiles for desert travel over the English makes, and when Philby offered to show him some he had, the King asked him if they came in that condition or "were they doctored at Jiddah?"

After dinner, the guests wash their hands and mouths and come back to the King to be perfumed. He sits with a jar of attar of rose in one hand and a wooden applicator in the other. Each guest opens his palm while the King dips the applicator and passes it over the palm of the guest who in turn rubs his hands together and passes the perfume over his beard, saying:

"Alhamdu-Lillah."

In bringing modernization to his country, Abdul Aziz has very frequently had to employ his native ingenuity to the fullest to win a point against deep-rooted prejudice. His efforts to bring about acceptance of the radio telephone is a good case in point.

In the face of isolation from the outside world for centuries, and an existence of hardship and scarcity, the religious reformation sank into the souls of the Ikhwan and took complete possession of them.

To them the world was made of good and evil—the good was in the Book, and with this they became familiar; the unknown was evil.

When Sultan Ibn Bajad entered the place of Hussein at Tayif, he saw an unfamiliar evil contraption on the wall and, with his own hands, he pulled it out with its roots and smashed it. That it was a telephone, connecting Mecca with Tayif, was incomprehensible to him.

Abdul Aziz had now builded a vast kingdom, difficult to traverse, and he had a free population that resented restraint, and shifted accordingly with the winds. It taxed all of his Najjabs (messengers) and their fast zaluls to reach him with belated news. I believe that it was Philby who sug-

[305]

gested the installation of the wireless telephone, and Abdul Aziz realized its importance to him in a flash, and ordered communication established between the principal districts.

To some of the Ikhwan, it was unbelievable that the instrument spoke: it was an innovation of the devil, for neither the Prophet nor his companions had spoken of it. Some kafir (infidel) like Philby, in league with Satan, was surely working his wiles on Abdul Aziz. Some of the Ikhwan watched the operators in the hope of catching them making sacrifices to the devil, others saw doom coming and wished for the good old days. They were not unlike, in their attitude, the Pilgrim Fathers of Massachusetts three hundred years ago.

Abdul Aziz became aware of the spreading rumors and, accordingly, called upon the religious teachers ("ulama") and a great number of the Ikhwan to set him aright, and counsel him.

When they assembled, he ordered the dial opened and the melodious voice of one of the best chanters at Mecca intoned the Fatihah, the first chapter of the Koran:

In the name of Allah, the Merciful, the Compassionate
Praise be to God, the Lord of creation
The Merciful, the Compassionate
Sovereign in the Day of Judgment.
It is Thou we worship
And of Thee we seek aid
Guide us in the straight path
The path of the recipients of Thy favor
Not those with whom Thou art displeased
Nor those who are gone astray.

When the reading was over, Ibn Sa'ud asked the gathering if they believed that this was the voice of Satan.

"Nastaghfrul-Allah!" ("We ask forgiveness of Allah!"),

[306]

they all chorused—and now, during the Hajj at 'Arafat and Mina, and in the very Haram at Mecca, amplifiers send the Khutbas (sermons) to the gathered thousands where no human voice could have reached before.

Many another new departure has subsequently been accepted, gratefully, by Ibn Sa'ud's people. The Man With a Purpose has telescoped centuries of progress into two and a half decades.

One is not surprised that Maj. Gen. Patrick J. Hurley, in his capacity as personal representative of President Roosevelt, said, after a conference with Ibn Sa'ud: "He is the wisest and strongest of all the leaders I have met in the Arabian states. He is a man of vision and executive ability, ready to lead his people in keeping pace with the progress of the world."

This is the man who started at Riyadh with forty men away back in 1902; the man who found himself in a land of scant promise, but who determined to make it thrive again. It was a hopeless task—so men said—but Ibn Sa'ud accomplished it. His job required unfaltering courage and patience, and a full fund of wisdom. It required well-planned strategy; a willingness to accept temporary setbacks and unwelcome compromises in the interest of the ultimate goal; and, above all, Faith.

It required, saying it another way: Abdul Aziz ibn Sa'ud.

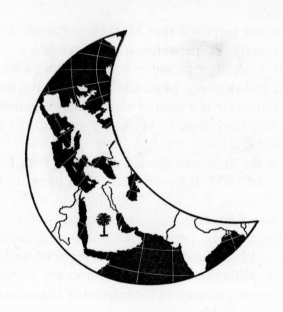